SAYING NO
IS NOT ENOUGH

"Nearly a decade after the first edition of this book appeared, I remain firm in my conviction that, although we live in a drug-filled society, parents can successfully help their children navigate these troubled waters."

—Robert Schwebel, Ph.D.

Praise for **Saying No Is Not Enough**

"[This book] may save your child's life; it could even save your own. . . . Dr. Schwebel correctly identifies tobacco as our most dangerous drug and provides valuable advice for parents on how to combat the pervasive influence of the tobacco industry."

> —Andrew W. Nichols, M.D., MPH, Professor and Director, Rural Health Office, University of Arizona Health Sciences Center

"I'm enormously impressed by the wisdom and humanity contained in these pages. If anything, the book is even more appealing than the very solid first edition. . . . With great sympathy for the burdens of parenthood . . . and enormous affection for and understanding of contemporary adlescence, Robert Schwebel tells us why simply saying no to alcohol, drugs, and the other lures of the teen years is not enough."

> —Peter E. Nathan, University of Iowa Foundation, Distinguished Professor of Psychology

"Even if your children are under two years old, read this book now and begin to establish the relationship and teach the skills that will strengthen their resistance to drug and alcohol abuse and other problem behaviors."

> —Rebecca Van Marter, Arizona Coordinator of the Southwest Regional Center for Drug Free Schools and Communities

"Full of wisdom and practical advice, this book will not only help parents deal more effectively with the issues surrounding drugs, but with all the other issues young people face growing up in today's world."

> —Lynda Madaras, author of The "What's Happening to My Body?" Book for Girls and for Boys

"An extremely important book for parents everywhere. . . . It places special emphasis on the importance of teaching children the dangers involved in drugs before they come in contact with them."

> —Parent Guide News

"Schwebel presents not only a blueprint for the prevention of drug and alcohol abuse, but also shows parents how to develop a close, warm, and loving relationship with their children built upon mutual respect, communication, trust, and confidence."

> —Lynn Max Tausig, M.D., President and CEO, National Jewish Medical Research Center, Denver, CO; Professor of Pediatrics, University of Colorado School of Medicine

"Essential reading. . . . Schwebel provides an excellent approach for all parents struggling to communicate with their teenagers."

> —Dr. Philip Cowan, head of Psychology Clinic, Psychology Department, University of California, Berkeley

"A strong tool . . . it supports families and is geared to helping build strong parent-child alliances from early childhood."

> —Charles B. Rangel, U.S. House of Representatives Select Committee on Narcotics Abuse and Control

"Saying No Is Not Enough stands out as a resource of practical, supportive ideas and strategies for parents, educators, and the community."

> —Linda Augenstein, Assistant Director, Comprehensive Health Education, Tucson Unified School District

SAYING NO IS NOT ENOUGH

*Helping Your Kids Make Wise Decisions
About Alcohol, Tobacco, and Other Drugs—
A Guide for Parents of Children
Ages 3 Through 19*

Robert Schwebel, Ph.D.

Updated Second Edition

NEWMARKET PRESS
NEW YORK

This book is published simultaneously in the
United States of America and in Canada.

Second Edition

10 9 8 7 6 5 4 3 2 1

Library of Congress Cataloging-in-Publication Data
Schwebel, Robert
Saying no is not enough : helping your kids make wise decisions
about alcohol, tobacco and other drugs—a guide for parents of children
3 through 19 / Robert Schwebel ; introduction by Benjamin Spock.
p. cm.
Updated second ed. of the 1989 ed.
Includes bibliographical references and index.
ISBN 1-55704-324-8 (hardcover). — ISBN 1-55704-318-3 (pbk.)
1. Teenagers—Drug use—United States—Prevention. 2. Teenagers—
Alcohol use—United States—Prevention. 3. Teenagers—Tobacco use—
United States—Prevention. 4. Drug Abuse—United States—
Prevention. 5. Alcoholism—United States—Prevention.
6. Substance abuse—United States—Prevention. 7. Parenting—United
States. I. Title.
HV5824.Y68S35 1997   649'.4—DC21   97-1938

CIP

Quantity Purchases
Companies, professional groups, clubs, and other organizations may qualify for special terms
when ordering quantities of this title. For information, write to Special Sales, Newmarket Press,
18 East 48th Street, New York, NY 10017, call (212) 832-3575, or FAX (212) 832-3629.

Book design by Joe Gannon
Manufactured in the United States of America

*For information regarding speaking engagements by the author,
call Dr. Robert Schwebel in Tucson, Arizona, at (520) 748-2122
or write to him care of Newmarket Press at the address above.*

CONTENTS

PART I
EMPOWERING YOUNG CHILDREN TO PREVENT DRUG ABUSE

PART II
TALKING WITH TEENS TO PREVENT OR INTERVENE IN DRUG ABUSE

PART III INTERVENTION

To my wonderful parents,
who empowered my brother and me
with love and understanding,
and to all parents
who want to empower their children.

Acknowledgments

Many of the ideas in this book grew from my work with Berkeley colleagues Hogie Wykoff, Becky Jenkins, Beth Roy, Michael Singer, Joy Marcus, Darca Nicholson, and especially Claude Steiner.

I had an opportunity to put the ideas into practice in Tucson with another set of colleagues who contributed more ideas: Craig Wunderlich, Rebecca Van Marter, Joan Meggitt, Joy Misenhelter, Linda Moreno, Chris Miller, Ginger Marcus, Anna Rascón, and Marilyn Civer. And I want to acknowledge colleagues in Phoenix: Nancy Hanson, Kris Bell, Steve Merrill, and Juanita Dressler.

Then there are my journalist friends in Tucson who taught me much about writing: Leo Banks, Nadine Epstein, and Mark Turner.

A first book is an opportunity to thank special teachers from the past such as Mrs. Stuart, Mrs. Helmcke, and Mrs. Skolnick in elementary school, Sam Baskin and the late Don Myatt in college, and Philip Cowan in graduate school.

Then there are family members who contributed in special ways: my wife, Claudia, and children, Frank and Henry; my brother, Andy, his wife, Carol, and their children, Davy and Sara; and my parents, Milton and Bernice.

Best friends Brian McCaffrey and Sylvia Yee were important in many ways. Also falling into this category are Bob Calhoun, Martha McEwen, Don Oberthur, Jeri and Richard Briskin, Mike and Susie Cohen, Betty Anne Krause, Alex Zautra, Ann Gaddis, Mary Morgan, Carol Schaedler, Chris and Hope Nealson.

From over the fence came support from my neighbors David Boomhower and Barbara Brown.

The National Institute on Drug Abuse funded much of the research that I found so helpful in understanding how to prevent drug abuse. The "parents' movement" helped stimulate action to bring the problem of drug abuse into the public eye.

I thank Al Zuckerman from Writers House and Esther Margolis from Newmarket Press for their confidence and commitment in making this book possible.

I have special thanks to give both to Theresa Burns, who is a gentle but strong and talented editor who started with this project and made important contributions, and to Keith Hollaman, also a strong, gentle, and talented editor who stepped in and added enormously to the quality of the book and the success of this project.

Being a Spock baby, my gratitude to Dr. Benjamin Spock extends back a lifetime. I thank him for writing his classic child-rearing book and for all he has done to help make this a better world for everyone. I know how he responds when people tell him that they are Spock babies: "Your parents should be very proud." So now I thank Dr. Spock for writing an introduction to this book and for his kind offer to review a previous draft. I hope that *he* is proud of the product.

INTRODUCTION
BY BENJAMIN SPOCK

Drug abuse, including abuse of alcohol, is a frightening threat to all parents these days, whether their children are teenagers or are still just babies, whether they suspect their adolescents are already involved or are quite sure they aren't.

One serious aspect of the problem is that adolescents (and particularly preadolescents) are more apt than adults to slip into abuse easily and rapidly. Another is that they consider themselves miraculously immune to addiction just as they consider themselves immune to pregnancy and serious diseases. (I still remember how amazed and indignant I was in my youth when I came down with a serious disease.)

But the greatest problem of all is teenagers' need to be independent, which makes them pooh-pooh the opinions of their parents and believe that it's their pals who know and speak the absolute truth. They fear that their parents will continue to try to dominate them. Therefore parents have to avoid condescension, avoid acting as though their greater age automatically confers greater wisdom. They should speak in an adult-to-adult manner, show respect for their children's opinions, and listen as much as they talk—listen not impatiently, with frequent interruptions, but with nodding head and remarks such as "I see what you mean." Parents don't have to surrender or hide their own points of view. In fact they must give their own conclusions in the end, and if these are not agreed to, they may have to impose them, out of love and the desire to protect, with no ranting and raving. Adolescents are often influenced by friendly, respectful discussion even though they can't admit it at the time and appear unmoved. It is the most important reason for starting your prevention work before your children reach their teens.

Robert Schwebel, an old friend and colleague of mine, has written this book to cover all aspects of the child drug abuse problem for parents. To me the most impressive aspect of the book is that he has worked in the field of child drug abuse for twenty years, worked with many hundreds of children individually and in groups, counseled many hundreds of parents. He is not offering theories. He is making detailed, practical suggestions that he himself has worked out and tested many times over. They have proved their effectiveness.

Dr. Schwebel is sure—as I am—that the best protection against drug use is for children to grow up in a close-knit, loving family in which certain strengths are naturally fostered: open, easy communication between them and their parents; self-esteem, which comes not only from love and regular opportunities to succeed but from receiving more approval than criticism; the ability to think clearly and reasonably, which comes from discussions with parents, meeting rules, and learning the consequences of poor performance; problem solving, which is developed out of opportunities to analyze difficulties and to work out remedies.

Parental love should be unconditional in the sense that children should know that they can count on their parents' devotion no matter what problems they may get into. This does not mean submissiveness to children's rudeness, deceit, or abuse, but a belief in their ability to measure up, a willingness to give them another chance.

Dr. Schwebel explains that children take to drugs not for mysterious reasons but, like adults, to relieve tensions, to gain pleasure, and to achieve social acceptance. This knowledge guides us in our search for cause and cure.

One of the author's basic convictions is that you, the parent, must not evade the issue of drug abuse, or pull the wool over your own eyes. And you should stick to the belief that drugs, including pot, are not for children—whether or not you can get agreement from your child. There should be no compromise on this.

I find most illuminating and valuable Dr. Schwebel's recordings of actual conversations, or suggested conversations, between teenagers and their parents. For much of the book deals with the tricky problem of how to talk with an adolescent who has been found to be using alcohol or other drugs and who, after lengthy discussions, is still unwilling to come to a sincere agreement to quit. He insists that his use of pot could not possibly be a problem for him, so there is no need to discontinue. How do you reach a meeting of the minds and a valid agreement? And if you can't, which happens more often with the older adolescent, how do you express your recourse to parental authority so that it will be acceptable and followed?

Dr. Schwebel suggests the exact words that the parent might use, to steer between authoritarianism on the one hand and ineffectual blind alleys on the other. He shows how you can be persistent, even penetrating, while remaining friendly and supportive. These suggested questions and comments cover the age range from preteen, through early teen, to late teen. They cover the child who has not even experimented with drugs, the one who has used them occasionally, the one who uses them regularly, the one who is showing harmful effects (in grades, moods, neglect of chores, withdrawal from family and friends), and the one who is definitely dependent, addicted.

For example, if the reasonable approach fails, you might say, "You think pot is harmless but I think it's risky and it is illegal. I'm unwilling to allow it. I wish you would think it over and we'll discuss it again in a day or two." If this is not successful—and only then—you can take a harder line, such as stopping the allowance, or restricting social life and after-school activities.

Dr. Schwebel discusses steps that might be followed when a child has made an agreement and broken it, from a serious talk and another chance, to withdrawal of various privileges and perhaps to a confrontation with a group of well-wishing friends and neighbors, to a refusal to let a defiant youth stay in the home.

This is not all by any means, but it should be enough to show you the wide scope and the positive spirit of this book.

Preface to the Revised and Updated Edition

Preparing the second edition of this book, ten years after writing the first, is an opportunity to reflect upon changes in the field and to respond to the changing concerns of parents. During this decade, statistics about the level of drug use have fluctuated a little but have remained high, as they will continue to do until we address the underlying reasons that compel people in our country to be such big consumers of drugs. Meanwhile, you, as parents, face the same challenge: raising children in a drug-filled society.

My basic recommendations for parents for preventing substance abuse remain unchanged: Start when your children are young. Create a family climate in which your children feel they can talk with you about anything, without fear, even if they have misbehaved. Help them understand the dangers of drugs. Empower them to feel good about themselves, to value good health, to take good care of their bodies, and to meet their needs in healthy ways, without drugs. Teach them how to make good decisions and how to resist peer pressure.

Strong rules protect young children and young teens from the use of drugs. With older teens, you need to establish a dialogue and an educational process so that your children make their *own* wise decisions. This is best accomplished by using the "exchange of information" method described in the second part of this book.

The original thrust of *Saying No Is Not Enough* remains the same, but the second edition contains some important changes. I have expanded the section about marijuana. Because the dangers of this drug have been consistently exaggerated, information about the real dangers has been discounted by many young people, who have come to see marijuana as both desirable (forbidden fruit) and safe. So I have attempted to distinguish the exaggerated dangers of marijuana from the real ones.

Although I wrote about tobacco in the first edition, this time I have added a full chapter on the topic. Tobacco is a dangerous, addictive drug too often overlooked in our prevention efforts. I believe that parents must develop an aggressive attitude to counteract the multi-billion-dollar advertising and promotional budgets of the tobacco industry aimed at getting our children to smoke cigarettes or chew tobacco.

Another development in recent years is that baby-boomers and younger parents are perplexed about what to tell their children about drugs because many of them had experiences, and even problems, with drugs. For that reason I have added recommendations about self-disclosure and about how to help your children make healthy choices without feeling hypocritical.

Those familiar with the first edition of this book know that I placed heavy emphasis on creating an open, trusting climate in a family. I believe that we greatly underestimate how much discussion is both needed and possible in a family to avoid serious behavioral problems. Nevertheless, in rereading the previous edition, I felt it was necessary to expand some of the sections about how to deal with lying and dishonesty in children, especially adolescents. We do not want to falsely accuse them of drug abuse. On the other hand, we must not be naive when our children mislead us. In this edition I have particularly stressed the importance of trusting intuitions and gut reactions, and being alert to unending excuses and explanations that don't quite add up.

Along these lines, I have added a section on drug-testing, an emotional topic, even more so as the home test enters the market. Because of the issues of personal liberty and dignity, I have been slow to embrace the strategy of drug testing youth. But I do see a place for it in extreme situations. I have worked with young people with serious drug problems and witnessed many instances where it was simply too late to create a climate of honesty and dialogue without forceful tactics. Too many bold-faced lies had been told, sometimes with quite imaginative stories that *almost* made sense.

Another change in this edition is that I have provided more help for parents whose children are *already* harmfully involved with drugs. In particular, I talk about how to take the initial steps to start a recovery process and how to respond to some of the roadblocks, such as when a drug-abusing youth says, "I'm just a teenager" (or "just a kid"), or "I want to party" (which means using drugs).

Nearly a decade after the first edition of this book appeared, I remain firm in my conviction that, although we live in a drug-filled society, parents can successfully help their children navigate these troubled waters.

R.S.
February 1998

PART I
EMPOWERING YOUNG CHILDREN
To Prevent Drug Abuse

1
WHY SAYING NO IS NOT ENOUGH

Thirteen-year-old Daniel has a choice to make. It's Saturday night. He's sitting in his kitchen with his two best friends. One of them wants to smoke a little marijuana that he got from his older brother. The other suggests they wash it down with a cool beer from the refrigerator. No adults are home. No one will notice.

This unexpected situation shocks Daniel, who has never seriously thought about using drugs. He is scared and confused. Although he has never discussed drugs with his parents, he knows from some of their comments that they would tell him to "just say no." In school he has attended programs about the dangers of drugs that told him he should "say no." Also, Daniel has seen scary television commercials suggesting that drugs "fry" your brain, although that message seems to be contradicted by his friend's older sister, who smokes marijuana, apparently without harm.

Beer doesn't scare Daniel. Marijuana does. But what worries him more is being called a "chicken" or appearing to be nervous about drugs. So he smokes the joint and drinks the beer.

Has Daniel turned into a "druggie" tonight? Certainly not. In fact, he gagged on the smoke and disliked the taste of beer. But the episode is significant because Daniel, at age thirteen, has broken the barrier of using illegal drugs and has also committed an act that he keeps secret from his parents.

Whether Daniel ever becomes harmfully involved with drugs in the future will depend to a great extent on his own personal development. The determining questions include: Will he become informed about drugs? Will he discuss drugs with mature and loving adults? Will he learn to meet his needs without drugs? Will he learn to resist peer pressure? Will he learn to make wise decisions?

Daniel's situation is similar to those faced by many of his peers. Like apples in the Garden of Eden, drugs are readily available to even the youngest and most vulnerable among us. Twelve-, thirteen-, and fourteen-year-olds, and often younger children, have important decisions to make. Even if they don't seek drugs, it's likely that something—marijuana, a can of beer, or a stronger drug—will be placed in their hands. Regardless of their parents' wishes, they will have to decide.

Most children, like Daniel, were not adequately prepared in their early years for decisions of this magnitude. Many decide about drugs without ever talking with an adult.

If you are frightened by this reality, you have plenty of company. Millions of parents are also frightened of what might happen, or has already happened, to their children. Although there is cause for concern, it's important not to panic and overreact, as some have done, assuming that *all* teenagers are using drugs and therefore *your* children must be using them. Many teenagers do not use drugs at all. Many of the teenagers who have already begun using drugs can be helped to avert harm. And even if drugs have caused harm, parents can still take effective action to minimize and correct the problem.

This book is written for parents who recognize the dangers of drug abuse and want to respond in a positive way. It is not, however, part of a "war on drugs," because drugs are not an enemy and certainly do not wage war. Many drugs are natural products that grow in the soil. Others are synthetically created by human genius and technology. Some drugs are used in religious practices, some for medicinal purposes, some in safe and socially accepted ways for fun and relaxation.

This is not an "anti" book to use in the fight against drugs. Rather, it is a positive book written to support you, as parents, in strengthening your children to help them learn to live healthy lives and make wise decisions. For young children, this will pro-

4

tect them from drug abuse and drug dependence. For children who have already used drugs, this will help prevent serious problems. And for children already harmfully involved with drugs, building their strengths will help with remediation.

If you are the parent of young children, you will find the first half of this book most helpful. The focus is on preventing problems before they occur. One part of the task is to help children understand the dangers of drugs. But the biggest challenge is *not* to scare them away from drugs. Rather, it is to prepare them for life so that they can meet their needs without chemical substances. We must raise healthy, competent, and informed children with positive attitudes about themselves and the world around them.

Children raised this way know how to lead happy and satisfying lives without drugs. They know how to have fun. They can communicate with others and form good relationships. They can solve problems. They have self-confidence. They can succeed in school. They feel good about themselves and their bodies. They do not *need* drugs to feel good, have fun, assert themselves, alter their moods, or change their feelings about themselves. Therefore, they are less likely to abuse drugs. Furthermore, children with self-confidence and positive values will not follow a crowd into doing something harmful to themselves or others. But take note: the development of these protective attitudes and life skills begins early in life, long before drugs are available to children.

There are two other important actions that should be implemented in early childhood for the prevention of drug abuse. One is making a clear statement that drugs are not to be used by children. With younger children, this means establishing and enforcing a rule that forbids drug use. The other important action is to establish open, honest communication in a loving family atmosphere. Children need to feel that they can talk with you, their parents, about anything, even mistakes they have made or behavior you might find objectionable. Later in life, when they face important and difficult choices, such as whether to use drugs, they will be able to discuss them with you. Creating an open climate of communication should not be postponed until a crisis occurs—when, for example, a child is considering whether to use drugs or is already using them. The best time to begin is early childhood.

The starting point for parents in preventing drug abuse is to be informed yourself. That is why Chapter 2 presents basic information about types of drugs and their effects, and also about how to evaluate drug use, abuse, and dependence.

For the parents of young children and preteens, Chapter 3 is about good beginnings in a family. It describes how to establish an empowering atmosphere in which young children learn the basic life skills and positive attitudes that "inoculate" them against drug abuse. Chapter 4 is a workbook of techniques and practical exercises that you can use to strengthen your children during the elementary years. It also offers guidance on how to talk with young children about drugs and other health issues, and how to create an open honest climate for dialogue in the family. Chapter 5 expands the discussion to the prevention of tobacco addiction.

The strategies for strengthening adolescents differ somewhat from those used with younger children. As with younger children, adolescents need solid information, guidance, and supervision. Whereas parents of younger children can make and enforce rules against drug use, the parents of adolescents cannot and should not control their children in the same way. Adolescents need to learn to think for themselves. They are preparing for adulthood. Empowering teenage children means giving them a certain amount of freedom, providing proper supervision, and expecting responsible behavior. The goal is to strengthen adolescents so that they strive for a positive lifestyle and make their *own* good decisions about drugs. Instead of dictating behavior, parents help their children learn to make wise choices.

The format for empowering adolescents is *discussion*. Dialogue between parents and children is especially important during this period. When parents can establish a dialogue with their teenage children, they will have influence on their drug decisions. When parents are shut out of the discussion they lose their influence, and peers become the main source of information influencing a young person's decisions about drugs.

If you are the parent of an adolescent, you will find the second half of this book most helpful. It tells how to empower teens to make wise decisions about drugs by engaging them in discussion, using what is called the "exchange of information" process. This process gives parents a forum for their input and encourages children to think for themselves. Chapter 6 is about opening the dialogue. Chapter 7 is about listening to one another. Chapter 8 is about making valid agreements and handling broken ones.

Some adolescents may already be using drugs when parents initiate discussion. Although this will change the content of what is discussed, discussion is still the most powerful influence parents can bring to bear against drug abuse.

If your child is *harmfully* involved with drugs, your task—strengthening your child to make wise decisions—remains the same. Because discussion is still your strongest weapon, Chapters 6, 7, and 8 are important for you. To make sure the drug problem is addressed in a serious fashion, you will also need additional strategies, which are discussed in Chapter 9. You will want to help your child learn other ways to meet his or her needs without drugs.

Too often, families are torn apart by discussion of drugs, especially if a child has already begun "using." It doesn't have to be this way. Discussion is an opportunity to help your children learn to think clearly and to develop a clear sense of personal identity. Good discussion about drugs can promote your child's personal growth and also family closeness.

Drugs are not just a family problem. The availability and acceptance of drugs in our communities is also a social problem, one that will not soon be solved. Long-term solutions include community action and changes in community standards. Until communities change, and while they do, you have to help your own children cope successfully with existing dangers.

Chapter 10 is about how families can work together in a community to create a positive social climate that encourages wellness, one in which drug use by teenagers is less accepted and less common. It is about families uniting to support one another and to improve their communities.

Throughout the book, true-to-life case histories are presented, along with sample dialogue between parents and children. The dialogue not only gives you a sense of what is effective and what is not, but also reveals the concerns of children. Generations who wish to move forward together must listen to each other.

The case histories and quotes are drawn from my own professional experience in the field of substance abuse, which began more than twenty-five years ago. At that time, I was a graduate student at the University of California at Berkeley and was working in the community with Claude Steiner, who was just then writing his book *Games Alcoholics Play*. It was coincidence rather than special interest that brought me into the field. But I was startled and concerned to see the prevalence of drug problems and the havoc they created in families. Since that time I have continued providing psychotherapy to people of all ages with alcohol and other drug problems, sometimes with their families and sometimes separately.

In working with adults with drug problems, I have noticed that their drug use generally began during childhood. Adults often link their drug problems to other problems earlier in their life, such as school failure, an inability to meet parental expectations, or problems in relationships with peers. I have watched these adults struggle—mustering power they didn't even know they had—to overcome their drug abuse or drug dependence. It's an uphill battle.

In contrast, I also work with teenagers who are having problems in school, or in meeting parental expectations, or in relating to peers, but are *not* yet using drugs. Often all they need is encouragement, or study tips, or some support about solving personal problems. This could turn things around for them. A little help in solving a personal problem could make a big difference. It could even prevent the development of drug problems. It is so much easier to prevent drug abuse during childhood than to face it years later, after so much suffering has occurred and so much damage has been done.

With adolescents who are abusing drugs, it is very important to face this problem *immediately* and not to wait until these young people become adults looking back at poor choices and wasted years.

In addition to my private practice, I have served for three years as the director of a publicly funded outpatient counseling center and substance-abuse-prevention program in Tucson, Arizona. From 1992 to 1997, I was clinical director of drug treatment services at a large treatment program with residential, day-treatment, outpatient, and hospital services for youth. Recently I have developed "The Seven Challenges," a widely used program for treating adolescent substance abuse, and have written *The Seven Challenges* and *The Seven Challenges Workbooks*. All along I have provided lectures, programs, workshops, and training for schools, families, mental-health professionals, juvenile-corrections personnel, and communities. I have also remained active in public-policy formation in the field of drug-abuse prevention and treatment.

ALCOHOL, TOBACCO, AND OTHER DRUGS

With all this talk about drugs, some readers might be wondering where alcohol and tobacco fit into the scheme of things. During my work in the field of drug-prevention and treatment, one of the most disturbing statements I have heard—and I have heard it often—was made by parents who breathed a sigh of relief as they said, "I'm glad to hear my child isn't involved with marijuana. He [or she] is only drinking alcohol."

Understandably these parents are pleased that their child is not using an illegal substance. (They are not especially concerned about the laws regarding the purchase or consumption of alcohol by minors.) However, alcohol is a drug, a powerful one to which millions are addicted. Parents should find little comfort in discovering that their young children are "only" drinking alcohol.

I have also seen parents roll over and accept that their children smoke or chew tobacco products, or accept the inevitability that this will happen, consoling themselves that it is not a more "dangerous" drug. They need to realize that tobacco is a very dangerous and addictive drug, and that it is referred to as a "gateway" drug because it is one of the first ones that children use. Each year in this country, there are approximately four hundred thousand preventable deaths attributable to tobacco, one hundred thousand attributable to alcohol, and only twenty thousand attributable to all the "street drugs" combined. The sale of tobacco products is reinforced by tobacco companies with billion-dollar advertising and promotion budgets, often targeting young people.

Like alcohol, tobacco is legal for adults to consume and therefore has gained considerable social acceptance. However, preventing nicotine addiction is a very important part of promoting the healthy development of children.

So when I talk about drugs in this book, I am referring to alcohol and tobacco as well. Sometimes I use the expression "alcohol, tobacco, and other drugs" to remind you that, although they have gained widespread social acceptance and are easily obtained, alcohol and tobacco products are dangerous drugs.

DRUG STATISTICS

Most books about children and drugs start with a drum roll and frightening statistics about youth, the most alarming ones that can be found to prove that our country is experiencing a crisis. I don't believe we need more hype about the drug problem. On the contrary, we need to be careful not to panic.

Most people are well aware that children have access to drugs and that this is a serious matter. Statistics will change from year to year. But the issue of preparing children to face a drug-filled world remains constant. What we need is not hysteria but a strong, calm, and reasonable response to the drug problem.

One statistic often cited is the age at which drugs are first used.[1] This statistic is important for communities dealing with prevention policy. But in your family it doesn't matter what the *average* age happens to be. What is important is that *your* children be prepared. It is important that they be informed about drugs and that they acquire the necessary life skills and attitudes they need to make good decisions. In your family you will want to maintain an ongoing, open dialogue about drugs so that your child receives the appropriate education *when he or she needs it*.

If you prepare your children to meet their needs without drugs, educate them about drugs, and have open communication in your home, I do not believe you have to be frightened. Drug abuse can be prevented. The best approach, of course, is to start early. But even if you got a late start and your children are already using drugs, there is much that you can do to minimize risk and harm.

A CLEAR MESSAGE ABOUT DRUGS

Because of the health risks associated with drug use and especially with the effects of drugs on youth, I think we should deliver a clear message: *The use of alcohol, tobacco, and other drugs is not for children.*

Not everyone who uses drugs is harmed by them. But drugs are certainly a health risk for adults and even more so for children. Children have not attained the maturity needed to manage powerful chemical substances and therefore are more vulnerable to drug problems. Drugs affect mood, concentration, and cognitive functioning, including memory. They can interfere with learning and impair school performance.[1] They can harm the body and disrupt healthy physical and emotional development.

One concern about young people is that they may have trouble setting limits for themselves. Many adults can limit their consumption of chemical substances to weekends or other carefully selected times when alcohol or other drugs will not disrupt their lives. They may, for example, drink only an occasional cocktail or glass of wine with dinner or at a social gathering. To be fair, it should be stated that some adults have trouble setting limits. But children have less self-control than most adults and therefore are even more vulnerable to problems. Once children decide to experiment with drugs, they may find it difficult to stop.

HOW DRUGS HARM ADOLESCENTS

The potential harm from drug use by *young* children is immediately obvious. The special risks with adolescents are less obvious but highly significant, especially when you consider what is supposed to happen during this stage of life. Adolescents are making the transition from childhood to adulthood. They are working to establish their sense of personal identity, which means separating from their parents and beginning to find their own answers to the questions: Who am I? What is important to me? Where do I fit into the world? Without a fully established sense of identity, adolescents are susceptible to peer influence and likely to "do what everyone else does." When friends are using drugs, they will be tempted to do likewise.

The process of establishing one's own identity necessarily involves exploration and experimentation, and can easily extend to drug experimentation. In a drug-filled world, *young* adolescents have to establish their identity in relation to drugs. In previous generations this was a decision that could be deferred until later in life. Now they are being forced to make choices about drugs when they are younger and less prepared to make wise ones.

Besides forming their own identities, adolescents are also involved in mastering the mental ability to think logically, to think through *all* the implications of *all* possible actions. Until they have mastered this logical ability, they are not yet fully equipped to think through *all* the implications of their own actions, including the use of drugs.

As a group, adolescents often "push the envelope" with risk-taking. Perhaps it is inexperience or poor judgment, or even lack of a strong sense of identity. For whatever reason, there is more of a tendency among youth than older people to get into a competition to prove who can hold the most alcohol, or "tweak" the most on speed, or take the most "hits" of acid (LSD).

Then there is the issue of denial. Drug abusers of all ages typically say, "I'm fine. There's nothing wrong. I don't have a problem." However, the risk of denial is greater among teenagers because, during this stage of development, young people have an exaggerated sense of invincibility. They believe that nothing bad can happen to them. This partially explains some of the dangerous risk-taking of adolescents.

One boy I counseled, Kenny E., age fourteen, denied his drug problem. Yet he smoked marijuana several times a day and recently began using cocaine and crystal methamphetamine (speed). He was known as someone who could outdrink or outdrug his peers. He rarely went to school and had been detained twice by the police in recent months. He was headed for serious trouble. Here is a small sample of his denial at work.

"Drugs haven't affected my life," he stated without equivocation.

"How about school? How are your grades?" I asked.

"D's and F's" he replied. "School is boring."

"When did you start using drugs?"

"Last year."

"What were your grades back then?"

"B's and C's."

"Oh, but you say drugs haven't affected your performance in school?"

"No."

Kenny would not admit to a problem. Next I asked him if he could stop using drugs.

"I can stop whenever I want."

12

"Have you tried?"

"Yeah."

"Were you successful?"

"Well, it was a bad time. My parents were hassling me a lot, you know. So I started doing drugs again. They were being impossible."

With denial, there is always an excuse for not stopping. Usually it is blamed on someone else, be it teachers, peers, or parents.

Kenny supported the denial by minimizing his drug use: "I don't smoke that much weed. I don't use that much coke or speed. It's not a problem." He exaggerated the drug use of his peers: "Everyone does drugs all the time," he said. "There's nothing wrong with me. It's normal."

His denial was further supported by a mistaken notion of what constitutes drug abuse. He thinks only of extremes, such as needle-popping addicts and skid-row bums. He does not understand that problems can be much more subtle.

One added risk for adolescents—and it was a factor with Kenny—is that they are shielded from the harmful effects of their drug use by virtue of being minors who have a roof over their head, the guarantee of food on the table, and the juvenile-justice system, which is much more forgiving than the adult system. Adolescents can dismiss their drug use, as they often do, as "just a kid thing." Meanwhile, their drug use escalates to dangerous levels before they feel the full impact of their actions, because they are being protected from significant consequences.

PREVENTING OR DELAYING DRUG USE

A clear message from parents that children should not use drugs does not guarantee drug-free children. Try as we might to prevent drug use, we need to recognize what we face and remember that this is a drug-filled, consumer-oriented society. Over and over again children receive the message, especially from the mass media and advertisers, that they should feel good, *right now*, on the spot: "If you feel bad, take this pill or that drug. If that fails, eat this food or buy that product." Supposedly this type of consumer behavior will make them feel good. They are constantly told that there is a quick fix for everything. No wonder children use drugs!

So, in a drug-filled world and during a period in life that calls for experimentation and exploration, it is not surprising that many adolescents start to use drugs. We can discourage this, but we must be realistic. Considering, too, the young age at which drugs are first used, it is not surprising that a substantial number of adolescents develop serious drug problems. Once this happens, the effects are devastating.

Drugs shield children from dealing with reality and mastering developmental tasks crucial to their future. The skills they lack that leave them vulnerable to drug abuse in the first place are the very ones that are stunted by drugs. They will have difficulty establishing a clear sense of identity, mastering intellectual skills, and learning self-control.

Teenagers with drug problems will not be prepared for adult roles. They will lose the benefit of important years of schooling, leaving them ill-prepared for the job market. They will not deal directly— that is, with a clear head—with the emotional and social issues of dating. This means that they will be ill-prepared to establish committed, loving relationships. In short, they will chronologically mature while remaining emotional adolescents.

Although a clear "don't use" message will not necessarily prevent drug use altogether, it could at least help to delay first use. This is important. Research has shown that the earlier a child begins to use drugs, the greater the number of negative consequences from drugs over the course of a lifetime. This is simply common sense. Younger children are over their heads when they start using drugs. They are headed for trouble. So we should at least aim to delay initiation of drug use.

SAYING NO IS NOT ENOUGH

Much has been said about the "Just Say No" campaign made famous by Nancy Reagan. Even before this particular campaign was launched, studies had shown that learning to say no was part of an effective way that children could resist negative peer pressure.[2] The former first lady used the slogan to rally public support against children's use of drugs and no doubt made a valuable contribution to public awareness of this enormous problem.

It is important that young children hear the "Say No" message, as in: "Do what we tell you to do. We know what is best. Say no to drugs." But young children need more than a slogan. They need positive role models. They need to feel good about themselves. They need to know how to have fun and how to cope with stress without drugs. In short, saying no is not enough. Young children need a broad range of experiences to help them learn positive attitudes and basic life skills. They need support in succeeding at home, in school, and in their social lives. By providing these experiences, parents go a long way toward assuring that their children are part of the vast majority of children—those who do not develop drug problems.

With adolescents, the "Just Say No" approach is entirely misdirected. Adolescents who are developing their own identities and learning to make their own decisions do not necessarily benefit from the campaign or take it seriously.

Teenagers need clear standards of behavior and an objective presentation of the facts. They need an opportunity to think for themselves and to discuss their thoughts. They need to learn to make good decisions on their own about drugs and, for that matter, all health issues. Instead, they are being served one-sided information—all the negatives about drugs—and therefore are not prepared when they start hearing the positives. And they are told what to do—"Just Say No." This is not very helpful advice, considering that rebelliousness is a major reason for drug use by teenagers.

Simply saying no is not enough. Children need to be empowered. Young children need an opportunity to learn positive attitudes and basic life skills. Teenagers need dialogue and discussion with their parents. Given an opportunity, all children can learn to make wise decisions about their health.

This book will help you, as parents, respond in powerful and effective ways to the drug problem. The idea is to take action as soon as you can, preferably long before your child has access to drugs. The goal is to empower your children.

In my experience working with families, I have noticed some pitfalls that diminish parental influence. One is a tendency to ignore and brush aside the drug problem. Another is called "enabling," which means taking actions that actually allow drug problems to continue. A third pitfall is authoritarianism, in which parents take powerful actions that, unfortunately, tend to breed rebellion. A fourth is overprotection. I discuss these pitfalls below and caution you about them, so that you can avoid them in your family.

PARENTAL PITFALL: IGNORING AND DENIAL

Many parents fail to notice or chose to ignore the problem of children using drugs. Some of them grew up in an era when drugs were definitely not an option and can't imagine that their children might have access to drugs. They are too far removed from today's youth, including their own, to recognize what is happening.

Some parents hesitate to bring up the topic of drugs because of the issue of trust. They say: "My kid is a good kid. I don't want him to think I'm suspicious of him."

The implication of this statement is that talking about drugs with children means accusing them of something, and that parents of "well-adjusted" children should steer clear of the topic. This is a false assumption. Discussion does not mean accusing or condemning a child. The purpose of discussion is to inform, to educate, and to empower. "Good kids" as much as any others need to be prepared for the tough decisions that lie ahead. They deserve support.

Another way that parents avoid the drug issue is by taking the "wait and see" approach. They hope that everything will be fine of its own accord: "I haven't yet heard about my kids getting in trouble with drugs, so I don't need to do anything." This is a dangerous outlook, because the parents are waiting for a crisis instead of taking preventive action.

Then there is denial, the same defense mechanism applied by drug users themselves and one of the most common ways that parents overlook drug use. Parents deny the existence of the problem by making believe that nothing is, or could be, wrong. Some denying parents know that children elsewhere are using drugs but say it won't happen in their community. Or they see it in their community but say it won't happen to their children. Or they see their children using drugs but reassure themselves that there is nothing to worry about: "If I ignore it, or don't think or talk about it, it'll go away."

An unsuspecting mother found a plastic bag filled with marijuana hidden under her fourteen-year-old daughter's bed. She asked her to explain.

Heather: "It's not mine. I'm just holding it for a friend."

Mom: "Oh, I'm glad to hear that you're not involved with drugs, because they're dangerous."

These are the words of a parent eager to be reassured. Although there's always the possibility that her daughter's explanation was true, there's also the possibility that it was not. It so happens that Heather had been having serious problems in school. She had become moody and irritable in recent months. Something was wrong. But Heather's mother dropped the subject of drugs like a hot potato. This is the psychological defense-mechanism of denial at work.

Still another way that parents deny drug problems is on the basis of an ungrounded and false sense of optimism. A composite of their wishful thinking goes like this:

"Kids will be kids. Teens will be teens. It's just a stage of life. Teenage behavior is always strange. My kids will grow out of it. They'll get over it."

Although many children who experiment with drugs manage to escape injury, others do not. There is no reason to panic, but, by the same token, there is no reason to presume that everything will be fine of its own accord. Children need help from their parents in dealing with drugs. Parents who ignore the issue cannot become an effective force in preventing problems.

PARENTAL PITFALL: ENABLING

Wishful thinking carried to its most destructive extreme is called enabling, which means doing what is needed to allow drug use to continue. On the surface, enabling does not appear to have much in common with ignoring, although they are indeed related.

Parents enable drug use by protecting their children from the consequences of their behavior. I counseled a wealthy family in which enabling had reached an unbelievable level before they sought help. When the son, Mark, started smoking pot, he began "ditching" school. His parents covered for him by writing notes to the teacher saying that he was ill. When Mark was caught burglarizing a home for drug money, his parents hired an expensive attorney to fight in juvenile court. The most amazing event occurred after Mark wrecked the family car while intoxicated—his parents bought him his own new car. By protecting Mark from the natural consequences of his behavior, they allowed him to keep on doing what he was doing. The drug problem got worse.

Enabling is similar to ignoring in its basic premise: "Just leave the child alone. He or she will do fine." But in addition, enabling parents clean up the messes of their children. They make excuses for them, sparing them the pain of consequences but not helping them become more responsible. This allows the drug use to continue.

In this day and age, when drugs are readily available, you cannot look away from reality. You cannot afford to ignore or minimize the dangers. Children need help and leadership. Parents who ignore or deny problems cannot possibly provide either.

THE AUTHORITARIAN APPROACH

Because solving the problem of drug abuse requires strong action, some parents attempt to dictate the behavior of their children. They rely on parental authority: "I'm the parent and I'll tell you what to do. I'm going to lay down the law under my roof." They impose strict rules. Children are expected to do as they are told, to behave as directed or else face serious consequences. Punishment or fear of punishment is supposed to keep children in line, to control their behavior. With the authoritarian approach, the emphasis is on obedience. It's not necessary that children understand the reasons for rules or that they participate in establishing them. All that matters is that they comply.

"Be home by ten," an authoritarian parent says to his daughter as she leaves for a friend's house on Saturday night.

"Why?" the fifteen-year-old girl asks.

"Because I said so," her father replies.

"But can you explain why it's important?"

"I don't have to explain anything to you," he says. "I'm the parent, and if you keep hounding me with questions, I won't let you go at all."

Authoritarian parents consider requests for an explanation to be an affront to their authority and feel no obligation to justify or even explain their position.

Authoritarianism is a powerful response to a serious problem. It has special appeal to panicked parents who recognize the dangers of drug abuse and want to take immediate and strong action.

Unfortunately, it is ineffective. Worse still, it often leads to the opposite of the desired effect—to a decline in parental influence. Authoritarian parents lose their ability to influence their children through reasoned discussion. This is a great loss, because teenagers are consumed with the task of forming their own independent identity, and they need the support of people they trust. If the family climate is one in which dialogue is seen as a threat to authority, they will be too scared to discuss what they think.

Because they are scared of their parents, teenagers will have to make difficult decisions, such as whether to use drugs, without the benefit of an open family discussion. They know that their parents would not support them in thinking through their *own* decisions but instead would lay down the law.

It could be argued that the loss of independent thinking by teenagers is a small price to pay for clear directives about appropriate behavior. In other words, teenagers will do as they are told without explanation and eventually understand the reasoning behind the directives.

This sounds good on paper. But in real life, when teenagers are struggling—as they should—to form independent identities, the typical response to authoritarian parents is rebellion. Younger children may jump into line when commanded to do something by their parents, but teenagers will not.

I was counseling a family with a fifteen-year-old son, Steve. When the mother mentioned that she had heard that some of Steve's friends were using drugs, the father turned red in the face, jabbed a finger toward his son, and issued an ultimatum: "If I ever find out that you've smoked pot, you'll be kicked out of the house for good. Mark my words."

Unfazed, Steve replied with a smirk on his face, "Don't worry, Dad. *You'll* never find out."

These are moves in the "Scare, Catch, and Punish" game played by authoritarian parents and their rebellious teenagers. It's an escalating power struggle involving strict rules, defiance, and harsh consequences. Parents impose strict rules that teenagers defy. Parents punish their children and see defiance as an indication of the need for stricter rules. Stricter rules lead to even more defiance and ultimately even more punishment. The result is angry and fearful parents pitted against their angry and fearful teenagers.

An unfortunate outcome of this power struggle is that at a certain point, when the stakes are high and the punishment is severe, the enraged teenagers finally pull the ultimate power play: "I don't care how you punish me. You can't control me. Take away whatever you want. Lock me up. Kick me out of the house. It doesn't matter. I'm still gonna do drugs and whatever else I want to do. I'll steal money and run away from home if I need to."

At this point the teenagers are out of control and the parents have lost all influence. On the surface, the teenagers look like rotten kids. But if you examine the interaction, their defiance can be seen as the predictable climax after a series of moves in the game of Scare, Catch, and Punish.

The authoritarian approach doesn't always lead to open rebellion. Sometimes the response is sneaky deception. At a workshop I conducted for professionals, a juvenile-court probation officer talked about his work with a troubled youngster, Tom, and his authoritarian father. With remorse and uncharacteristic tears in his eyes, Frank, the father, had described his son's secretive rebellion to the officer. It was a story about deception. Frank laid down the rules, very strict ones. Tom said he would obey. For several years Frank boasted about how well his son behaved and advised all his friends to get tough with their kids. "You gotta play hardball" were his exact words. He pointed to his son's behavior to demonstrate the truth of his pronouncement. Secretly, however, his son broke all the rules. Frank learned the truth about what had been happening for the past four years of his son's life only from the juvenile court after the boy was picked up for burglary. By that time, Tom had a serious drug problem.

It's not pure folly that makes the authoritarian approach so widely practiced. Authoritarian parents recognize the drug problem and the need for high standards. The problem is not the standards but the process by which they are established, one that deprives children of understanding and self-respect. Authoritarian parents attempt to *control* the behavior of their teenage children when they should be helping them learn to think and make their own decisions. Limits are important, but children need to have room within the limits to make

20

some choices. They need an opportunity to explore and think for themselves, and to talk with adults who listen.

Recent studies have shown that parents who rely heavily on obedience, even when motivated by the best of intentions, actually harm their children. One study found that the ability to reason is impaired by parents who believe that children learn best when they "just listen to what they are told" and obey whomever is in authority. This approach to child rearing squelches curiosity and stunts a child's ability to think. Children in such families are distractable and uncreative, have little intellectual curiosity, and do poorly on tests of basic intellectual skills.[3]

PARENTAL PITFALL: OVERPROTECTION

Another response to the drug problem, somewhat related to the authoritarian approach, is parental overprotection. Overprotective parents shield their children from the harsh realities of the world. Like authoritarian parents, they attempt to control the lives of their children, but the method of control is different. Whereas authoritarian parents use rules and punishment to try to tame the "animal" energy of their children, overprotective parents present themselves as allies. They see the world as a threat, communicate this fearfulness to their children, and then rescue them from dealing with reality. These are the parents who, instead of helping their children understand difficult homework assignments, actually do the work for them.

The overprotected ten-year-old girl who goes to summer camp is frightened her first day and calls home to be rescued. Her parents drive about a hundred miles to pick her up that evening and take her home. She never learns coping skills.

Although most teenagers will eventually feel their oats and try to break free from the overprotective nest, the likelihood that parents will maintain control is greater with this method than the authoritarian one.

The big problems come later in life. When parents do all the thinking and decision-making, children never have an opportunity to think and make decisions for themselves. As young adults, they have to face the harsh realities of the world without any preparation. They lack experience and tend to panic in stressful situations.

A POSITIVE MODEL: EMPOWERMENT

In our drug-oriented society, children need the powerful support of their parents. However, too often ideas about power are limited to the cruder and more forceful manifestations, such as raised voices, threatening gestures, popping veins, and pounding fists. There is a better way. You can have a powerful influence over your children without going to these extremes. The alternative is cooperation. It is not exercising power over other people. It is sharing power.

Parents, by virtue of age, knowledge, experience, and material resources, have more power than their children. You can use this power to protect your children and at the same time to strengthen and empower them—that is, assist them in becoming stronger, smarter, and more competent in their own right. That's what we are talking about in this book. A helpful way to think about empowerment is in terms of a transfer of power, a concept that is important to bear in mind when working with your children to prevent drug problems.

TRANSFER OF POWER

Transfer of power refers to parents using their own power to help their children become strong individuals. This process is best understood by considering the entire span of child development, from birth, when an infant is totally dependent, to approximately age eighteen (the age varies in different cultural groups), when the goal is to have helped the child become an independent young adult.

The parental role is most clear at the extremes of the continuum. With infants, parents have total responsibility. With young adults, parents recognize the need to allow their children to make their own decisions and to take responsibility for their own lives. Parents are available for support.

In between the extremes, the parental role is more difficult to define. Parents continually assess the readiness of their children to assume responsibility. As children grow older, parents gradually relinquish control. It is a transfer of power, with children gaining ever more freedom, responsibility, and decision-making opportunities. Parents provide guidance and support to their children, and expect increasingly responsible behavior. It is a philosophy of trust. Children will make mistakes, but that's part of the learning process. Parents help their children learn from their mistakes. In this process, children are empowered to become wiser, more responsible, and more mature.

The same continuum applies to decision-making about drugs. Parents forbid their young children to use drugs. Gradually, over many years, parents stop trying to control their children's behavior. By the time the children become young adults, they need to be making their own wise decisions.

Even babies need respect and a measure of independence. For example, they should be given an opportunity to fall asleep alone or to struggle to reach a toy. Parents who believe that their babies can't be happy without Mom and Dad in their presence deprive their infants of the opportunity to form relationships with friends, babysitters, and other relatives.

As children begin to understand language, parental decisions should be explained. Young children are given options and allowed to make some choices. Older children are allowed to make increasingly important decisions on their own and are consulted about other ones.

At a certain age, a child is allowed to cross the street at a major intersection, to have a say about bedtime, to receive an allowance, to take public transportation, to date, and to drive the family car. At a certain age an allowance is given, a child is allowed to take public transportation. No formula clearly states when to give these responsibilities. Variations occur because of the unique individual involved and the particular set of circumstances.

One important difficulty for parents in managing a successful transfer of power is that the process itself is uneven. In particular, the child's demand for freedom and his or her ability to cope with it accelerate greatly during the teenage years. Suddenly, many young adolescents seek independence and a significant role in making decisions that affect their own lives. The challenge for parents is to respect the drive for independence by providing learning opportunities, yet to maintain legitimate limits.

This challenge is complicated by parental fear. A child's need for freedom increases greatly during adolescence, at the same time as interest in sex increases and drugs become available. Out of fear, many parents clamp down and start setting tighter restrictions on their children. This is developmentally inappropriate. Children need experience with freedom, supported by adult supervision. Empowering children through the transfer of power is a delicate process in which parents challenge their children, but with challenges that are appropriate.

In the previous section, it was pointed out that many parents try to protect their children from drugs but go overboard and overprotect. Similarly, some parents overprotect their daughters from boys. Consider the example of a girl who was not allowed to date. When she left home at age eighteen, unprepared for the social pressures that lay ahead, someone likened it to "throwing her to the wolves."

Rather than saving this girl from teenage males with overactive hormones, it would have been far better if her parents had empowered her, giving her freedom, responsibility, and support. This would have meant allowing her to go on dates with a curfew as a teenager and providing her with an opportunity to discuss the different situations that arose. She would have learned from her parents' guidance and supervision. Gradually the curfew could have been extended, and less discussion would have been necessary. By the time she became a young woman, she would have been ready to handle romantic relationships on her own.

An entirely different set of problems is created by the other extreme of child-rearing, permissiveness, in which excessive freedom is given without adequate controls or support, or at a level that a child cannot yet handle. Under these circumstances, children fail and feel bad about themselves.

An extremely harmful form of permissiveness occurs when children are raised without sufficient discipline and control. The children are too free. They do whatever they want. Misbehavior such as temper tantrums and rude and aggressive behavior is tolerated. It is tolerated because parents underestimate their children and set low expectations, or because they want to be "nice" to them, or because they have given up on controlling them. Permissiveness *always* backfires. Children raised permissively do not learn self-control and eventually get out-of-control. They are especially vulnerable to getting out-of-control with their drug use.

Permissiveness is sometimes a parenting style that needs to be corrected and is sometimes merely a result of miscalculation. I know a mother and father who decided to let their ten-year-old daughter pick her own bedtime. To their dismay, every night she watched "The Tonight Show." It put her in a good humor before bed but left her tired and grouchy in the morning. The parents hoped she would realize what was happening and go to sleep earlier, but she kept her late bedtime for almost three weeks. Finally, the parents realized they had given the girl freedom that she was not yet ready to handle. Fortunately, they had the presence of mind to take responsibility for the error so that the girl didn't blame herself for failing. They explained their mistake to their daughter and selected a reasonable bedtime. The girl was relieved when they took back control.

As you will see in the following chapters, preventing drug abuse is part of the transfer of power whereby you teach your children important life skills and positive attitudes so that they can make wise decisions on their own.

ROLE MODELS

I remember being six years old and standing next to my father at the sink. He would lather up his shaving cream, and I would do the same. Then he would start shaving, and I would rub my face with a plastic razor. At the end, he applied witch hazel to his face and to mine. It is a very fond memory. Aside from enjoying the company of my dad, I also was learning what men do from my role model and teacher.

All children learn the same way I did. We watch what our parents do and then copy it. Even now, more than forty years later, I still shave with a safety razor—the way my father taught me—although long ago he switched to an electric one.

Because parents teach by example, their drug-taking behavior will certainly influence their children's.

When Mom is grouchy and says, "I can't get up in the morning without my cup of coffee," the children take notice. When she savors a cigarette after dinner, they notice that, too.

When Dad has a drink to "chill out" after work, the kids see it happen. They watch what he drinks, why he drinks, how much he drinks, and how he behaves afterward.

When parents reach for medications at the slightest hint of illness and don't even read the labels, children get a message.

When parents drink alcohol or smoke marijuana to self-medicate against stress, children notice. And they notice when parents take Valium, Prozac, or whatever the miracle drug *du jour* happens to be. This isn't to say that you should never have a beer or glass of wine. In fact, children raised in families practicing moderation have less drug abuse than those raised in abstinent families. The most important issue is to think of the examples we set and to avoid substance *abuse*.

It's not just drug-taking behavior that parents teach by example. Children notice how parents have fun, how they deal with stress, how they cope with problems. Children notice how parents deal with peer pressure.

In drug-prevention workshops and books, these harsh realities are sometimes sanctimoniously brought to the attention of parents, who then believe that they have to be saints to save their children. I have heard speakers say, "How do you expect to help your kids if you yourself . . . ?"

Because most of us are not saints, many parents feel guilty and worry that one false move will ruin the lives of their children. Although expecting perfection is unfair and unrealistic, there is no escaping the reality that children learn by observing their parents. And if you want to do a good job of helping your children steer clear of drug abuse, you will want to set a good example.

As you read the next chapter, think about your own drug use.

If you or your spouse has problems with drugs, it will be important for you to make personal changes, for yourself and for your children.

What Do You Tell Your Children About Your Own Past?

Let's assume you are raising open-minded, bright, inquisitive children. Let's say you have honest communication in your family. One day your child, whom you have told, "Drugs are not for children," asks if you ever smoked marijuana. Many parents who have smoked marijuana or used other drugs are confused about what to do. They have two concerns. One is maintaining honesty and openness. The other is not wanting to appear hypocritical.

For the parents of young children, I urge great caution. Be aware that your children may have seen scary public-service announcements on television about drug dangers or attended drug-prevention programs in school. They may be very frightened by the truth of your drug use and too immature to understand any explanations you attach to your story. In my view, they should be protected from this reality when they are young. With older, more mature children you may want to discuss your own experiences, assuming you have resolved any problems you had with drugs. If you are currently abusing drugs, you certainly will lose credibility.

"Do As I Say, Not As I Did"

Parents who themselves smoked pot or used other drugs often fear being accused of hypocrisy. Their children may ask, "If you did it, why can't I?" Is it hypocritical for a parent to say, "I did it, but don't you do it"?

My answer is that you, as parents, must stick to your guns. Whatever you may or may not have done in your life does not change your primary responsibility, which is to help your children make wise choices. Drugs are a health risk, especially for children. The message to children should remain the same.

You should not defend your stance against drug use by children on the basis of your own experiences. You should defend it on the basis of its own merit. If, however, you have an open exchange about your own drug use with mature adolescents, you should be prepared to discuss why you want your children to behave differently from the way you did. You might point out important differences between the current era and earlier generations. In particular, I would note these three points: (1) Due to the way it has been cultivated over the years, marijuana has become a much stronger drug than it was in the sixties, seventies, and eighties. (2) Children are using drugs now at a younger age than in previous generations. Much of the experimentation in the sixties was not initiated until the college years. (3) More kinds of dangerous drugs are available at an earlier age.

POSITIVE ATTITUDES AND LIFE SKILLS

As you read the following chapters about the positive attitudes and life skills that strengthen children and prevent drug abuse, think of where you stand with these attitudes and skills. It will be an opportunity to consider such issues as how you cope with stress; how you find outlets for good times, excitement, and recreation; and how you respond to peer pressure.

Remember, you are living in a drug-filled and sometimes troubled world, just as your children are. You're not immune to the same problems and pressures that affect them. You need the same life skills they do and may discover some deficiencies of your own.

Many people have the ability to love others but have trouble giving that same love and concern to themselves. Maybe it takes reading a book for your children's sake to stumble upon areas of personal concern that can make your own life better. If that is so, then consider it a gift from your children. Helping them grow to be strong and competent people is an opportunity for you to grow, too.

As you read on, remember that the threat of drug abuse is no match for the power of parental love and education. You can take action to prevent drug problems in your children before they occur and to solve them if they already exist.

2
DRUGS AND THEIR USE, ABUSE, AND DEPENDENCE

Sometimes I begin a lecture or workshop with a riddle. I tell the audience that a common definition of a drug is "any substance that in small amounts produces significant changes in the body, mind, or both."[1] Then I say I'm thinking of a particular substance, a powdery white one, that can produce significant changes in the mind and body.

"What substance is it?" I ask.

"Cocaine," someone says.

"Good guess, but that's not what I'm thinking about."

"Heroin," someone else says.

"Another good guess, but sorry, that's not what I'm thinking about."

Usually, by now an audience member guesses right, but if not, I give the answer anyway: sugar.

They get my point that it is sometimes difficult to distinguish between food and drugs. Then I ask if anyone in the audience is a chocoholic. Those who regularly seek a chocolate "fix" probably have a vague understanding of addiction, although most of them don't realize that chocolate contains caffeine, an addictive drug, and also another chemical closely related to caffeine.

"What about coffee?" I ask. "Is it a drug?"

To further complicate matters, I suggest they consider the classification of alcohol. What is it? The body burns it as a fuel. In that sense it's a food. In another sense, because people use it to get high, we think of it as a drug. But in very large amounts, alcohol is a toxin. It is poisonous.[2]

What I'm trying to do in these lectures is to promote open-mindedness in thinking about drugs. The topic is so emotional and political that people tend to get locked into rigid thinking. They have opinions, usually strong ones. But they confuse opinion with fact. Usually they are overcommitted to their opinions and underinformed about drugs.

Even when people start with identical information, they can reach entirely different conclusions. This happens often in everyday life—the topic doesn't have to be drugs. Consider a husband and wife who have been married for sixteen years. They each know their income, their expenses, and how much money they have in the bank. They agree on the facts. But she wants to go to Europe with their savings, and he wants to spend the money on practical household repairs such as a new roof. He wants something tangible that will last a long time. She says they will have a lifetime of memories from their trip abroad, and they can leave a bucket under the leak. It's all a matter of how they choose to interpret the facts about their financial situation. It's a matter of what is important to them. The same is true in drug discussions. Facts are only part of what people consider in forming their opinions.

This chapter will prepare you for discussing drugs with your children. It gives an overview of how drugs, in general, affect the body. It gives additional information about the specific drugs most often used by children. Also discussed are the stages of drug use—from experimental to dependent—and the signs and symptoms of a drug problem.

But before getting to the facts, let's look some more at people's opinions. Below is an exercise that will help you clarify your own thoughts about drug use, abuse, and dependence.

GOOD DRUGS AND BAD DRUGS

People make their judgments about drug use, abuse, and dependence on the basis of facts and interpretations of facts that are strongly influenced by values. What is acceptable to one person may not be acceptable to another.

Opinions about drugs vary in different cultures and in different historical eras. Early Muslim sects used coffee in religious rites but had prohibitions against alcohol. It was the opposite in Europe. When coffee was first imported in the seventeenth century, the Roman Catholic Church opposed it as an evil drug. Yet wine was used as a traditional sacrament in Catholic masses.[3]

Attitudes about drugs change over time within a given culture. When tobacco was introduced into Europe, it provoked such strong opposition that the authorities in some countries sought to impose the death penalty for its use. Soon tobacco use was widely accepted and even encouraged, in the belief that it made people work more efficiently.[4]

In this country, alcohol has a checkered history. Early Americans were exceedingly heavy drinkers, which led, in the second half of the nineteenth century, to an active Temperance Movement. The movement succeeded first in persuading some local governments to ban alcohol, and eventually achieved the passage of the Eighteenth Amendment. This allowed Congress to institute Prohibition in 1920, under which the sale and manufacture of alcohol became a federal crime. Prohibition was repealed by the passage of the Twenty-First Amendment thirteen years later, returning control of alcohol to the state and local governments where it remains today. While it may be legal, alcohol probably brings more distress to more people than any other substance.

Within homogeneous groups, such as a nation or a religion or an ethnic group, there tends to be more agreement on attitudes than there is *between* different groups. Those in the same age group are usually more in agreement with each other than with the overall population, creating what has sometimes been called a "generation gap."

But even among similar people—all teenagers, all parents, all Christians, all Jews, all school administrators, all teachers—there are great variations about what is considered good and bad. Within a single country, various groups may have different opinions about particular drugs. This is evident in the United States with marijuana. Although many people strongly condemn its use, others use it freely and believe it should be legalized.

Different judgments about drugs are well demonstrated in an exercise I sometimes conduct in workshops, called "Use, Abuse, and Dependence." It challenges people to clarify their own opinions. It helps them see that other people have different ideas. It also helps them learn to differentiate facts from opinions. You can do this exercise at home as you read this book.

As you read about the drug situations described below, ask yourself whether the drug use described constitutes use, abuse, or dependence. In workshops, after describing a drug situation, I ask for a show of hands. Invariably, opinion will be divided among the three options. After the vote is in, I ask for an explanation. Why is it an example of drug use? Why abuse? Why dependence?

Let's start with an example involving a hardworking man who comes home from the office and has two cocktails every night after work. If his wife is there, they drink together. If not, he drinks alone. He says it relaxes him. He enjoys the feeling. Is this use, abuse, or dependence? Think about it yourself and then read some of the responses from workshop participants below. First, what is your opinion?

Now here's what other people have said:

"I'd say it's use, because he uses it to relax."

"In my opinion, it's abuse, because there are better ways to relax than by using booze."

"I disagree. I think it's dependence, because it sounds like he needs it. He does it every day after work and even does it alone."

"Yeah, but nobody is hurt by it. He's at home. He doesn't drive drunk. I'd say it's use."

"But it's not good for his liver. I'd say it's abuse."

"Wait a minute. Some medical studies say it's good to drink in moderation in order to relax. I'd say it's use."

"But there are better ways to unwind. In my opinion, it's abuse, because it's a habit. He can't go without it."

How about this example? A woman wakes up cranky every morning. She uses a coffee maker with a timer that turns on automatically before she even wakes up. Her family steers clear of her until she has had her two cups. Is this use, abuse, or dependence? What's your opinion?

Here is what other people have said:

"I'd call it dependence, because she has to have it every day."

"It's use, because it's only two cups. It's kind of a nice luxury."

"I agree. Some of us drink coffee at the office. Others drink it at home."

"It sounds like abuse to me. She's probably not addicted, because she could stop. But she uses it to wake up every day."

"I say it's dependence, because she's cranky unless she has the caffeine. Her mornings sound like they focus on coffee. Therefore, she's dependent on it."

How about the twenty-year-old college student who smokes marijuana occasionally on weekends? He enjoys himself, never gets into trouble, and behaves quite well when under the influence.

"It's abuse, because marijuana is illegal."

"It's illegal to speed on the highway, and people do it all the time. I don't see that as abuse. I'd say that in this situation it's drug use, because it doesn't harm anyone. It just helps him relax. If he harmed someone, I'd call it abuse."

"It's just for fun. I'd call it use. It's not any worse than drinking a beer."

"I'd say it's abuse, because it's bad for his body, especially his lungs."

"It's abuse, because it keeps him from finding drug-free ways of enjoying his weekend."

One of my favorite vignettes in the "Use, Abuse, and Dependence" exercise is the example of a woman whose physician knows her well and has essentially given her an open-ended prescription for Valium. He has told her to take the medication only when she is under a great deal of stress and not at other times. She has held to the agreement and has used the medication on only three occasions during a full year.

Most audience members call it use, but a few will disagree.

"I think it's abuse. Anytime you use drugs to deal with problems you are abusing them."

"I think it's abuse, too. Taking tranquilizers only masks feelings. I think the woman should feel her feelings and learn to deal with reality. She could learn to tolerate stress or how to change her situation so that she feels better."

"I agree. It's abuse. She could learn yoga or find some other way to relax."

These opinions inevitably bring out some people who believe that the doctor can do no wrong:

"It's just use. The doctor prescribed it. She takes the pills only when she's under severe stress—only three times. It's not like she's hooked on them."

Then I start teasing: "What if she takes Valium five times per year? Seven times? Fifteen? Twenty? Forty? Sixty? Where do you draw the line?"

Here's a wild one to think about. What would you call it when a sixty-three-year-old woman tries cocaine once, and only once. Her granddaughter thought she was "cool" and gave it to her. The older woman hardly felt the effects at all. She said it was maybe like drinking one martini.

"I'd say it's use, because she is just trying it once—no big deal."

"I'd say it's abuse, because by trying it she is approving of what her granddaughter is doing."

"It's abuse, because it's a dangerous drug."

"But no one was harmed."

"Maybe she *was* harmed. Drugs are more dangerous with old people."

How about the person who smokes a pack of cigarettes every day, enjoys it, and has no desire to quit?

How about the parent who smokes marijuana infrequently for recreation and lets a teenage son try it once at home?

How about the thirteen-year-old who sneaks one beer with a friend?

The differences that emerge in the "Use, Abuse, and Dependence" exercise make it abundantly clear that people can arrive at different conclusions about drug situations. And so I sometimes tease an audience of adults: "If you can't agree with each other, how do you think you'll ever be able to agree with your children?" Then I get serious and talk about how important it is for husbands and wives to discuss their values with each other and to reach a common understanding so that they are not giving their children mixed and confusing messages.

Some of the biggest differences I have observed when doing this exercise occur with groups who include both parents and teenagers. Parents are often very adamant about the drugs they fear their children might be using, especially marijuana, LSD (acid), cocaine, and amphetamines (speed). And children come down harder on alcohol, typically their parents' drug of choice. As baby-boomers have aged, there is increased tolerance of marijuana by parents. This exercise helps the different generations understand each other's point of view better.

The more you and your spouse think through your own opinions about drugs, the better-prepared you will be to address the topic with your children. With teenagers in particular, with whom discussion and dialogue are the main instrument of parental influence, you will want to be informed with facts, and clear about your opinions— what they are and how you formed them. Your ability to reach conclusions about drug use, through systematic analysis, will serve as a good example for your children.

In forming opinions, most of the factual information falls into several main categories, listed and described below. These categories give reasons for opinions and a basis for comparing differences of opinion. Too often we have opinions because we *know* they are right, but can't discuss the reasons in an articulate manner. By using the categories described below, you can demonstrate good reasoning to your children while also giving them a framework for systematically thinking about drugs.

EVALUATING USE, ABUSE, AND DEPENDENCE

Below are nine categories for evaluating drug consumption: drug pharmacology; legality; quantity, frequency, and length of use; changes in patterns of use; methods of ingestion; setting; personality, age, and health of user; reasons used; and effects of use.

Drug Pharmacology

The *pharmacology* of the drug itself has a bearing upon opinions about use, abuse, and dependence. Important considerations include:

- Does the drug create dependence? How easily?
- What is the potency of the drug?
- How does the drug affect the body? The mind? A person's health? A person's behavior? With small doses? With large doses? With prolonged use?
- What drugs are being combined? Some drugs combine in a synergistic way, meaning that the total effect of a combination is stronger than adding the effects of each drug taken independently. In other words, $1 + 1 = 3$. A good example is Valium and alcohol. When they are combined, the potency of the two is far greater than might be expected if they were combined linearly, $1 + 1 = 2$. Other problems include dangerous, unwanted effects that could arise from combining "street drugs" with prescription medication.

You don't need to be an expert in pharmacology to talk about drugs with your children. On the other hand, it is important to be informed. Later in this chapter you will find basic information about specific categories of drugs

Legality

Legality is an issue when evaluating drug use, abuse, and dependence. The possession or sale of some drugs, but not others, is legal.

Legality also has a bearing on other considerations in drug use.

For example: How accessible is the drug? What does it cost to procure it? Illegal drugs are sold at inflated prices. Heroin is a good example. When the opiates, of which heroin is one, were made illegal in 1914 under the Harrison Narcotics Act, the cost of the drug greatly increased. In order to support an expensive habit, most users of this substance had to commit crimes and engage in a criminal lifestyle.

Legality also has a major bearing on purity and potency. When drugs are manufactured in clandestine laboratories or acquired through underground channels, the consumer has no way to evaluate the product. Most drug dealers "cut" their drugs—they adulterate them in order to gain greater profit from sales. Because the consumer cannot reliably estimate the potency or judge the chemical composition of street drugs, there is an increased risk of overdoses and "bad trips."

Quantity, Frequency, and Length of Use

How much of a drug is used? Is it one beer? One six-pack? One case? Is it one gram of cocaine? Several grams?

Body weight is a factor in evaluating the amount of a drug dose, as is age. Children and elderly people are more sensitive to drugs and will have more pronounced responses.

How often is a drug used? What is the interval between doses? One case of beer over a week? A six-pack every night? Smoking marijuana once in the evening? Smoking all day long? Using amphetamines (speed) for several days without stopping?

Another consideration: What is the *length* of use? Has the person been smoking cigarettes for a month, a year, ten years, or more? Is the use experimental? Is it habitual? (You will find more on how to evaluate this when we discuss the stages of drug use later in this chapter.)

Changes in Patterns of Use

Has the pattern changed? Is the quantity increasing? Is the frequency increasing? Is it remaining the same? Increase in quantity and frequency could indicate that *tolerance* has developed—that more is needed to create the same effect. Increase in frequency could indicate the development of dependence and an effort to avoid a *withdrawal syndrome*—the body's negative reaction to not having the drug. Change isn't necessarily negative. A person might be using drugs more often without necessarily suffering any adverse effects.

Methods of Ingestion

How is the drug administered? Is it inhaled through the nose (huffed), smoked, sniffed through the nose (snorted), injected under the skin? Does one eat it? Drink it?

Drugs that are swallowed tend to be slower-acting, whereas injected drugs enter the bloodstream immediately. The same drug can have very different effects, depending, in part, on how it enters the body. For example, the effects of cocaine are influenced by the method of administration—whether it is snorted, injected, or smoked.

Illegally injected drugs may involve the use of contaminated needles, which carry the considerable risk of spreading hepatitis, the HIV virus, and other infectious diseases.

Setting

One very important consideration in evaluating drug use, abuse, and dependence is the *setting*—the physical and social environment. Use that may cause problems in one setting—let's say drinking beer at work—may be entirely acceptable in another, such as at a ball game. The critical questions are:

Where is the drug used? At home? At work? While driving? At school?

When is the drug taken? First thing in the morning? At school? After work? At work? Before going to bed? On weekends?

With whom is the drug taken? With colleagues at work? With fellow students? Alone? With a spouse?

Personality, Age, and Health of User

Drugs affect people differently. Their effects are related to the psychological state of the individual and to what he or she wants the drug to do and expects it to do. This is sometimes referred to as the "psychological set"—the way in which an individual's mind is set to respond to the effects of the chemical. If there is anxiety associated with use, it is possible that a drug will create panic or that the pharmacological effects will be muted. Attitudes play a part in determining drug effects.

A single cocktail can make one person funny and charming, another bitter and angry, a third one sleepy, and a fourth one sad.

What you expect from a drug can influence its impact. In a classic experiment, subjects were told that they were drinking alcohol but were actually given a placebo (an inactive substance). After consuming the beverage, they behaved as if they were under the influence of alcohol. Their expectations, not the drink itself, influenced their behavior.[5]

In evaluating drug use, health problems should also be considered. Certain chemicals interact negatively with existing health problems, such as alcohol drunk by a person with a liver problem.

Reasons Used

Why is the drug used? People use drugs for medical reasons, to have fun, to avoid boredom, to relax, to cope with stress, to fall asleep, to escape reality, to suppress feelings, to release feelings, to generate extra energy, to create excitement, to satisfy curiosity, to defy authority, to be accepted by a particular social group, to alter consciousness, and for many other reasons as well.

Most drugs can have varied uses. For example, alcohol is used for almost all the reasons listed above. Codeine can be used medically as a painkiller or recreationally to get high.

In evaluating drug use, one consideration is whether a drug is the *only* way a person has to satisfy a particular need. If this is so, there is a greater risk of becoming dependent on the drug to meet that need. In this regard, the age of the user is important, too. At certain ages people have particular developmental tasks. For example, teenagers are learning about romantic relationships in preparation for adult loving relationships. If they cope with the anxiety of dating by getting high all the time, they will not succeed in maturing properly. They will become chronological adults but remain emotional adolescents.

Effects of Use

The immediate *effects* of a drug depend upon a variety of factors, such as the amount taken, the psychological set, the setting, the individual's biochemistry, the individual's level of tolerance and physical dependence, and the way the drug enters the body.

The relevant questions are: How is a person's physical and emotional health affected by the use of the drug? How does the person behave under the influence of the drug? Does he or she engage in dangerous or high risk behaviors, such as driving under the influence of drugs, or participation in high risk sexual behavior?

For evaluating the effects of drug use over an extended period of time, the important questions about consequences are: How has a person's life been affected? Have there been positive effects? Have there been adverse effects? Has drug use caused problems at work? Behavior problems at school? Grade and achievement problems? Has it caused conflict in relationships with friends? With family?

Has drug use become the only way, or one of many ways, to avoid boredom? To deal with depression? To have fun? To deal with stress? Has it given a person more energy at times when it is needed? Has it depleted energy? Has it caused health problems? Financial problems? Legal problems? What will the effects be if use continues at the same level? What if use increases?

Is the user *aware* of how the drug is affecting him or her?

Drug Use, Abuse, and Dependence

What, then, constitutes drug use, abuse, and dependence?

Drug use generally refers to the use of substances without substantial harm or risk. It usually would include an "experimental" drug user, who is just "trying" drugs to see what they are like, and a "light" user, who does not engage in high-risk behavior while under the influence. It should be pointed out, however, that even light or experimental drug users could cause harm to themselves or others—for example, causing an automobile crash while under the influence. Also, the use of some drugs is illegal, therefore involving legal risks.

Drug abuse is generally considered to be using drugs in harmful or potentially harmful ways. You can think about it in terms of health—whether drugs have damaged, or could damage, the body or mind, or have interfered with personal growth, development, and fulfillment. Harm could be caused by a single use of drugs—for example, causing an automobile crash while driving under the influence, or combining drugs dangerously, or overdosing on drugs. Harm could result from ongoing use, such as long-term health consequences. A pamphlet published by the National Institute on Drug Abuse uses this definition: "Drug abuse is the use of a drug for other than medicinal purposes which results in the impaired physical, mental, emotional, or social well-being of the user."[6]

Sometimes drug abuse in adolescents is best understood by what does *not* happen that should be happening. Adolescents should be preparing for the future and learning about life. But, while getting high, many of them do not do such things as: go to school and prepare for a career; learn to feel comfortable with male and female friends without being high; learn to solve problems; learn to cope with stress; learn to cope with pain, anger, and other strong feelings; learn to have fun and excitement without drugs; figure out what they believe in and where they want to go in life.

Another consideration is whether drug use conflicts with community-accepted standards of behavior. Clearly, judgments such as these depend upon personal values. Some say that if a drug is illegal, then consuming it is abusive. Some say that legality is irrelevant—that drug use is a personal choice, and our society's laws are not necessarily rational.

Drug dependence is a step beyond drug abuse. It is said to occur when a person needs a drug. His or her life centers on drugs. The individual is either using drugs or thinking about attaining and using them most of the time.

Whether a particular incident or pattern of drug consumption constitutes use, abuse, or dependence is to some extent subjective. People can interpret the same events differently. However, we can at least provide a framework for reasonable discussion by considering the nine categories for evaluating drug consumption in the previous section and the general descriptions of use, abuse, and dependence stated above.

ADDICTION, TOLERANCE, AND DEPENDENCE

The concept of addiction is a controversial one. In Roman law, to be addicted meant to be bound over or delivered to someone by a judicial sentence. It meant a form of legal slavery. For instance, a prisoner of war would be bound over to a member of the Roman elite. In sixteenth-century England, the meaning was the same. It was said that a serf was addicted, or bound over, to a landowner. But a new use of the term later emerged. Previously a legal term, it came to be used more loosely to describe any form of bondage. For example, one could be addicted to a person, a vice, or tobacco. If you are a slave to something, then you are addicted to it.

The medical theory of addiction that developed over the years was much more narrow than the general use of the term. A drug was said to be addictive if it created both tolerance and a withdrawal syndrome.

Drug *tolerance* is a physical or behavioral condition that develops in users of certain drugs under certain conditions. It creates the need to increase the amount of drug taken in order to achieve the same effect. In other words, after using certain drugs for a while, the user must take larger amounts to achieve the same effect. The body is able to tolerate more without being affected. Some drugs are quicker than others to create tolerance.

The other component of the medical definition of addiction is that an addicted person will experience a physical reaction when drug use is discontinued, suffering from what is known as a *withdrawal syndrome*. The most common symptoms are vomiting, chills, nervousness, and muscle tremors. They may persist for a few days or a week. Only certain drugs, such as opiates (for example, morphine, codeine, and heroin), depressants (alcohol, minor tranquilizers, and barbiturates), and stimulants (tobacco, cocaine, and amphetamines) create a withdrawal syndrome. With some drugs (alcohol and barbiturates), under some conditions, withdrawal is dangerous, and reduction of doses should be gradual and medically supervised.

In recent years it has become clear that the narrow medical definition of addiction is too limiting. An individual can be a slave to a drug for psychological as well as physiological reasons. Anyway, with some drugs it is difficult to determine whether the addiction is physical or psychological in nature. Often both kinds of addiction occur together.

People psychologically *dependent* on a drug feel that the drug is necessary for their well-being and have a compulsion to seek and use it. Drug use becomes the center of their lives. Attempts to discontinue use lead to extreme anxiety or depression and can cause physical reactions such as insomnia, restlessness, headache, irritability, and appetite loss.

Because of the difficulty in distinguishing psychological and physiological reasons for the compulsive use of drugs, it makes sense to think of addiction in more general terms, encompassing both motives. To avoid confusion, some people now use a different term, *dependence*, to describe a person's psychological or physical need to have a drug.

Broadening the definition of addiction by using the concept of dependence helps avoid misunderstandings in which drug users say, "I have no problem with this drug—it's not physically addictive." Any drug has the potential to be abused, and many of them can cause dependence. Psychological dependence is no easier to avoid than physical dependence.

The distinction between physical and psychological dependence is important primarily in ensuring that the withdrawal process is handled safely. And with modern treatment, physical withdrawal can be handled with a minimum of discomfort and risk. The major task in overcoming any drug dependence is dealing with the psychological dependence—the perceived need for a drug.

THE DRUG-USE CONTINUUM

Most teenagers who use drugs do not develop lasting problems. But some do, and the problems can be devastating. One way to think about drugs is in terms of four stages, or levels, of use along a continuum. The first stage is experimental use; the second is seeking the mood swing; the third is harmful, regular use; and the fourth is dependence. Drug use can stop at any stage.

Many people experiment with drugs just to see what they are like. The majority stop at either stage one or two. Only a small percentage of drug users develop serious problems in important life areas—family, school/work, friends, the law, psychological/emotional health, personal finances, and physical well-being—and move on to stages three and four.

Most parents do not want their children using alcohol or other drugs. However, their response to drug use should be different according to the stage of use. With experimental use, they need to have an honest, open, and serious discussion. With dependence, they need to seek professional help.

If drug use is in stage one or two, most parents want it to stop.

However, they must at least do what they can to prevent the use from progressing into stages three and four.

Although most parents want their children to completely avoid drug use, delaying initiation can, at a minimum, provide some protection against harm. Statistics show that the earlier drug use begins, the greater the risk of eventual problems.[7] This makes sense. Young children have less maturity than older children and less experience with self-control.

Stage One: Experimental Use

Children in this stage are curious and want to try drugs to see their effects. They may be responding to peer pressure. They may try to obtain a drug or simply use it when it becomes available. Once their curiosity is satisfied, they may discontinue use, or take the drug when it becomes available again, or move to stage two and begin to seek the drug.

Stage Two: Seeking the Mood Swing

Aware of the effects of drugs on their moods, children at this level integrate drug use into their lives. More time, money, and forethought go into drug use. However, usage remains casual, mainly in social settings, and does not interfere with normal functioning on a daily basis. Individuals in this stage experience drugs as mostly positive. They feel good when under the influence. Adult "social drinkers" fall into this category.

Stage Three: Harmful, Regular Use

In this stage, children use drugs on a regular basis, sometimes to cope with problems of living. Daily functioning is affected. Responsibilities are neglected. School performance deteriorates. They may miss school, embarrass themselves in public, mistreat friends, and lie to cover their misbehavior. They may steal money to pay for drugs, get into trouble with the law, or begin to experience negative physical effects.

Many of these children spend their time with drug-using friends, often discarding old ones. A central focus of activity with these friends is acquiring and using drugs. These children may believe that they could stop using drugs, but generally they will discontinue use only for brief periods of time and then resume again with the first motivating event, whether it is stress or "a great party."

The guilt associated with the misbehavior in this stage will damage self-esteem, contributing to more stress and possibly leading to increased drug consumption.

Family members sometimes rescue their children during stage three. They take over responsibilities neglected by their drug-using children and lie to protect them in school or at work. This is called enabling, and it is harmful because it supports the continuation of drug abuse.

Stage Four: Dependence

This is the extreme of harmful use. Drugs dominate the lives of people in this stage. They feel compelled to use them. Drug use takes priority over many normal and necessary daily activities. The dependent person is isolated and alienated, feels very bad about himself or herself, and uses drugs to "medicate" against these feelings. Physical, psychological, and social functioning are severely impaired, although the physical consequences may not be as obvious in young people as in adults. The bodies of dependent people are accustomed to the drugs. Drug use at this point probably provides little or no pleasure because the substances are taken as an escape from discomfort or from the pain of withdrawal. Chances of staying in school or maintaining employment are marginal. An apathetic, secretive, and noncaring attitude prevails. Some dependent people realize that they have lost control. Others continue to insist that they could easily stop, although all the evidence indicates otherwise.

How to Tell Whether Your Child Is Using Drugs

Casual drug use by children in stage one or two will be very hard to recognize, unless they tell you about it. That is why open discussion is the key to preventing drug abuse. Recognizable signs of drug use come late in the chain of events, usually during stages three and four.

In order to know whether your children are using drugs, you need a baseline—you need to know their normal behavior. Then you can watch for substantial changes. Some of the changes may be normal and healthy. Some are problematic. Of the problematic changes, only some will be drug-related. Regardless of cause, if your child has experienced important negative changes, you will want to address them. They need your attention. Although you should avoid hasty conclusions, drug abuse could be the cause of seemingly unexplainable changes in your child.

Below is a list of the signs and symptoms that could indicate drug use or possibly other problems.

School

- increased truancy and tardiness to classes
- drop in grades
- behavior problems in school
- negative attitude about school

Social life/friends

- dropping out of old activities
- dropping old friends and making new friends who are drug users
- strange-sounding phone calls with covert communication about drugs

Emotional life

- basic personality changes—was outgoing, now withdrawn; was withdrawn, now outgoing; was relaxed, now fidgety
- incidents of inexplicable mood changes—euphoria followed by tenseness and edginess; excessive suspiciousness or paranoia
- caring less about everything—school, sports, other activities
- appearing listless and "hung over"
- increased forgetfulness

Family

- very secretive (do not confuse this with a need for privacy)

- estrangement from family
- less responsible at home
- more conflict at home

Physical effects

- red eyes
- deterioration in personal hygiene
- weight loss (for certain drugs)
- sleep disturbances
- fatigue or hyperactivity

Also, there are various types of *physical evidence* that suggest possible drug use:

- drug paraphernalia
- use of incense (possibly to cover the smell of marijuana)
- beer or liquor supply unaccountably diminished
- money or other valuables missing
- prescription drugs of family members disappearing
- items that can be inhaled disappearing (see page 60)

A note of caution: Some of what are called signs of drug use can be caused by a variety of reasons besides drugs. Some can possibly be normal teenage behavior.

I once had parents bring their daughter to my office, convinced that her bloodshot eyes were proof positive of drug use. The poor girl was suffering from allergies and wouldn't go near alcohol or any other drug.

Many changes that alarm parents may simply be part of normal adolescent development. Most teenagers begin to find new friends, spend less time with their families, and challenge adult values.

Behavior changes can be caused by problems unrelated to drug use—emotional, family, and relationship turmoil is quite common at this age. Any changes are, however, cause for consideration and worthy of your attention.

TYPES OF DRUGS

Sometimes it seems as though you would have to go to medical school for five years and then live around a school yard for another couple of years in order to begin to learn about all the drugs that are available. And you would need an incredible memory.

When I first entered the field of drug prevention and counseling I was overwhelmed by the dizzying array of names and nicknames for the drugs. But I've been in the field long enough now to say two things that you will probably find reassuring: (1) There is a sensible way to organize the multitude of drugs into categories, so that to be an informed person you don't have to know details about every single substance. Knowing the types of substances will give you a basic level of understanding of all drugs. The categories make logical sense and are therefore relatively easy to comprehend and remember. (2) You don't have to be all-knowing about drugs to be helpful to children. You just need to be informed and know where to look if you ever need more than a basic understanding. In the following section you will find plenty of information to begin working with your children to prevent drug abuse. Most of the pharmacological and historical information was gathered from sources 1, 8, and 9, listed in the references for this chapter. If you want or need more detailed information, you can refer to these sources or to a wide variety of other publications on the topic available in bookstores and libraries. Another option is to call the National Clearinghouse for Alcohol and Drug Information at 1-800-729-6686 which provides a wide array of free publications and other resources.

Most drugs that are abused fall into six basic categories: stimulants, depressants, narcotics, hallucinogens, cannabis, and inhalants. I have added anabolic steroids to the list because they have become another type of drug that is abused.

The easiest way to remember drugs is by the purpose for which they are taken.

Keep in mind that drugs are used to modify moods and behavior. Start with this assumption. We live in a busy, rushed society with many pressures and many stresses. In order to meet the demands of the society, people take certain drugs to speed themselves up. These are called *stimulants*.

One effect of living under stress is that it creates tension and anxiety. To relieve these feelings, people take drugs that slow them down and also help them forget their troubles. These are called *depressants*. In slowing people down, one of the first actions of these drugs is to slow the part of the brain that controls inhibitions. So another effect of depressants, in low doses, is to help people relax, "get loose," and have fun.

Another category of drugs that slows people down is called *narcotics*. These potent drugs are opiates. That is, they are made either from the opium poppy or are synthetic derivatives. Because of their potency and the dangers associated with them, until recently they have not been widely used by children.

Another effect of living in our high-pressure society is that many people focus so much on success and "making it" that their fantasy lives and imaginations are shut down. It makes sense that they would want a drug that radically alters their perceptions and imagination, or, in the lingo of the recent past, "blows their minds." These are the *hallucinogens*.

Cannabis, of which marijuana is the major derivative, is in a category of its own. Sometimes its effects resemble those of a stimulant and sometimes those of a depressant. Like a hallucinogen, it can also alter perceptions. Because of its wide range of activity, it is a popular drug.

Inhalants are not widely discussed by adults, but they are important drugs for you, as parents, to know about. These are volatile substances—that is, substances that become or emit a gas at room temperature, such as glue, gasoline, paint, and nitrous oxide. Children sniff (huff) these drugs for the effect of being light-headed or drunk. Inhalants are very dangerous. They are also the easiest drugs for young children to obtain and therefore "the drug of choice" for many in this age group.

Returning to the theme of a hurried and competitive society, we see that intense competitiveness has entered the sports world. Therefore we have drugs known as *anabolic steroids*. Although hazardous to the health of athletes, they are frequently used because they give a competitive edge. They are starting to be used by young children.

So there you are: a simple way to remember drug types. Those that speed you up (stimulants); those that slow you down and loosen inhibitions (depressants and narcotics); those that alter perceptions (hallucinogens); those that give a broad range of effects (marijuana); those that even young children can easily obtain to get "drunk" (inhalants); and, finally, those that give athletes a competitive edge (anabolic steroids).

These types of drugs are discussed below in a little more detail, and a select group of specific drugs—those favored by children—are also examined.

Stimulants

These are drugs that speed up the central nervous system. They usually reduce appetite and make a person feel less tired, more alert, and more energetic. Some people respond to these substances by feeling happy. Others feel anxious and jittery. In taking certain stimulants, people feel stronger and smarter, as their bodies are pushed beyond normal capacity. The logical aftereffect of such a demand on the body is to feel sluggish and tired. The sleep cycle is disturbed.

Some stimulants are plants found in nature, and others are chemicals created in laboratories. Cocaine, caffeine, nicotine, and amphetamines (sometimes called "speed") are all stimulants. Another type of stimulant is called a "lookalike." These drugs are made to look like speed, have similar effects, and are sold legally. Diet pills are among these. The major ingredient in many of these drugs is caffeine.

Cocaine. Cocaine is a stimulant derived from the leaves of the coca shrub, which grows in South America. For nearly five thousand years, Peruvian Indians have chewed on the leaves of this plant for the mild stimulation it provides as well as the appetite-suppressing effect. They have done this without apparent damage to their health.

The drug did not become a health hazard until 1860, when European scientists succeeded in extracting the cocaine alkaloid from the coca leaf. At first, this product, cocaine hydrochloride, was hailed by physicians as an excellent anesthetic. It was used as a local anesthetic and in cough medicines, nasal sprays, and a variety of other medications. It was an ingredient in many teas, extracts, and wines and in the original recipe for Coca-Cola. Sigmund Freud promoted cocaine as a treatment and substitute for morphine addiction. Only later did the problems of overdose and dependence become evident. Federal legislation outlawed the drug in the early part of this century.

Illegally, cocaine is used to create a rush of euphoric excitement. It is sniffed through the nose ("snorted"). Cocaine is also water-soluble and can be injected into the bloodstream. And it can be altered to a substance suitable for smoking ("crack").

Cocaine increases pulse rates, raises blood pressure, and creates feelings of energy and euphoria, promoting better performance of certain mental tasks. Fatigue is decreased. Occasional users who snort cocaine sometimes have a stuffy or runny nose from the drug.

One serious danger under any circumstance is overdose. In large enough quantities, multiple seizures can occur. Cocaine can trigger sometimes fatal cardiac arrhythmia or respiratory paralysis.

Cocaine smuggling is a billion-dollar business. Pure cocaine is diluted ("cut") with various adulterants. Because it is a street drug, the user can never be sure of the purity or concentration of the substance.

Because of the intense pleasure of cocaine, people can become highly dependent upon it. With serious dependence, users report a preference for cocaine over food, sex, family, and friends. Chronic excessive use eventually leads to depression and flattened emotions. Some people use cocaine almost continuously in order to avoid the depression and fatigue of "coming down."

Regular users of high doses of cocaine are restless, irritable, and anxious. They may have difficulty sleeping, which can lead them to use other drugs such as alcohol, marijuana, sedatives, and heroin in order to compensate.

Chronic users of cocaine experience withdrawal problems, including intense anxiety and depression. Even after the initial depression subsides, an ongoing emotional numbness known as "the coke blues" can persist for months.

In extreme cases, longtime users of high doses of cocaine may become paranoid, may hallucinate, or may suffer from what is called "cocaine psychosis," a state that resembles schizophrenia.

Each means of administering cocaine has its own set of risks. Snorting causes nasal membranes to crack and bleed and may destroy the septum (the cartilage separating the nostrils).

One danger of injecting cocaine is the same as the danger of any drug that is taken by injection—the risk that unsanitary needles may cause hepatitis, HIV, or other infections.

A type of smokable cocaine, known as crack, is a less expensive form of the drug sold in small "rocks" that give the user a five-to-twenty-minute high. Because it is smoked, it reaches the brain in less than ten seconds. A euphoric high is followed by a crushing depression, creating a cycle of ups and downs that reinforces the craving. Dependence can develop within a few weeks of first use. Although a single dose does not cost much, the high is brief, and the need for more and more of the drug becomes very expensive. Crack users are energized, active, and often paranoid in their quest for the drug.

Caffeine. Caffeine is probably the world's most popular drug. It is a bitter, crystal-like substance found in coffee, tea, cacao, and kola plants. It was named after the coffee plant, from which it was first isolated in 1821. It is also an ingredient in many over-the-counter medicines, especially cold remedies and cough syrups.

Arab goat-herders discovered coffee around A.D. 850 after observing the energy of goats that had eaten the berries of coffee plants. Coffee was introduced to Europe and America during the sixteenth and seventeenth centuries and was a very popular drink during the Renaissance, when many artists claimed it provided inspiration and insight.

Caffeine is a natural component of kola-nut extract, used in cola and other soft drinks. Additional caffeine is added to these beverages. Caffeine is also found in the cacao tree, from which we get chocolate.

Body temperature and blood pressure increase after using caffeine. Other effects include decreased appetite and delayed sleep. In some people, intake of more than 250 milligrams of caffeine can cause nausea, diarrhea, sleeplessness, trembling, palpitations, headache, and nervousness. An average five-ounce cup of brewed coffee contains 100 milligrams, a twelve-ounce cola drink between 30 and 46 milligrams. One tablet of No Doz, an over-the-counter stimulant, contains 100 milligrams. Tolerance may develop with the use of 500 to 600 milligrams per day (about five to six cups of coffee). Caffeine intake has also been related to a higher risk of certain types of cancer and to peptic-ulcer disease.

The use of caffeine by children is a serious health concern. Children consume most of their caffeine in soft drinks. Based on body weight, they consume it at a level near those that are known to cause central-nervous-system impairment in adults.

Nicotine. European sailors and explorers arriving in the New World found the Indians smoking rolls of dried tobacco leaves. They tried this drug, liked it, and soon were addicted to nicotine, the chief active substance. Sailors who smoked tobacco craved the drug and carried the leaves and seeds with them, spreading the tobacco plant around the world.

At first use, most people do not like the taste of tobacco. But they learn to enjoy the energy rush. Smoking cigarettes causes an increase in heartbeat and a rise in blood pressure. It is hard on the cardiovascular system. Smoking first stimulates and then reduces the activity of parts of the brain and the nervous system. Some regular smokers experience diminished appetite and an increase in metabolic rate, and many experience a decrease in physical endurance due to a decrease in their lungs' ability to exchange oxygen.

Cigarettes are a causal factor in coronary heart disease, vascular disease, chronic lung diseases such as bronchitis and emphysema, and cancer of the lungs, larynx, mouth, and esophagus. They are also associated with other forms of cancer and many other health risks. Respiratory infections are more common and more severe in smokers.

Smokeless tobacco is also a health threat. Absorbed through the lining of the mouth, nicotine from smokeless tobacco enters the bloodstream more slowly than nicotine from cigarettes. But the average blood concentration of nicotine in regular users of smokeless tobacco is the same as in smokers.

Smokeless tobacco is associated with an increased risk of several types of cancer, including lip and gum cancer and cancer of the esophagus. Prolonged use causes discolored teeth, bad breath, and gum disease. It interferes with the sense of taste and smell.

Young males between eighteen and thirty are the typical chewers ("dippers") of smokeless tobacco. This is probably why tobacco companies use sports stars to promote it in advertisements.

The use of nicotine is likely to produce dependence. More than half of all adult smokers would like to stop. But nicotine is an extremely tough habit to break. Withdrawal symptoms include anxiety, irritability, lethargy, and weight gain due to a change in metabolic rate.

Amphetamines. Amphetamines were first synthesized in the nineteenth century but were not widely used medically until the 1930s, when the drug was introduced as an ingredient in decongestant inhalers. Drug companies saw the stimulant properties of amphetamines, as did thrill-seekers, who used the drug recreationally and started calling it "speed." Amphetamines became medical wonder drugs of sorts, enabling users to go for long periods of time without sleep or rest. For the next forty years, two closely related drugs, dextroamphetamine and methamphetamine, were widely prescribed as antidotes for depression, lethargy, and fatigue and, especially in the 1960s and 1970s, as diet pills.

As health hazards were identified, fewer amphetamines have been produced and prescribed. But clandestine labs now produce both the drug and lookalikes with similar effects.

Amphetamines can be injected, "snorted" through the nose, or taken in pill form. They increase heart and breathing rates and blood pressure. They decrease appetite. They may cause dry mouth, sweating, headache, blurred vision, dizziness, sleeplessness, and anxiety. Users report feeling restless, anxious, and moody. Higher doses intensify moods. Extremely high doses can cause rapid or irregular heartbeat, tremors, loss of coordination, and even collapse. Amphetamine injections increase blood pressure and can cause death from stroke, high fever, or heart failure.

In long-term users, speed exhausts the body. Tolerance develops, and more of the drug is needed for the same effect. Addicts feel that the drug is essential to normal functioning and take it to avoid the down mood. Possible problems with long-term use include malnutrition (and diseases associated with it), skin disorders, ulcers, sleeplessness, weight loss, and depression. It's a tough habit to break, with strong withdrawal symptoms.

Large amounts of speed over a long period of time cause "amphetamine psychosis," in which the user suffers from hallucinations and delusions. People who become paranoid from the drug may also become violent.

Crystal methamphetamine ("crystal"; "crystal meth"; "ice"; "tweak") is an inexpensive, long-acting form of speed with highs that last from six to ten hours. This drug has become popular and can cause serious harm. People who use it like the energy burst that keeps them alert and awake for many hours ("tweaking" or "getting amped"). Sometimes people take the drug to lose weight, especially girls reacting to social pressures to be thin. The high from the energy is matched by a low that follows, the "crash." To avoid the low, people take more crystal, making this drug highly addictive. The human body can endure a great deal; some people run marathons. But with crystal meth, it is as if a person runs a marathon (taking the drug) and, instead of resting, runs another one (taking the drug again). It is dangerous and extremely unhealthy. Crystal users sometimes stay awake for several days before coming down. Some users experience hot-headed highs and commit violent crimes under the influence. Some get psychotic. People do lose weight from the drug. But they do not accomplish their goal of looking better, because they lose muscle mass and get acne and body sores.

Another stimulant used by young people is ecstasy (MDMA), a designer drug formulated from amphetamine. Though technically a stimulant, the drug has a psychedelic effect. It is found at high schools, universities, and wild dance parties known as "raves." Taken by mouth in small doses, it rarely causes bad trips. However, at high doses, and in combination with other drugs, it does cause adverse reactions. There is conflicting evidence about damage to the brain from this drug and about other negative effects, both physical and emotional.

Depressants

Depressants, sometimes referred to as "downers," slow down the mind and body. In our rushed and hurried society, they provide a chemical means to calm down, relax, and fall asleep. Side effects include slowed reaction time and sometimes slurred speech. These drugs are most familiar in certain forms: alcohol; Valium, Xanax, and other minor tranquilizers; barbiturates such as Nembutal and Seconal; and sleeping pills.

They depress the central nervous system, slowing heartbeat and respiration. They sedate people and are sometimes known as sedatives.

Depressants, including alcohol, are especially dangerous in combination, because they combine with each other synergistically. In other words, if you combine two of these drugs, you get more than twice the impact.

Depressants lead to both tolerance and physical and psychological dependence. Withdrawal from dependence on a depressant can be very dangerous and should be medically supervised.

Barbiturates. The first barbiturate, phenobarbital, was introduced in 1913. Barbiturates are still used for medical purposes, including seizure control. They are, however, very dangerous because overdoses can be fatal. Sometimes people accidentally overdose, taking a small amount at first but then, being groggy, taking more and losing track of how much they have consumed.

Tolerance develops quickly with barbiturates, and the amount needed to induce sleep can eventually equal the lethal amount. Withdrawal from barbiturates, as from all depressants, is serious and potentially hazardous. Symptoms include restlessness, insomnia, and anxiety. Withdrawal can result in convulsions and even death, and therefore should be supervised by a physician, who will administer other drugs and/or gradually reduce the dose. It is dangerous for a dependent person to suddenly "go cold turkey."

Benzodiazepines. Another class of depressants is benzodiazepines, the best-known of which are the minor tranquilizers Valium and Librium. These are among the most widely prescribed drugs. Although introduced by pharmaceutical companies as a miracle cure for anxiety, they are simply another type of depressant, carrying the same risks of adverse effects and dependence. Too often they have been prescribed as the remedy for the stress and difficulties of everyday life.

Alcohol. This depressant is one of the most popular and widely abused drugs in the world. It has been around since earliest recorded history. Alcohol forms naturally when fruits or juices ferment in warm places. In the fermentation process, microorganisms that live on the skin of the fruit feed on the sugar, making the alcohol.

From the beginning, alcohol was used for medicinal purposes, at celebrations, and in religious rites. The alcohol used in beverages is grain alcohol. Its chemical name is ethyl alcohol.

Nondistilled alcoholic beverages include wine, beer, and hard cider. Distilled alcohol, known as spirits, dates back only a few hundred years, when wine was heated and then cooled, with the vapors being condensed in another container. The initial idea was to concentrate wine into a smaller volume to make it easier to ship overseas. Then water would be added. However, people found that they liked the taste and effect of the distilled beverage; this led to the production of scotch, bourbon, rum, gin, and vodka.

The Eighteenth Amendment to the Constitution became law in 1920, forbidding the manufacturing and sale of intoxicating beverages. It was repealed by the Twenty-first Amendment in 1933.

Alcohol is a depressant that slows down the central nervous system. Small doses generally produce good moods and feelings of energy and warmth. They lower inhibitions and reduce anxiety. People seek these effects, but many have difficulty staying in this pleasurable zone and take too much. They go from the pleasurable zone into the trouble zone.[10]

The effects of the drug vary greatly according to the amount of alcohol in the blood, the personality of the person drinking, and the mental set and setting in which the drug is used. The same dose affects people differently. It also appears that there are individual differences in the body's ability to metabolize alcohol. For some, this means fewer unpleasant side effects, increased preference, and possibly greater risk of addiction.

The effects of excessive amounts of alcohol are apparent in drunken behavior: slurred speech, impaired coordination, and sometimes misbehavior. Another serious risk is that the drug produces a subjective experience of competence and alertness that does not match reality. Alcohol slows the body, slows reaction time, and diminishes judgment. Yet it may increase confidence in performance. This false confidence is one reason that people drive and take other risks under the influence of alcohol.

Another effect of excessive drinking is a hangover. Consuming additional alcohol relieves the immediate effects of a hangover but can contribute to a developing dependence.

One of the reasons that alcohol is such a problem is its social acceptability. It is advertised extensively, sold widely, and given as a gift. It is served on airplanes, at theaters, at ball games, and even in some work settings. It's a drug that's hard to avoid.

Tolerance develops with alcohol, as with all the depressants. It is estimated that about one in ten drinkers, or approximately twenty million Americans (including over three million teenagers), are alcoholics. Alcoholism wreaks havoc in the life of an individual and his or her family. It is an economic burden to society in terms of both the cost of treatment and the link to crime and automobile accidents. Withdrawal from a serious drinking problem causes major emotional and physical distress and can even be fatal.

The long-term dangers of alcohol include cirrhosis of the liver, which is a common result of overuse. Alcoholics may also suffer brain and central-nervous-system damage. Used during pregnancy, alcohol can cause fetal alcohol syndrome, a condition involving irreversible physical and mental birth defects.

Narcotics

Some people think that all illegal drugs are narcotics. However, only certain types of drugs, those derived from opiates or synthetic copies of opiates, are actually narcotics. The origin of the name is the Greek word *narcos*, which means "sleep." These drugs relieve pain and make a person drowsy. They slow a person down and create feelings of euphoria. They are most familiar to us as the pain-killing drugs that dentists and doctors prescribe, such as codeine, Demerol, morphine, and Percodan. The illegal drug heroin is also a narcotic. Recently, heroin has been available in a cheaper and purer form. This, combined with publicity about its use by celebrities in music and other arts, has spurred an increase of heroin use by youth.

Hallucinogens

As the name implies, these are the drugs that create hallucinations—imagined voices, visions, or feelings. Hallucinogens also change perceptions of time, experience, and distance. The effect can be mild or intense, depending on the drug and the dose.

Some hallucinogens are produced by the plant kingdom, such as mescaline from the peyote cactus, and psilocybin from a species of mushrooms referred to in the drug culture as "magic mushrooms" or, more recently, "shrooms." The practice of incorporating hallucinogenic mushrooms into religious ceremonies dates back to around 1500 B.C. in Mexico and Central America.

One risk with hallucinogens is "bad trips," when users become anxious and panicky about their altered state of consciousness. Another problem is flashbacks, when the effects of the drug recur, sometimes long after use, creating unpleasant intrusions and sometimes panic. Still another risk is the possibility of drug-induced psychosis.

LSD. One of the most widely used hallucinogens, lysergic acid diethylamide (LSD; acid), was accidentally synthesized in 1943 by the Swiss chemist Albert Hohmann, who was working for Sandoz, a pharmaceutical company. Four years later Sandoz made the drug available for two purposes—to aid in releasing "repressed material" in psychotherapy and "to induce model psychoses of short duration." American psychiatrists were interested. The CIA was also interested in this drug that could possibly drive people crazy.

In the 1960s, many of the human guinea pigs in tests of LSD found that they liked their experience on acid, and they spread the word, thereby promoting recreational use of the drug. Alarmed lawmakers made possession of LSD illegal.

PCP. Another hallucinogen, phencyclidine (PCP; angel dust), first synthesized in the 1920s, was hailed in the early 1960s as a non-narcotic anesthetic agent with analgesic properties. But it was found to produce too many adverse side effects, and its use by humans was made illegal. Its only legal use now is as an anesthetic for animals. In the late 1960s people started using this "animal tranquilizer" for recreation. Its extreme potency and unpredictable effects make this drug particularly dangerous.

Inhalants

These are volatile chemicals that produce intoxication when inhaled or sniffed ("huffed"). Sniffing makes a person feel "drunk" and creates a wide range of emotions ranging from funny and happy to fearful. Inhalants include glue, gasoline, nitrous oxide (used by dentists), fingernail polish, typewriter correction fluid, paint, freon, fumes from spray cans (certain paints, deodorants, and hairsprays), water-based Magic Markers, and butyl nitrate (sold in small glass bottles in "head shops"). Most of the substances sniffed are commercial preparations that are safe when used as directed for their intended purpose. But they are very dangerous, even fatal, when abused.[11]

Sniffing can cause stomachaches and fainting. With prolonged use, sniffing can harm the nerves, liver, and kidneys. It can harm the lungs and cause brain damage. Some children suffocate from inhaling fumes from bags. Some people suffer heart failure from sniffing.

Inhalants are cause for grave concern because they are the drugs most accessible to young children. Because parents do not suspect that their young children could be using drugs, many inhalant abusers escape detection until the problem is very serious. This means that early detection is essential. You can watch for the warning signs, which include:[12]

- product containers of substances huffed or paraphernalia, such as bags or rags (fumes are sniffed from inside bags or off of rags soaked in the product)
- suspicious trace odors
- facial rash around the mouth, nose or lips (or even paint, if that is the product "huffed")
- persistently runny nose and unexplained coughing
- irritated eyes and dilated pupils
- extreme mood swings, often accompanied by grandiose speech, bizarre risk-taking, anger, or violence

Children sniffing inhalants may appear to be drunk, confused, or light-headed. They may slur their speech. They often become nauseous and vomit, and experience headaches.

Marijuana

The most popular of all illegal drugs, marijuana (pot; bud; weed), consists of the crushed leaves and stems of the hemp plant (*cannabis sativa*). The intoxicating ingredient is delta-9-tetrahydrocannabinol, commonly referred to as THC. The current crop of marijuana has been cultivated to contain much more THC than in the past and therefore has far greater potency. To produce sinsemilla—the Spanish word for "seedless"—the marijuana grower disrupts the growth cycle of the plant so that the seeds do not form, leaving a higher concentration of THC in the leaves. Normally, the THC would go toward producing seeds.

Hashish is made by taking the resin from the leaves and flowers of the plant and pressing it into slabs. It contains more THC than marijuana.

People use marijuana to get high, to relax, to alter their consciousness. It can temporarily improve one's mood by lifting depression, diminishing anger, or helping one to forget problems. It can loosen inhibitions and put a person into a dreamy, sometimes sleepy, state. The drug induces a faster heartbeat and pulse rate. Reddening of the eyes, dry mouth, and dry throat also occur.

Because marijuana reduces the ability to concentrate and affects short-term memory, it can interfere with learning and academic success. Its use, in some cases, can contribute to diminished motivation to succeed in school. Also, the lifestyle of young people using marijuana is often associated with "ditching" (school truancy).

Despite subjective feelings to the contrary, smoking marijuana impairs driving ability and is a risk factor for motor-vehicle crashes. Some users, frightened by the effects of altered consciousness, panic when they are high, making their experience a negative one.

A particular risk for children using marijuana is that some of them come to see it as the solution to their problems, often without even realizing what is happening. They find with marijuana that they are able to forget what upsets them, cope with stress, reduce their anger or anxiety, and socialize comfortably. Marijuana can provide relief from their secret fears of facing new, difficult situations. They use drugs to deal with life instead of learning how to deal with life through their own inner strengths.

Longtime users of *large* amounts of marijuana develop psychological dependence. They are high so much that they begin to have problems with relationships, work, and school.

Marijuana smoke irritates the lungs and is a risk factor for lung cancer. Users of this drug inhale deeply and hold the smoke in their lungs. Many marijuana smokers also smoke tobacco, thus combining health risks.

The "amotivational syndrome," in which a person seems to lose ambition, has been attributed to marijuana. Opinions differ on whether it is drug-induced or just a contributing factor. However, "burnout" is a non-medical term, developed by marijuana users themselves, to describe people who have smoked heavily over a prolonged period of time. A burned-out person is slow, dull, and inattentive.

Despite the impressive list of possibly harmful effects of the drug, marijuana is often seen as a "safe" drug. This partially explains the recent increase in the use of marijuana by children. Clearly, the well-documented risks of the drug merit concern. However, I believe that adults, overeager to prevent drug use, have exaggerated dangers and sometimes made unsubstantiated claims of harm. This has caused a loss of credibility among youth, who then dismiss even the *real* risks associated with marijuana.

Much of the research on marijuana has been conflicting. The tentativeness of the discussion is reflected in the following excerpt from a pamphlet published by the National Institute on Drug Abuse (with my emphasis added):

> Some research studies *suggest* that the use of marijuana during pregnancy *may* result in premature babies and in low birth weights. Studies of men and women who use marijuana have shown that marijuana *may* influence levels of some hormones relating to sexuality. Woman *may* have irregular menstrual cycles, and both men and women *may* have a temporary loss of fertility. These findings *suggest* that marijuana *may* be especially harmful during adolescence, a period of rapid physical and sexual development.

Anabolic Steroids

Drug use by athletes has a long history. As early as 1865 there were reports of swimmers and cyclists taking drugs. In 1904, U.S. Olympian Tom Hicks collapsed after winning the marathon. He had taken highly poisonous strychnine in combination with brandy. In the 1954 weight-lifting championships, U.S. weight-lifting physician John Ziegler learned of the Soviet use of testosterone. He then developed Dianabol, the first anabolic steroid in the United States.

Steroids are a synthetic form of the male hormone testosterone. Although available as a prescription drug for certain medical disorders, these drugs are easily attainable in most gyms and are widely abused. Coupled with exercise and a high-protein, high-calorie diet, they produce a state of euphoria, diminished fatigue, and increased bulk, power, endurance, and aggressiveness in both sexes.

The use of anabolic steroids is laden with risks. Misuse of these drugs has been associated with personality changes and mood swings, infertility, abnormal liver function, increased cholesterol level, high blood pressure, premature cessation of bone growth, bleeding ulcers, jaundice, and premature death. More muscle and tendon injuries are apparent among users.

Taken by healthy men, steroids shut down the body's production of testosterone, causing breasts to grow and genitals to shrink.

Large doses in women trigger masculine changes, such as lowered voice, increased body and facial hair, changes in sex drive and menstruation, and increased aggressiveness.

With the enormous dangers inherent in their use, why do athletes take anabolic steroids? Apparently, many athletes will do anything for a competitive edge. In 1967, when one hundred runners were asked whether they would take a drug if they knew it would help them win the Olympics but would kill them in a year, more than half said they would take it.[13]

The use of anabolic steroids by males is probably also a response to this society's preoccupation with physical appearance and the desire for the muscular look.

THE SCARE APPROACH

In the 1950s, the 1960s, and the early 1970s, children were exposed to much information about the dangers of drugs. The idea was that this information would serve as a deterrent and scare them away from drugs. However, these programs failed to decrease drug use and in some instances actually increased it by arousing curiosity about the "forbidden fruit." Another problem with these programs was that some of them gave false and exaggerated claims of danger, which led to a loss of credibility and eventually the counterargument, also inaccurate, that "drugs are harmless." A third reason these programs failed is that information about drugs can be ignored or denied. Such knowledge is not potent enough to counter the needs or desires that motivate drug use. This is clearly evident with tobacco. Look at the number of adults who smoke tobacco despite what is known about the health risks.

The failure of informational approaches to drug prevention does not mean that children should remain uninformed. Recent thinking is that information should be given but not exaggerated, and that it should be supplemented with other programs. The modern approach to preventing drug problems includes: (1) providing reliable information about both the dangers of drugs and the benefits that people seek from them, and (2) teaching skills and attitudes that provide alternative ways of meeting the needs that would otherwise be met by drugs.

Now you have a solid base of information about drugs and drug use, abuse, and dependence. The next two chapters are about how you can provide reliable information about drugs to young children and teach them the attitudes and life skills that empower them to meet their needs without drugs.

3
THE EMPOWERING FAMILY

Paul, age twenty-three, had a serious cocaine problem when he came to me for help.

His wife, Janet, had just kicked him out of the house. She was tired of his lies, hostility, and extreme moods. Although Paul was making a substantial income selling electronic equipment on commission, he was in debt, constantly borrowing to pay for cocaine and lying to Janet about where their money was going. He was also in danger of losing his job. Nevertheless, Paul had great ambitions about saving enough money to go back to school, earning a business degree, and becoming the success everyone had expected him to become. But the way things were going, it was pie in the sky.

Paul came from a high-achieving family. His father was a respected physician and his mother an engineer for a computer company. His older brother had studied law at the University of California at Berkeley and his younger sister excelled in high school and was class president.

To all the world, Paul seemed like a bad apple, an irresponsible young man who was hurting everyone he loved. Most people had no idea of the underlying causes of his drug abuse, the seeds of which were planted during childhood. Paul, like many children, never had an opportunity to learn the attitudes and life skills that could have protected him against drug problems. In the course of therapy, we uncovered some of the roots of his early drug use.

Paul had been successful in elementary school, made friends, and seemed to thrive. Good report cards were rewarded with praise, but recognition for school achievement was about all the encouragement that he received. He remembered wishing that his parents would spend more time with him but feeling guilty because he knew they were "important people."

In junior high he started to have minor academic problems, in part because of the turbulence of adolescence. "We expect better grades," he remembered hearing his father say sternly. And Paul was frightened. He had been doing his best, didn't know what was wrong, and didn't know where to turn for help. In the next few months his grades continued to decline slightly. His father again pressured him to do better, established stricter homework rules, and limited Paul's social time. But Paul didn't understand the cause of his school problems and therefore didn't know how to solve them.

He remained unhappy, confused, and scared. He was angry that his parents were not more supportive. He couldn't cope with his father's pressure, which only seemed to make him more tense and caused greater decline in his academic performance. Paul felt hopeless about reversing the downward trend and gaining his father's approval. As his confidence dwindled, he clearly remembered having one particular thought: "Dad thinks I'm a bad kid. He should see what the other kids do. If he wants to see bad, I'll show him bad."

Soon he started drinking alcohol and smoking marijuana, and so his drug problem began. Some would say that this was teenage rebellion, and certainly there was an element of that. But something else was happening. He was under stress and didn't know how to cope. Drugs were an escape, a release from parental pressure. They were also a way to express anger toward his dad and, most of all, a way to feel good instead of discouraged and scared.

Why Children Use Drugs

Paul used drugs for the same reason that many adults use them— to "solve" problems, to escape from pressure.

Linda, age fifteen, had a similar motivation: "I get high because I hate school and my parents drive me crazy. Instead of feeling bad, I feel good."

In general, most reasons that teenagers use drugs are the same as those that motivate adults.

"I smoke weed for fun," said John, age fourteen, to his parents. "Everything's more fun when I'm high. I love the feeling."

"All the kids drink," said Brian, age fifteen. "I'm no different from my friends. Only the schoolboys [bookworms] and the nerds don't drink."

In terms of motivation, the words of these children are consistent with what common sense indicates and scientific studies have shown: children use drugs for three main reasons.

For positive experiences. Children want to feel good and have fun. They are seeking sensations. They want to alter their consciousness, have bursts of energy, or even experience hallucinations. They want something new, exciting, and risky. They are curious. They dread boredom.

To relieve stress. Drugs provide an escape from reality, a mood-altering experience. Children use drugs to relax or to stay calm in tense situations. Drugs are a way to cheer up or to avoid feeling sad or angry.

Drugs are also used to reduce tension or calm fears. For example, in a dating situation, teenagers take drugs to lower inhibitions and relax. In a school situation, teenagers use them to calm jittery nerves before taking exams.

In response to social influences. Many teenagers use drugs because they consider it "cool." They want to belong and be accepted by peers. Another social influence is the model set by adults. Children see adults using drugs and imitate their behavior in order to be more adult.

The mass media, which often portray drugs as glamorous, are also an important influence. Advertisers use the media to promote the use of the legal drugs, tobacco and alcohol, suggesting that getting high is part of the good life.

PREVENTING DRUG PROBLEMS

The public is aroused, and rightfully so, about convenience stores conveniently selling alcohol to minors. Our government officials are very busy trying to combat the massive flow of drugs into our country. Sometimes it's tempting to see the whole problem as "out there," where the drugs are manufactured and sold, and not "in here," where they are consumed—at home, in our country, in our communities, and in our families.

We can eliminate one or many of the sources of drugs, but as long as the demand remains, the supply will be forthcoming. And the demand is based on *real needs*. Children turn to drugs to meet these needs. Until they find other ways and choose to use them, they will continue using drugs. Therefore, any effective effort to prevent drug abuse must identify the needs that are met by drugs and help children learn healthier and less risky alternatives.

There are many ways to have fun, excitement, pleasure, and adventure in life without drugs. There are many ways to minimize stress and alleviate tension without drugs. There are many ways to socialize with other people and be part of a group without conforming to a drug-using norm. Children who are empowered to meet their needs in these ways, without drugs, will be far less likely to abuse drugs than will those who lack the necessary life skills.

What I'm describing is not a quick fix to the drug problem. It may not sound as powerful and impressive as "waging a war against drugs," but it works. With consistent effort, parents can prepare children to resist drug abuse. Drug prevention is child promotion. More than saying no to drugs, it's saying yes to children.

This chapter is about helping children learn positive ways of meeting their needs—helping them learn to enjoy life, solve problems, cope with stress, resist peer pressure, and form positive relationships. Your home is the classroom. The curriculum is a set of positive attitudes and life skills. The lesson plan is to establish a home climate that empowers children.

If Paul, discussed at the beginning of this chapter, had come from an empowering family, he would have been able to turn to his parents for support in solving his school problems. He could have discussed the pressure to succeed that he felt. His "important" parents would have been more available to him, or, at least, Paul could have discussed his impression that they were unavailable. In an empowering family, Paul would have been able to improve his life, and therefore his mood, and would not have had the strong need for drugs that eventually led to his cocaine problem.

THE CURRICULUM

The curriculum of life skills and positive attitudes that allow children to resist drug abuse has four major components: high self-esteem, clear thinking, problem-solving, and positive relationship values and skills. The rationale for this curriculum is explained below.

Self-Esteem

At the top of the list is high self-esteem. It is the foundation upon which children develop. Children with high self-esteem are less likely to abuse drugs because:

- They respect their bodies and won't damage them by harmful involvement with drugs.
- They respect themselves and want to achieve their goals. They won't engage in activities, such as abusing drugs, that could be detrimental to their success.
- They feel competent and confident. They are willing to take and meet challenges without needing drugs to feel secure.
- They know their strengths and are motivated to work hard to attain their goals. They feel good about success. They minimize failure and therefore reduce the need to rely on drugs to hide the pain of failure.
- They feel lovable and don't feel as much pressure to conform in order to win approval, as children do sometimes, by taking drugs to be accepted by peers.
- They know and respect their own feelings. They will take their own needs seriously and learn to meet them, and won't have to rely on drugs for feeling good.

Clear Thinking

Clear thinking is a core component of the curriculum to prevent drug abuse in an empowering family. Children who think clearly are less vulnerable to drug abuse because:

- They can evaluate experiences and learn from them, thereby gaining mastery and self-esteem.
- They are thoughtful in formulating their own values and opinions, including those about issues such as drugs. They are less likely to make bad decisions.
- They have a sense of how the world works. They can think through the advantages, disadvantages, benefits, and consequences of various ways of behaving and make good choices. They can make good things happen in their lives and don't have to rely on drugs to feel good or to kill pain.
- They have good judgment in choosing friends, selecting those who will not be negative influences.
- They can think through the short-term and long-term effects and risks of using drugs.

Problem-Solving

Children with problem-solving ability are less vulnerable to drug abuse because:

- They can identify and solve problems that could cause stress.
- They can plan to make good things happen in their lives: to attain goals, to create positive situations, and to avoid bad ones.
- They approach decision-making systematically, not impulsively or haphazardly. They are less likely to make bad decisions about drug use or behaviors that could lead to drug use. They are more likely to attain their goals.
- They can figure out positive ways of coping with stress, anger, or sadness. They don't need drugs to take away pain.

Positive Relationship Values and Skills

Children with positive relationship values and skills are less likely to abuse drugs because:

- They have respect for others and therefore behave respectfully.

- They have the ability to make friends and maintain good relationships. These friendships will contribute to their well-being, reducing the need to take drugs to feel good.
- They will not select negative peers out of loneliness and needing to belong.
- They have independent minds and are not necessarily followers of the crowd. They are assertive enough to go against peer pressure.
- They have the ability to communicate feelings and therefore work out differences with family members and peers.
- They have the ability to solve relationship problems with friends and family members and do not need to use drugs to escape difficulties.

Now that we have described the curriculum, we will talk about the lesson plan, which is also the description of an empowering family.

GIVING AND ASKING FOR STROKES

At first glance, the lesson plan for building self-esteem—a core component of the curriculum for an empowering family—seems obvious: good, down-home, mushy love. You've read it over and over again: Praise your children. Hug them. Kiss them. Tell them that you care. Show it. Unfortunately, there is a problem in the love department, a set of culturally accepted rules that keep families from freely sharing their affection.

The problem has been called "the stroke economy" by psychologist Claude Steiner.[1] Strokes are defined as affection in any form. They are compliments such as:

"You're a great kid."

"You're very smart."

"You did a great job."

"I love you."

They are also physical expressions of affection such as kisses, hugs, and pats on the head.

All people need strokes to survive, just as they need food, shelter, and water. If strokes were freely shared, everyone could feel loved and appreciated. But we have accepted a set of rules, the stroke economy, that limits the free exchange of strokes and leaves almost everyone emotionally deprived.

Two of the most destructive rules are: (1) You can't give the strokes you feel, and (2) You can't ask for the strokes you want.

Typical reasons for not giving strokes include believing that:

- The other person doesn't care about what I feel.
- I would look foolish giving compliments.
- If I gave one, then I'd have to keep on giving.
- If I gave compliments freely, it would cheapen their value.

Because of these reasons and others like them, we learn to withhold affection.

An equally damaging rule is that we do not ask for strokes because we believe that:

- It would put the other person on the spot and make me seem too demanding.
- The other person will think I'm needy or weak.
- I shouldn't need anyone else's attention. I should feel good without it.
- If I have to ask, the other person won't be sincere.

Because of the stroke economy, children do not get enough strokes, cannot develop self-esteem, and will go to great lengths to get attention, sometimes even getting into trouble just for recognition. Their logic is simple: "If I can't get attention by being good, then I'll get it by being bad."

Stroke-deprived children are emotionally needy and vulnerable to peer pressure. They will conform and do what the in-crowd is doing, including using drugs, in order to be accepted by their peers.

In an empowering home, parents have to overcome the rules limiting the free exchange of strokes. Besides promoting self-esteem, freely exchanging strokes helps to promote positive feelings within the family. This builds goodwill and is the basis for other important aspects of family life, especially for dealing with problems, negative feelings, and constructive criticism.

You may want to review your own stroke practices in your family. Consider these issues:

The importance of expressing deep affection and respect. These feelings often go unstated. Do you say things such as "I love you" and "You're great"? These are much-needed affirmations.

The importance of physically expressing your love. Do you give physical strokes such as hugs and kisses?

The tendency to detract from appreciation by attaching a secondary and unnecessary message. Do you give pure, uncontaminated strokes? Beware of these forms of contamination:

- A stroke combined with a demand: "I think your schoolwork has been great. Now keep it up."
- A stroke combined with criticism: "You might not be good at math, but at least you're a creative person."
- A stroke combined with a criticism from the past: "You never were so sweet to Grandma before. You used to ignore her. I like the change." (This would be better stated as "I really liked seeing how sweet you were to Grandma during your last visit with her.")

The tendency to focus on only a narrow range of "worthy" behaviors, such as good report cards. Do you try to keep a broad vision of what you appreciate in your children? In giving strokes, try to be expansive in what you appreciate, praising diverse qualities and actions such as cooperativeness, intelligence, creativity, effort, productiveness, imagination, warmth, humor, friendliness, special competencies, physical appearance, compassion, emotional strength, physical prowess, and joyfulness.

The tendency to give but not to ask. Do you ask for the strokes you need from your children? For example: Do you ask for appreciation, affection, and compliments? Do you let your children know about some of your own emotional needs? Doing this sets a good example. Also, it is a way to teach children the importance of giving as well as receiving affection.

Showing interest in and paying attention to what your children feel and think. Do you take your children's emotions and opinions seriously? Are you a good listener? Do you empathize with what your children feel? Do you ask for their opinions?

Part of the lesson plan for self-esteem is to break the rules of the stroke economy and to freely exchange affection in your family.

BUILDING SELF-ESTEEM WITH UNCONDITIONAL LOVE

The connection between the love of parents and self-esteem in children is widely understood. But it's important to discuss a certain type of love that is absolutely crucial to the empowerment of children and therefore to the prevention of drug problems—that is, unconditional love.

This quite simply means that no conditions are placed upon your love. You show your affection, and it remains constant. It is irrevocable. It is not: "I love you *if* you . . . "

Unconditional love means: "I love you no matter what, even when you have problems at school or at home, and even when I'm angry at you. I will not withdraw my love under any circumstances."

This type of love is the building block of self-esteem. When children feel loved unconditionally, they are able to love themselves. Unconditional love promotes two other components of self-esteem: self-acceptance ("I'm fine the way I am") and self-confidence ("I can be successful at what I do").

Unconditional Love and Self-Acceptance

In an environment of unconditional love, people are free to be themselves, to say what they think and feel without fear.

In contrast, children who are worried about losing their parents' approval hide their inner thoughts and feelings, especially the negative ones. "If I get angry," they fear, "my parents will stop loving me. I'd better not let anyone know what I *really* think or feel." Under these conditions, hurt, anger, and other emotions fester beneath the surface and create stress in the family.

One of the best ways to show unconditional love and to teach self-acceptance is to encourage and respect openness by asking children for their opinions and asking them what they feel. Even as adults, we have sometimes had the experience of feeling something we couldn't quite allow ourselves to say. Children need extra encouragement, or permission, to speak out. This permission can be a very simple but loving statement: "What's the matter? What are you feeling? It's okay to tell me, whatever it is."

Anyone who had this encouragement as a child remembers it fondly.

To increase self-esteem, you must provide unconditional love.

Later in this chapter, you will read about communication methods that you can teach your children, so that even negative emotions, suspicions, and criticisms can be expressed and handled constructively.

Unconditional Love and Self-Confidence

The "I love you no matter what" attitude of unconditional love promotes self-confidence in children, the sense that they can be successful in meeting all challenges.

Throughout the years, you want to help your children accept new challenges and learn from them. The learning process inevitably involves mistakes and setbacks, but unconditional love provides security. You never waver in your affection. You trust in your children's ability to gain competency. Children who are not trusted in this way are afraid of making mistakes and losing their parents' approval.

Sometimes children need gentle encouragement to take challenges and lots of support to persevere, just as we adults do. The first time ten-year-old Peter was allowed to take a bus across town with his best friend, to go to a movie, they transferred at the wrong place, got lost, and were an hour late returning home. In some families, Peter might have been ashamed about what happened and punished. He might have feared criticism and invented a story to explain his tardiness. Instead, he and his parents openly and lovingly discussed the experience. His parents showed him a map and helped him learn more about the bus routes. Their confidence helped Peter maintain his own confidence that he could eventually master the transit system. Self-confident children believe in themselves, learn from their experiences, and master the challenges they face. They are not defeated by setbacks.

I cannot overstate the importance of unconditional love that allows children to go to you when they are having problems or allows you to go to them to offer help, not punishment and not a threat. Most of the adolescent drug-abusers I have counseled had school or other problems *before* they began using chemical substances. They didn't know what to do. They didn't turn to their parents for help. They turned to drugs.

When children are having problems in school, or anywhere, the message of unconditional love is: "You can make mistakes, have problems, and suffer setbacks, but I'll still be here for you." It's tragic if children feel they must hide their difficulties from their parents. If they do hide them, where will they get the support they need?

Unconditional Love and Constructive Criticism

The attitude of support and unconditional love is reflected in the way that criticism is expressed. Ideally, criticism should be of a child's behavior, not of his or her basic character.

When Susan left her dolls and other toys scattered throughout the living room, her mother harshly criticized her character: "Susan, you're a little slob. Go pick up your stuff and put it in your room."

It would have been far more constructive to say: "Susan, you left a mess. You left your toys scattered around the house. Please remember that you are supposed to put them away after you use them. Please put them away now."

The latter response allows Susan to maintain her self-esteem while being reminded of her responsibilities.

Seven-year-old Katy has a mom who helps her learn from mistakes without attacking her character.

Katy went to a friend's house after school and forgot to call home. Her mother was frightened and tracked her down. She did *not* say: "What a stupid and irresponsible thing you just did." Instead, she said: "I was frightened and upset that you didn't call. You're supposed to call to let me know what you're doing. Why didn't you call?"

"I forgot," Katy answered. "I was so excited about seeing Sandra's new dog, I just forgot. I'm sorry."

"I expect you to call in the future," her mom said. "What do you need to do to make sure you don't forget even when you're excited about something?"

"I don't know, Mom."

"Why don't you think about it for a while, and we can talk later."

At dinner Katy volunteered a solution: "Mom, I think I need to be *doubly* careful to call when I'm excited and having a great time. I'll remember next time."

"Good for you, Katy."

When nine-year-old Matt's academic performance declined suddenly, his mother didn't respond with punishment. She didn't accuse him of being lazy or stupid. Instead, she showed unconditional love and asked him what was happening. He was upset and said he couldn't concentrate in school.

"Why not?" his mother asked. "Is something bothering you?"

"No. "

"Are you sure?"

"Well, I don't know. Maybe."

"Is it the divorce?"

"Yeah, I think so. Things have gotten worse. Dad doesn't take me on weekends like he used to."

"And that's pretty upsetting, right?

"Yeah. "

"And it's been on your mind?"

"Yeah."

"And you think it's affecting you in school?"

"I think it is, Mom. I've been having trouble concentrating."

This discussion clarified at least part of the problem. Matt's mother needed to help her son deal with the divorce and his father. Then she needed to see what else was contributing to the school problem. If Matt had fallen behind in his schoolwork, he might need help catching up. Once the problems were addressed and he did catch up, he would undoubtedly go back to his previous level of school achievement.

As you can see, unconditional love and constructive criticism are alternatives to responding to every problem with blame, punishment, and harsh criticism. It is a building block of self-esteem, based on the idea that children can learn from experience. Children who feel loved unconditionally develop self-confidence, which allows them to face their problems and solve them.

When they become teenagers, children who are loved unconditionally are not afraid to discuss alcohol and other drugs with their parents. Because they are not afraid to say what they really think and feel, they will be able to benefit from such discussions.

Preemptive Unconditional Love

One way to show unconditional love is to refrain from blame and put-downs. A related way is to take *preemptive* measures that prevent children from blaming themselves for events they did not cause. By preemptive measures, I mean something done *before* problems occur in situations that, if ignored, could cause problems.

For example, children tend to blame themselves for an alcoholic parent. "If I had been a better child," they think, "my dad wouldn't be drunk, and he wouldn't treat me this way." Children also tend to blame themselves for a divorce. They have seen their parents fighting, sometimes over them, and believe they have caused the conflict.

With preemptive unconditional love, children are reassured. In counseling, I suggest to divorcing parents that they each make statements such as the following to their children:

"You are absolutely not responsible for this divorce at all. It is entirely the responsibility of your mom [or dad] and me. We were not able to work out our differences. You are not to blame at all, and we will both continue to take loving care of you."

Building Self-Esteem Through Mastery and Success

After talking about unconditional love, it may seem like a contradiction to talk about the *need* for success and achievement in self-esteem. But there is a connection. Although unconditional love is a good starting point, *success and competency also contribute to how we feel about ourselves. Constant failure detracts from self-esteem.*

To promote self-esteem in children, it's important to arrange conditions to maximize mastery and success in school, at home, with friends, as community members, and in the special interests of children, whatever they may be.

This means giving your children freedom and responsibility. It means encouraging them to take up challenges, to set attainable goals, and to achieve them. You don't want to push too hard, but you also don't want to underestimate what your children can do.

As you will see in this chapter, mastery of the other parts of the curriculum for empowerment—clear thinking, problem-solving, and positive relationship values and skills—will contribute to your children's success and therefore their increasing self-esteem.

Clear Thinking for Empowerment

Thinking is a skill that requires cultivation. With sufficient practice and experience, all children can become clear thinkers. They won't necessarily become Einsteins, but certainly they can become individuals with good judgment, prepared to make wise decisions of all sorts, including decisions about drugs. *In an empowering family, clear thinking is a core component of the curriculum to prevent drug abuse.*

As a parent, you have an enormous opportunity to promote thinking skills and to support your children in gaining an understanding of the world. You can help them feel confident about their thinking, learn to focus their thoughts, define a thinking task, and carry it out successfully.

In empowering families, the home atmosphere is conducive to thought-provoking conversations, with topics ranging from the most philosophical to the most personal. There is a "let's talk" feeling. Anything that interests a family member is discussed. It could be a critique of a film that everyone saw or a brainstorming session about where to go on a family vacation. In these conversations, everyone is urged to formulate an opinion and express it. No subject is taboo, not even a family crisis such as illness, divorce, or the loss of a job. No one is punished or criticized for sharing personal thoughts.

Aside from the considerable educational benefits of these discussions, when it's time to talk about drugs with teenage children, it helps to have had a longstanding history of openness.

In discussions at home, it is not so much *what* children think that matters. The essential idea is that they are encouraged to think, to form opinions, to listen to other opinions, and to practice logic. They need a chance to think for themselves and, through dialogue, to see a variety of different ways of looking at an issue.

You can promote discussions in your home with your own personal openness and by asking thought-provoking questions. Many of the questions will arise spontaneously, in keeping abreast of each other's activities:

> "What do you think of your new teacher?"

> "What's happening with Sara's brother who is spending a year as a foreign-exchange student?"

Questions can be about community issues and current events:

> "What do you think of the new highway they're building nearby? How do you think it will affect us?"

> "What do you think about the upcoming elections?"

You can also be playful in your questions:

> "If you could visit any country in the world, where would you like to go? Why?"

> "What are your five favorite things to do for fun?"

Thought-provoking conversations are an important link to the formation and clarification of values. By focusing on value-laden topics such as religion, sex, grades, proper behavior with grandparents, and, of course, drugs, you help your children think through their values.

Another important topic for discussion is media presentation of drugs. As families watch television programs together, it is a good opportunity to point out ways that alcohol and other drugs are sometimes romanticized, as in the cheerful, sexy, festive scenes that are used to sell beer. Media awareness of this sort is excellent preparation for dealing with negative social influences.

Clear Thinking About Goals

In your discussions, it's important to help your children learn how to think but not tell them *what* to think. For example, in a discussion about school, you might be tempted to talk about the importance of good grades. But children benefit more if they are drawn out and given a chance to reach their own conclusions. Ask them: "What would you like to achieve in school? What are your ambitions?" Then ask them why. Afterward, you can add your own ideas and opinions to help expand their thinking.

Children raised in a supportive and thinking environment will feel good about themselves, have self-confidence, and understand much about the workings of the world. Without being pressured, they will choose to strive for positive achievements. They will want to be loving and contributing members of a family. They will want to succeed in all aspects of life.

Family dialogue can also be used to encourage children to think about the future. For example, ask directed questions such as: "What do you want to be when you grow up? What do you need to do to achieve these goals?"

The ability to think about the future helps children make wise decisions, which is especially important later in life, when drugs are the issue.

Drugs feel good when used, but children need to be able to project into the future and see the dangerous long-term effects.

Clear Thinking About Rules

One goal children strive to achieve is to be loving, responsible, contributing, and respected members of their families. Their responsibilities include, for example, calling home when they are supposed to, returning home at the designated time, and handling a fair share of household duties. Success earns them praise and gives them a sense of importance, belonging, and self-esteem. It feels good to be part of a cooperative and respectful family.

This doesn't mean that children are little angels. They need rules, limits, and controls. They often want to stay up past their bedtimes. They want to ride their bicycles to places they are not allowed to go. They may want to go out in the evening when you believe their safety is at risk. Part of their learning experience includes gaining an understanding of the reasoning behind rules, learning to accept reasonable authority, and realizing that they cannot do whatever their impulses dictate. *Parents control the behavior of children with clear and consistent rules until children have learned enough self-control to do it themselves.*

Open discussions are an important part of the process of setting rules and making agreements at home, and of establishing the division of household responsibilities. To promote good thinking, the reasoning behind rules is explained, and, whenever possible, children are involved in the decision-making process. Children realize that rules are set up to protect them and help them succeed. This awareness is important later, when rules are set about drugs and other teenage issues.

For example, setting a bedtime is a great teaching opportunity. Bedtimes are not set, as children sometimes think, to prevent them from watching their favorite television shows. Open discussions help them see that bedtimes are set to ensure that they get enough sleep to be rested in the morning. This awareness promotes forethought and self-control. Children will realize that they may not feel tired at their bedtime, but they must go to sleep in order to be rested the following day.

Children often perceive rules as obstacles to their happiness. You can help them understand the good reasoning that underlies family rules. Below is an example of two different ways of explaining to a child why he or she is not being allowed to ride a bicycle to a particular park. The first leaves out important details and doesn't address the feelings of the child:

"No, you can't ride your bike to the park. It's not safe."

The second is much more informative and loving:

"I'm sorry. I wish you could ride to the park. I know you want to go, but there's a lot of traffic on Congress Street, and I don't think it's safe. When you're older and have more experience, I'll let you ride to the park. Meanwhile, you can ride in our neighborhood, and we can take some longer bike trips together."

Clear Thinking About Consequences

One of the best ways to help children learn good thinking skills is nature's way, giving them an opportunity to observe cause and effect—or, as psychologists put it, teaching through natural or logical consequences.

Let's say that your son consistently forgets to bring his lunch to school. This is an open invitation for you to rescue him by hopping into the car and delivering it yourself. You wouldn't get a tip, as the pizza-delivery boy would, but your son would see, as he probably wants to, that you care and that you will do things for him. He also would see that you believe he can't be responsible for himself and that he doesn't need to be responsible, because someone will bail him out.

A better alternative is to make an observation: "I notice you've been forgetting your lunch a lot lately." Then ask a question to start a discussion: "What do you think is going on?" Finally, offer problem-solving assistance: "What can you do to remember to bring your lunch?"

This shows that you care. You've noticed the problem. It also shows that you believe your son is capable of remembering and does not need to be rescued.

If he continues to forget to bring his lunch, you should resist the temptation to deliver it. Instead, explain that you respect him too much to treat him like a baby, and that you know he is capable of re-membering. If he forgets again, he'll have to buy his own lunch with his allowance or go hungry.

The natural consequence of forgetting is that he may be hungry for a day, but he will quickly learn his lesson. In many situations such as this, nature will work wonders. You can let children learn for them-selves.

Sometimes children "forget" as this boy did, or break rules of one sort or another, as an "experiment." They are not bad kids. They are merely curious, trying to find out how the world works. This boy might be wondering: "Will Mom really not bring my lunch? I'm going to find out." Once he finds out, he'll probably start remember-ing.

Sometimes we have to help nature along. Either the natural con-sequences are too severe—you don't let your child cross a dangerous intersection to learn from the natural consequences—or the lesson is too complex. The supplement to natural consequences are logical consequences. These are consequences that logically fit the problem behavior.

For example, one mother drove her two children to school to save them from a very long school-bus ride across town. Her ten-year-old son began picking on his five-year-old sister, consistently ruining the trip for everyone. His mother warned against such nastiness and said that she would refuse to go to the trouble of driving him around town if he would not be respectful of his sister. This was a logical consequence.

The boy persisted in his bullying behavior. Next day he was on the bus, an hour and a half each way. He learned fast. That was the last time he bullied his sister in the car.

A good example of combining natural and logical consequences involved a girl who was not performing one of her household responsibilities, emptying the dishwasher. First her mother asked her what the problem was and tried to solve it through discussion. That didn't work. The natural consequence of the continued misbehavior was that other family members became angry at the girl. They expressed their resentment in a disciplined and constructive way. That didn't help. Finally, the mother established some logical consequences:

"You'll have to do your own laundry this week. I don't feel good about doing it for you when you won't do your share around the house."

Then she added—and this is very important:

"This is not the way I want it. I would prefer cooperation. But when you don't do your share, I eventually grow weary of doing mine. I want you to learn about being responsible. I look forward to the near future, when I hope you'll do your share of the chores and I can feel good about doing mine."

A week of doing her own laundry helped the girl better understand the importance of sharing household responsibilities. From then on, she did a much better job of emptying the dishwasher.

As you can see, children are not helped by being spared rules or by being protected from the consequences of misbehavior. They need the rules and limits to learn self-control. They need the consequences to learn from experience. It builds judgment.

As children get older, self-control and good judgment are important life skills that protect against drug abuse. Children who are good thinkers about consequences will see the risks of using drugs.

In using rules and consequences, the idea is to take the meanness out of child-rearing. Children can learn all the valuable lessons they need without being mistreated, threatened, or severely punished. Natural and logical consequences are educational.

SETTING UNPOPULAR LIMITS

Some parents who themselves grew up with authoritarian parents who set harsh rules and used severe punishment may tend toward permissiveness. "I don't want to be like my parents," they think, so they avoid setting limits and making rules, or, if they make them, fail to follow through with enforcement. This is a serious mistake. Children who grow up in such an environment will tend to be out of control. They need parental control in order to develop inner control.

I worked with a single mother in therapy whose eleven-year-old daughter, Monica, was very bright but was doing poorly in school. Her grades were near failure because teachers subtracted credit for homework that wasn't completed. Monica said she was too tired to do assignments at the end of the day, after practicing with the soccer team, doing her household chores, and eating dinner. A very reasonable discussion with Monica didn't seem to help. Her mother was not persuasive enough to convince her to take control over her school destiny. I suggested that soccer participation could be made contingent on the completion of homework. It would not be punishment, but if Monica was too tired to do school assignments, the time that would have gone to soccer would be better spent on homework. Her mother would essentially be saying that school has a higher priority than sports. When I suggested this, she said to me: "I want to be a good mom. I don't want to deprive her of anything."

"Tell her that," I said. "It's great that you feel this way, that you don't want her to miss anything. You want her to play soccer. You don't want to take it away from her. But if she doesn't do her homework, you will need to take action to protect her from failing in school."

She did lay down the law and, miraculously, Monica found that she had the energy to do her schoolwork every day after soccer practice. By using her authority with love and firmness, Monica's mother helped her daughter develop much-needed self-discipline.

There is an art to maintaining parental authority with grace. When you have to establish a "bottom line" that your children find objectionable, you can let them know that you're sorry they're disappointed, that you don't like disappointing them, but that under the circumstances you find it necessary.

PROBLEM-SOLVING

Clear thinking, as discussed above, encourages children to pay attention to their thoughts and opinions, to develop their reasoning ability, and to reflect on their experiences. *Problem-solving is a special type of clear thinking and a crucial component of the curriculum to prevent drug abuse in an empowering family*. It involves an attitude of accepting problems rather than ignoring them. It also requires the skill of finding solutions.

Problem-solving is as basic to the prevention of drug abuse as learning to swim is to drowning prevention. Children with problem-solving skills know how to:

- have fun
- prevent negative feelings
- cope with stress and frustration
- find friends with positive lifestyles
- deal with negative peer pressure

Parents tend to think of problem-solving as it applies to existing problems with their children. For example, it could be misbehavior at home, a bad report card, poor eating habits, or trouble getting along with friends.

But problem-solving abilities should also be used to plan for success. That is, children are given an opportunity to set ambitious goals for themselves and then to use problem-solving skills to devise a plan to attain these goals.

Problem-solving also has an important place in prevention—that is, the problem to be solved is how to prevent future problems. For example, you can help your children with problem-solving *before* they enter a new school by discussing what to expect and how to handle it. Similarly, *before* the family moves, you can talk about potential problems concerning the new home and neighborhood. And you can prevent potential drug problems by discussing drugs *before* your child has been exposed to them and is tempted to experiment.

Another type of problem-solving is early intervention. For example, you may notice that your son is not socializing with other children. Before he feels depressed about his isolation, you can bring the problem to his attention and help him make some changes.

I had a personal experience as a child that I think illustrates how parents can help with early intervention. During the summer between third and fourth grades, I transferred to a new school. The children in my new school had learned tumbling in physical education the previous year. In gym class I was frightened when we lined up to do forward somersaults. I don't remember the exact details of what happened, only that I came home and explained that I was very upset because I couldn't do what everyone else was doing. My parents went into the "you can solve this problem" mode. I can still remember my mother saying, "You can do anything you want to do."

That weekend we moved some mattresses into the attic, and they gave me lessons. I practiced in the safe confines of my own home. Instead of dreading my return to gym class and fearing humiliation because I couldn't tumble, I proudly went back, convinced I could master any challenge and solve any problem. My parents had done a good job of early-intervention problem-solving.

Teaching Problem-Solving

One way that children learn about problem-solving is by observing their parents. It's a good idea to make a self-evaluation of your own efforts as a role model: How do you approach problems? Do you set a good example by taking a positive problem-solving approach to family life and other problems of day-to-day living? Do you ignore problems, hoping they will go away? After problems are identified, do you use a systematic problem-solving approach, or do you respond haphazardly or impulsively?

I found it interesting to do therapy with a family in which the oldest son had an impulse-control problem with drugs. He didn't go looking for drugs, but if they showed up, he couldn't turn them down. His parents had a similar impulse problem, not with drugs but with their credit cards. They never saw a home-improvement item or electronic appliance that they didn't want to buy. They never heard about a vacation adventure that they didn't want to take. As a consequence, they were in debt and forever digging themselves in deeper. In their family-therapy sessions we had some excellent discussions about how to face problems and resist temptations.

Another important assessment you can make as a parent is whether you observe and address problems that are occurring in the lives of your children. Also consider whether you encourage your children to take a problem-solving approach. Problem-solving is an activist way of life. If your child is having problems in school, this shouldn't be ignored. If your child seems moody and upset, find out what's happening. If your child doesn't seem to have friends or is having problems with peers, talk about it. If your child can't openly discuss feelings, help him or her learn to do this.

Children need support in recognizing and solving problems. You provide this support both by serving as a good role model and by teaching your children to understand and use the problem-solving process. This process is described below and illustrated with an example.

1. Look for indications of problems.
2. Identify a problem.
3. Assess the cause of the problem.
4. Pick the goal.
5. Identify available resources that could be used to attain the goal.
6. Now that the goal is clear and the resources are defined, think of all the possible alternative solutions.
7. List the pros and cons of each possibility.
8. Choose the best action or best combination of actions.
9. Make an action plan and carry it out.
10. Evaluate the outcome and revise the plan as needed.

This process was used by the Sherman family shortly after they moved to a new home in a different city during the summer. In late August the parents noticed an indication of a problem—their seven-year-old son, John, was agitated. They assessed the source of the problem and found that he was nervous in anticipation of his first day in a new school.

John and his parents set the goal of making it easier for him to get a good start. Available resources included John's parents and his new friend who lived down the block. John and his parents brainstormed a list of possible actions to take and evaluated the pros and cons of each of them. Then John decided what to do. He had his parents take him to the school building before the first day of school to make it feel more familiar. He talked with his friend to find out more about the school. He arranged to walk to school on the first day with his friend. He discussed his fears with his parents and got reassurance. By successfully carrying out the plan, he gained a valuable lesson in coping with stress and taking control of his own life.

Problem Solving About Behavior After School

Two problems about her nine-year-old son, Paul, concerned Mrs. Bowen. First, he spent almost all of his allowance on junk food. Second, every day after school he came home to watch television alone instead of playing with friends. When Mrs. Bowen returned from work, she would find Paul in front of the television munching Hostess Cupcakes and surrounded by empty potato-chip bags. At dinnertime it was small wonder that Paul had no appetite.

Mrs. Bowen started with her own problem-solving, listing all the alternatives. She had several. She could ignore the problem and hope it would go away of its own accord. She could punish Paul or lecture him. She could tell him what to do. She could try to control his behavior by cutting his allowance—no money for junk food—and disconnecting the television. Or she could talk it over with Paul and invite him to think it through for himself, which is what she finally did.

Over the course of several weeks, mother and son had excellent discussions about nutrition, exercise, and friendships. Mrs. Bowen realized that Paul had some favorite shows he didn't want to miss and that part of the fun was snacking. But Paul began to understand the importance of changing his lifestyle and even started to joke about "couch potatoes." He said he wanted more friends but that he was shy and didn't know how to make them. He asked his mother for advice. One suggestion he liked was that he join a basketball team, which he did, thereby getting more exercise and cutting down his television time. Mother and son also figured out ways that Paul could have friends sleep over on weekends. Gradually Paul cut back on junk food and began to save his allowance for, in his own words, "better things."

"After all," he said, "I get free food at home. Why should I waste my allowance on junk?" Mrs. Bowen had helped her son solve a problem and laid the groundwork for a healthier lifestyle.

Problem-Solving About Boredom

Mr. and Mrs. McClain had recently read an article, linking boredom and drug abuse, in which a teenager was quoted as saying that she used drugs for fun and that getting high was the only way she knew to "entertain" herself.

When the McClains' eleven-year-old daughter, Karen, said she was bored, they became alarmed and brought her to my office. I reassured the family that this was a problem that could be easily solved. The parents resisted the temptation of criticizing Karen or lecturing her about all the wonderful things you can do in the world. They also decided against serving as her social director. Instead, they helped Karen brainstorm her own list of fun activities. Then they helped her implement them, including making arrangements for the piano lessons she wanted and transporting her to various recreational activities. When Karen complained of being bored, which was still a habit of hers, her parents directed her to her own list of activities. They calmed themselves down and empowered Karen to find joy and pleasure in life.

Solving problems about how to have a healthy lifestyle, as Paul did, and about how to overcome boredom, as Karen did, are constructive measures toward the prevention of future drug problems.

POSITIVE RELATIONSHIP VALUES AND SKILLS

In an empowering family, a core component of the curriculum to prevent drug abuse includes learning how to have good relationships.

The best place for children to learn positive values about relationships and important relationship skills is at home, with the family. Most of these values and this knowledge are acquired in day-to-day living, when children are given positive attention, unconditional love, encouragement, support, and affection. If parents are calm, respectful, and patient, then children will learn to be that way. If families are cooperative in sharing the work around the house, then children will learn to be cooperative. Thus, all of the skills we have talked about in this chapter will help children learn to value positive relationships and to maintain them.

The home climate of an empowering family is one of close contact and openness, allowing for great involvement in the lives of your children. Part of a close relationship includes keeping up to date with routine discussions of everyday events. These discussions occur after school, after work, at the dinner table, before bedtime, and during other special times together. You can talk about your day and your children can talk about theirs. It's a gold mine of opportunities to help your children gain greater awareness of themselves and the world around them.

When your daughter says she's bored or your son says he was chased home by bullies, you can teach problem-solving skills.

When your child is worried about an exam or has had a very frustrating day, you can teach coping skills.

When your child heard about crack for the first time or wants to know about AIDS, you can teach thinking skills.

On countless occasions you can increase self-awareness and self-respect by encouraging and praising your children.

Inevitably, conflict will occur in *every* family, even with the very best of relationships. People have differences. Conflict is normal. To minimize conflict and to resolve it when it does occur, good communication and negotiation skills can be practiced at home and taught to children.

Using a few basic relationship skills at home and teaching them to your children can enhance the quality of family life and will provide a strong foundation for your children's relationships with others. These skills—expressing resentments and other negative feelings, communicating suspicion, expressing constructive criticism, and negotiating differences—are described below.

Expressing Resentment and Other Negative Feelings

Repressed anger is a major motivation for drug use. Children must learn disciplined ways to express their anger.

In my lectures and counseling, I recommend a simple fill-in-the-blanks sentence for the communication of resentment and other negative emotions within the family. The sentence goes like this: "When you did A, I felt B." With this format, A describes an observable action. For example:

"When you left dirty dishes on the kitchen counter . . . "

"When you didn't help clean the garage yesterday . . . "

"When you left your books and papers and school materials on the living room floor . . . "

"When you raised your voice to me while we were watching television this morning . . . "

In the first part of each sentence, the idea is to be as specific as possible in order to facilitate understanding. Instead of saying, "When you waste electricity," make the meaning more specific, such as: "When you leave your bedroom lights on even though you're not in the room . . . "

The second part of the sentence describes one or more feelings:

" . . . I felt annoyed."

" . . . I felt resentful."

" . . . I was very angry and hurt."

Putting it together, you end up with a sentence such as this: "When you left dirty dishes on the kitchen counter, I felt annoyed."

In using the recommended format, you want to be careful not to insert judgments into either part of the statement. In the above example, judgments could wrongly have been used in either the first or second phrase, as illustrated below:

"*When you acted like a slob*, I felt annoyed."

"When you left dirty dishes on the counter, *I felt that you were being a slob*."

Note that in this last statement, even though the words used were "I felt," what followed was a judgment, not a feeling.

Another precaution is against exaggeration, especially the use of words such as "always" and "never." These extreme words often make a description of a behavior inaccurate. For example, before saying, "You *always* come late to our family meetings," think about whether that person really has not been on time even once.

The elegance of this format for expressing emotions is that the resulting statement is indisputable. It describes how a person felt when a particular event occurred. It is not a judgment about the event or the person. In a cooperative household, people want to know the impact of their actions and don't want to make others feel bad unnecessarily. In families and other close relationships, the respectful communication of feelings is preferable to an argument, lecture, or demand.

Communicating Suspicion

One very important but seldom discussed communication skill is the communication of suspicion. When people are lacking information about a situation, they creatively fill in the gaps with their intuition and imagination. When they imagine something negative, they are said to be suspicious. Once suspicion arises, one option is to assume that the intuition is correct. This can cause serious problems. For example, a parent might punish a child for something he never did. Another option is to assume that the suspicion is wrong. But this causes problems, too, because the suspicion lingers until it is disproven. I recommend a third option for dealing with suspicion: withhold judgment until more information is gathered. Thus, a suspicion is stated tentatively to help determine its validity.

Many misunderstandings in families can be avoided by an agreement to check out suspicion. Very important questions will come to the surface. It's not uncommon, for example, for parents to say: "I don't believe you've told me everything. Have you?"

Children have their own suspicions: "Since you won't let me go away with my friends for the weekend, I think you believe that I use drugs or that I might do something crazy. Is that true?"

The temptation in responding to a suspicion such as this is to be quickly reassuring and to deny hard-to-admit realities. This would defeat the purpose. The ideal response to a suspicion is to find the validity in it, even if it is just a kernel of truth:

"Son, I don't think you use drugs, and I don't think you would do something crazy. But, frankly, I think that if you went with your friends, there might be pressure to drink alcohol and experiment with drugs. I don't think you're ready yet to handle that pressure."

The boy might be disappointed to hear this, but at least there is now greater understanding and the possibility of further dialogue.

Expressing Constructive Criticism

Those of us who have not yet attained perfection—even if we deceive ourselves and think we're almost there—can most definitely benefit from constructive criticism. That's how we learn. Children learn from the constructive criticism of their parents. It is equally true that adults benefit from constructive criticism, sometimes even from children. *Family members need a form for communicating their critical thoughts in a loving and supportive way.*

The tone and purpose are crucial. The purpose is to build each other up, not to tear each other down. The tone therefore should always be loving, in the spirit of unconditional love, as described earlier in this chapter. Name-calling and put-downs are inappropriate.

Constructive criticism falls into two basic categories. One type is about issues that affect the rest of the family. For example:

"You said you would pull the weeds in the front yard, and you haven't."

"When you were on the phone with Grandma, you sounded impatient with her hearing difficulties."

"I've noticed that you haven't been returning the keys to the car after you've borrowed them."

A second type of criticism is about the well-being of the person criticized:

"Son, you seem to rush through your homework at night. I'm concerned about whether you're learning your lessons when you rush this way."

"I've noticed that you don't make arrangements to see friends on weekends. Is it difficult for you to do that? Can I help you? Do you want to talk about it?"

"You don't seem to be getting any exercise lately, especially since you stopped riding your bicycle to school. I think physical activity is important. What do you think?"

Criticism of any sort is most constructive when it is specific. Generalizations are supported by specifics that clarify the meaning:

"You haven't been very nice to your younger sister lately. This morning, when she asked for help, you said, 'Get lost.' You don't have to help her, but you could at least be polite in turning her down."

Constructive criticism is best expressed in humble terms, acknowledging that other people may have a different view of reality:

"This is how I see things. How do you see them?"

To avoid misunderstandings, differentiate fact from opinion:

"Twinkies and all those sugary foods you eat almost every day have little nutritional value and lots of calories [fact]. I think you eat too much of that stuff [opinion]. What do you think? [What's your opinion?]"

By calling an opinion an opinion, you allow room for differences of opinion. This promotes dialogue and understanding.

Negotiating Differences

One of the best ways to promote good relationships within families is to cooperatively settle differences through negotiation. This is based on the premise of equality, which means that all family members have an equal right to have their needs met and that everyone will make an effort to take care of each other. Good communication starts with everybody stating their desires. Then differences are settled by negotiation. Solutions can be compromises (we'll meet each other halfway), trade-offs (you get your way this time, and I get my way next time), and creative solutions (let's find a brilliant solution that satisfies everyone).

In negotiation between equals, people try to meet each other halfway. But parent/child negotiation is not between equals. Parents have the ultimate authority and sometimes have to lay down the law. Still, the process of negotiating should be based on mutual respect, and the goal is to empower children by giving them ever more say in decisions about their lives.

With younger children, negotiating might involve giving them opportunities to participate in particular activities under specified conditions:

"You can play with your friends as long as you are home and washed up in time for dinner at six o'clock."

"You can stay up late and watch the television show tonight as long as you take a nap during the day and finish all your homework."

Family discussions about the division of housework responsibilities should include active participation by children, who should be allowed to state their preferences and lobby for them. Similarly, children should be involved in discussions about family vacations and recreation.

Teaching young children to cooperatively negotiate differences prepares them for adolescence, when a reasonable negotiating process in the family is a crucial requirement for preventing drug abuse. If you want a more-detailed discussion of communication and negotiation skills in family life, I suggest you read my book *Who's on*

Top, Who's on Bottom: How Couples Can Learn to Share Power (New York: Newmarket Press, 1994).

THE EMPOWERED FAMILY AND REPORT CARD WARS

Because school problems often precede drug problems, this chapter concludes with an example of how parents can empower children in school situations and how empowerment contrasts with the ever popular carrot-and-stick approach.

We start with the carrot. In some families, report-card time is a game played for expensive rewards, almost like "Wheel of Fortune." Two A's equal an evening of miniature golf. All A's earn a trip to Disneyland. What, no sports car? That will have to wait until a varsity letter is also earned.

The intention of parents is to encourage excellent school performance. Eager schoolchildren work hard for their cash prizes. But ask them why they strive for good grades and the answer is, "To get a trip to Disneyland."

What's the real message? "Good grades are important to Mommy and Daddy." School seems very important to parents, but there is little understanding of why it might be important to children. Bribed youngsters don't recognize the inherent joy of learning, or discover that mastery of schoolwork is a fine feeling in itself.

This reminds me of something I have heard teenagers with a marijuana or alcohol problem say about their parents: "*They* [my emphasis] should be happy that I don't use cocaine."

It's the same confusion. Whose life is it, anyway? The satisfaction of school success is first and foremost for children themselves. The pain of drug problems may be heartbreaking for parents, but first and foremost it is the child who suffers.

The reward, or carrot, approach to school success not only confuses children about the joy of learning but also creates three other problems. One is that monetary rewards begin to lose their appeal as other factors become more important to children. Another is that some children begin to resent the bribery: "If my parents *really* love me, why do they show their appreciation only when I get high grades?" A third is that it creates an extra burden of pressure.

Children vying for parental rewards and approval are sometimes scared by the pressure. Overanxious, they have trouble in school.

A better way to motivate children is to allow them to discover for themselves the joy of learning and the good feelings that accompany school success. This is easily accomplished in a home that encourages clear thinking. Children's natural excitement about education is encouraged by parents who ask them what they have learned in school during the day. Children recognize that they are engaged in an important activity—gaining knowledge and mastering skills.

You can ask your children how they feel about grades. Most of them will say that they want to achieve good grades without being bribed. Better yet, let your children bring it up themselves spontaneously. Children love it when their parents listen to their exuberant reports of school success.

In open discussions, children sometimes reveal doubts about their abilities. This is an opportunity to encourage them and to give them whatever support they need for school success, such as teaching them study skills, helping them understand subject matter, or arranging for a tutor.

If there are problems in school, you can help with problem-solving. School, like any other type of work, sometimes can be boring or frustrating. Children sometimes have to endure bad teachers. When children are anxious, discouraged, or frustrated, you can help them learn to cope. This, like mastery of the subject matter itself, is an inherent reward that money can't buy.

With the carrot-and-stick approach to education, when the rewards have failed and school grades are substandard, the other side of the equation—punishment—comes into play:

"You haven't done your homework. Therefore, you can't play with your friends this weekend."

Punishment such as this is premature and prevents understanding of the problem. A valuable learning opportunity is lost. A child could be asked why he didn't do his homework today. It could turn out that he had a good reason. For example, it could be that he didn't understand the consequences of missing assignments and falling behind in class. Rather than punishing a child, the empowering parent wants to help him learn to think clearly about the effects of his action, whatever it may be, so that he can become self-motivated to make changes.

When grades decline in school, "report-card wars" are fought in many American families, as the punitive force of parental punishment is pitted against the cunning maneuvers of children.

A ten-year-old boy forges his mother's signature on a bad report card. Four months into the school year, his father steps into the picture:

"Where's your report card, son?"

"Well, Dad, the computer broke down. There won't be report cards for a few more months still."

"I'm gonna call the school."

"I don't feel well, Dad."

"You're busted, son."

The sad truth is that children who are having difficulties in school often are afraid of their parents, usually with good reason. When parents discover low grades, the response is a punitive one: "You can't go out weekends. You can't socialize. You won't get your allowance for a month."

Such a response essentially pits the parent against the child. Generally, the assumption is that the child has been lazy, that he or she hasn't been doing enough homework. More effort is needed. Grades will improve if adequate parental pressure is applied. Therefore, part of the punishment is loss of autonomy: "You will come home directly from school and do three hours of homework every day." In other words, the parent says to the child: "You are unmotivated. I'm going to make you work harder."

What is lost in this interaction is the fact that children themselves, given an opportunity, would very much like to succeed in school. They may not know how to do it. They may not feel that they can do it. They may be discouraged. They may give up. They might even hide their discouragement by claiming that school is boring. Children need help, not punishment. They need problem-solving assistance.

Parents who take a punitive approach to a poor report card fail to tap a child's inner motivation for success. They fail to help a child understand the real reasons for substandard academic performance.

A much better response to poor grades is to be on the same side as the child: "I imagine you feel pretty discouraged about your report card. Let's talk it over and figure out where the problem is. I'd like to help you improve your grades."

Usually a discussion between parent and child, in a loving atmosphere, can uncover the underlying problems. Sometimes the answer can be found simply by asking a child what he or she thinks the problem is.

A child might know exactly, for example, "I get scared when I take tests." Often the child doesn't know. In these circumstances, parents can help by asking questions such as these: "Do you have trouble concentrating when you do schoolwork? Which subjects cause you problems? How do you study for exams?"

It may be found that children are upset about something, even a problem at home, that is distracting them from concentrating. They may need help in developing study habits, such as finding a quiet place to do homework and picking a time to work without distractions. They may not understand how to prepare for tests. They may have lost confidence in their own abilities.

Solutions will not necessarily be simple, but identifying the real cause of poor grades is at least the first step in problem-solving. It's a far cry from engaging in report-card wars.

We began this chapter with a discussion of Paul, the young man whose grades fell in junior-high school. As you may recall, his father took the punitive approach. He sternly reprimanded his son for poor performance, pressured him to get higher grades, and set up strict homework rules. This response only increased Paul's frustration, made him angry, and led to worse failure. It eventually led to serious drug abuse. When Paul began having problems in school, he did not need harsh criticism and severe consequences at home. What he needed instead was an empowering family that offered loving support and some solid help with problem-solving.

4

WORKBOOK FOR
EARLY DRUG PREVENTION

The roomful of children have been primed for a guest lecturer: me. I walk into the third-grade classroom, look around, and then ask, "Who in here has ever taken drugs?"

A wave of nervous giggling spreads through the room, followed by silence and eventually a protest about such a silly question. "Of course we don't use drugs," they say.

"You don't?" I reply, pretending shock. "What about Tylenol? Haven't any of you ever taken one? What about cough medicine?"

Everyone laughs.

"I bet you use other drugs, too. Who in here has ever had a Coke or a Pepsi, even once? Raise your hands."

All hands are up, including mine.

"What's the drug in cola drinks?"

Usually someone in the class knows about caffeine.

The children are smiling, amused, and interested, a good way to begin a drug discussion. Too often such discussions begin with a drum roll, setting a nervous tone. Look at the embarrassment and resulting dishonesty that we have in parent-child discussions about sex. We can avoid the same pitfall with drugs if we lighten up and confront the issue with a little less pomp and a lot more humor.

I know about the drum-roll approach to drug information from firsthand experience, as I'm sure many of you do. I remember those scary drug movies we were shown in school, with innocent teenagers, intoxicated by marijuana, jumping out of tenth-story windows. And I can picture those sinister men who came into play-grounds armed with needles to stick into the arms of little children.

For me it was lots of smoke but no fire. They could have been showing *The Invasion of the Body Snatchers*. It seemed just as unreal compared to my experiences but far less entertaining.

Those sorts of lessons in school did nothing to prepare me and my generation for having meaningful drug discussions with our families. At worst, they promoted overly serious, rigid, and agonized encounters.

This chapter is a workbook of sorts that should be used in conjunction with the curriculum and lesson plan for preventing drug abuse presented in the previous chapter. It will be most useful for working with younger children and preteens.

As you know, part of the lesson plan is to teach drug information. So the first part of the workbook covers that topic. I assure you that the approach is gentle and nonhysterical.

The other part of the lesson plan is to teach positive attitudes and basic life skills. As you saw in the last chapter, children need self-esteem and the ability to create positive experiences in their lives *without* drugs. They need to learn to cope with stress, when it occurs, *without* drugs. And they need to know how to make good friends and resist negative peer pressure. The second part of this chapter is filled with activities you can do with your children to help them master these challenges.

STARTING DRUG DISCUSSIONS

When you discuss drugs with young children, I recommend talking in very relaxed ways and using spontaneous situations to broach the topic. Many opportunities present themselves in everyday life.

One such opportunity is following media exposure—for example, after viewing a television commercial, television show, or feature film involving drugs.

Simple questions are all it takes:

"What did you think about the movie? Do you think it was a true picture of how drugs might affect someone?"

Simple observations can be made in a humorous rather than "scare the children" tone:

"It sure looks like everyone has a great time in that beer commercial. I think they leave out some details, like the man who's drunk and vomiting in the bathroom, or people who drink and then drive home drunk. They could wreck their cars and kill or injure themselves or innocent people."

You can use tobacco advertisements in magazines to show that they depict slim, attractive young people enjoying cigarettes in the great outdoors. Somehow they always seem to imply you will be happier, healthier, and more relaxed, and have more friends and more fun, if you smoke cigarettes. You can ask your children what they think of these advertisements.

Another opportunity for drug discussions is in the context of real-life experiences—for example, when a friend or relative becomes intoxicated at a party or in your home.

Casual discussions about drugs can take place at the dinner table as part of the normal flow of conversation:

"I've been reading in the newspaper about young kids using drugs. Do you ever hear about kids using drugs in your school? I'm curious."

The tone is very important here. The parent is not cross-examining the child. Rather, the spirit is one of interest and involvement. It's part of what happens in close families. It's part of getting to know each other.

In that same spirit, your bright and alert children might ask you: "If drugs are so harmful and dangerous, why do you drink wine with dinner and beer during football games?"

This is a good, thought-provoking question. Children have a way of keeping you on your toes. I'd answer by saying: "Some drugs are legal and can be taken safely by adults. Taking drugs is like flying an airplane or, better yet, making parachute jumps. It requires maturity. Adults are supposed to have enough maturity to make good decisions about drug use. The truth is, not all of them do."

I hope that you can honestly say that alcohol, as you use it, doesn't harm you. However, if you have a drug or alcohol problem, face it: your children have raised an important issue. If you want to do everything you can to help them, you'll have to confront your own problem.

In most families, if people aren't censoring their thoughts, discussions about drugs will occur spontaneously. However, if you find some barriers in your family, or if you want to add a new dimension to your discussions, you can play a word-association game. In this game, all family members write the first five thoughts about alcohol, tobacco, marijuana, and cocaine that come into their minds. Then they talk about those thoughts. This is a good way to get a sense of your children's attitudes and current level of knowledge. Your children will also get insights into your thinking.

WHEN TO START

At workshops and lectures, parents often ask when they should start to talk with their children about drugs. They are referring to alcohol and illegal drugs such as marijuana.

I explain that drug education begins at a very young age, shortly after children begin to master the language. But it doesn't begin with discussions of tobacco, marijuana, or alcohol. It begins with discussions about what we put and don't put into our bodies. Teaching about poisons, such as ammonia and other dangerous cleaning agents that are kept out of the reach of children, is part of the discussion. Teaching about nutrition, about what foods and which combinations are healthy and which are not, is another part.

Even at three years of age we should begin to help children understand the different types of foods we put in our bodies, such as protein, carbohydrates, fruits and vegetables. We can teach what good things we get from each type of food. We also should talk about why we do not eat unlimited amounts of certain types of foods, for example sweets and desserts. This is an important way to introduce the idea of taking care of our bodies. Nutrition discussions should begin long before little kids overdose on Twinkies. They are part of an ongoing dialogue about what is a balanced diet and how food helps your body grow and stay healthy.

Teaching your children to think wisely about what they eat is preparing them for later decisions about whether they will take psychoactive drugs into their body.

One of the first opportunities to talk specifically about drugs with children is when they are taking medication, whether it's a cold remedy or a prescription drug. You can inform them about different types of medical preparations, such as pills, ointments, sprays, drops, liquids, and shots. You can talk about the directions and precautions printed on the bottles or containers. Explain that a person takes only the right amount at the right time and that misuse can mean that benefits are lost or, worse, that harmful and sometimes dangerous reactions can occur. Children need to know that they should take medicine only when it is given to them by you or another responsible adult. These early discussions make it clear that people have to be fully informed in order to decide whether to take medicine, how much to take, and how often. At some point, you can explain about prescription medication: that they are taken only under a doctor's supervision and only by the person for whom they are intended.

Even as you have these discussions with your children, you can reflect on the examples you are setting. It wouldn't be a good idea to go rummaging through the medicine cabinet every time someone has the slightest symptom. This gives the appearance of casualness about taking medication.

The ideal time to start talking about illicit drugs is before age ten. Preteens are old enough to think about many adult subjects yet still young enough to accept parental guidance. Usually they have not used illicit drugs and will agree with you that cigarette smoke is gross and stinks up a room, and that people who drink alcohol sometimes get obnoxious. Most children under ten think that the idea of smoking marijuana is "icky."

By fourth grade some children report that alcohol is a big problem for their age group. By sixth grade many children are already beginning to feel the pressure to drink. It makes sense, therefore, to start discussions early, when you and your child are more likely to agree about non-use. It is easier to reinforce a non-use norm than to try to change someone who has already decided that drug use is acceptable.

Another important reason to have discussions at this young age is because children's "expectations" about drugs are established early, and positive expectations go hand in hand with future use. Surprisingly, expectations about alcohol are usually established by age ten. Many children who drink expect that alcohol will improve their functioning. Some of the expectations are inaccurate, such as the belief that "it'll help me think better while taking an exam." Other expectations correctly identify potential benefits ("It'll make me more relaxed, funnier, and braver at parties") but don't recognize the risks, such as addiction, public embarrassment, or failing to learn to cope with social situations without drugs. Therefore, long before children actually begin to drink or use other drugs, it's important to talk with them about what they believe happens when these substances are used. You can clear up some of the widespread myths.

Keeping Your Cool

The unpanicked approach to drug discussions can take place even when you are a little shocked about how the topic arose. I'm sure my dad was a little shocked many years ago when I first discussed tobacco with him.

I was in fifth grade. A friend of mine had stolen a few cigarettes from his mother. We smoked them in his "clubhouse," a shack in his backyard.

The filter broke off the cigarette that I had puffed on. (I didn't even know what it meant to inhale.) My friend said that I would catch tuberculosis because the cigarette had no filter.

"What about non-filters?" I asked.

"That's different," he answered. "You get tuberculosis from smoking filter cigarettes when the filter breaks."

In terror, I confessed my terrible wrongdoing that night, hoping I could still be saved. My father reassured me about my particular health concern and then asked what I thought of cigarettes. "Pretty gross," I said. He agreed. He said that my mother and he didn't smoke because "we think they're gross, too," and if I ever wanted to hear more details about why they didn't smoke, I could ask. That incident is one of many reasons that I don't smoke now, so many years later.

I suppose my parents could have punished me. But I didn't need to be punished. My father helped me think through the issue of tobacco in a way I could understand. He showed me that I could talk with him about drugs without fearing the consequences. Nothing was taboo. The message was: "I'm glad you could share that with me. Let's talk it over. If there's a problem, let's solve it together."

WHAT TO SAY

The most important message to communicate to children about alcohol and other drugs is that these substances are not for them to use. This message should be communicated unequivocally. You can acknowledge that many children in this country do use drugs and that perhaps their parents have not explained as clearly as they should have about the potential dangers. But you want to make it clear: Drugs are not for children.

Does this mean that when a child asks to taste your wine at dinner, you have to deny the request? In my opinion, that's being a little too rigid. Of course, you'll use your own values to decide what to do, but a taste, out of curiosity, is very different from the experimental use of drugs for the mind-altering effects. You can give a taste but still make it clear that only adults have the option of really drinking alcohol. As you may recall from your own experience, most children who try alcohol find the taste to be unpleasant.

Much of what you choose to discuss with young children will be determined by your own values, the interests of your children, and the flow of the dialogue. Below I have highlighted some of the most important material you will probably want to include in a thorough "introduction to drugs" discussion. The quantity of information presented here couldn't effectively be communicated in one or even several sittings. Consider it part of the curriculum for the preteen years.

BASIC DRUG INFORMATION

You'll want to define "drug." As mentioned earlier, one definition is: substances that in small amounts produce significant changes in the body, the mind, or both. A few examples will illustrate this: People use drugs to make a headache go away, to clear a stuffed nose, or to change their moods.

Sometimes, however, people take drugs for one purpose, but they experience side effects. For example, cold tablets relieve cold symptoms, but they also make you drowsy and thirsty.

Some drugs, you can point out, are accepted for use in our society, and others are not. Just because a drug is legal does not mean it is harmless to your health. For example, tobacco and alcohol can be very dangerous.

Why do people take street drugs, or use tobacco or drink alcohol? This is an important issue to address. Let your children provide their own answers at first. They probably know many of the reasons. You can add others: to feel good, because their friends do it, for fun, to be popular, to escape, to forget bad things, to sleep, to stay awake, to relax, to not feel nervous.

Your children may ask: "People use drugs to make friends, to feel good, or to not feel bad. So what's the problem?"

The answer, in my words, goes like this:

"Sometimes people do benefit from drugs. But there are many dangers in using them. One danger is that when people rely on drugs to feel good or make friends or deal with life in one way or another, they *don't* learn how to do these things without drugs. They don't really grow up, and they always need to have drugs. This can cause other serious problems and even ruin lives. In this family, we will help you learn healthy ways to deal with life and enjoy life, without drugs."

This provides an opportunity to introduce the concepts of abuse, dependence, and drug tolerance.

ABUSE, DEPENDENCE, AND DRUG TOLERANCE

Even very young children can understand the concept of "abuse" if it is presented in a simplified form. Ask them what they think it means. They may have ideas such as "being mean to a friend," or "when you kick the cat." They may have heard of child abuse.

Young children don't understand drug pharmacology or, in that sense, drug abuse, but they can be prepared for such an understanding by putting "abuse" into terms that make sense to them, such as *ice-cream abuse*:

"What if I had one scoop of chocolate ice cream after dinner? If it was real good, should I have another one? How many? What if I had six scoops and got so sick I threw up? How about two scoops right before dinner?"

This gives children an idea of abuse, meaning excessive use—taking too much of something at the wrong time, or taking something that is bad for you.

This same reasoning can be carried over to alcohol: "What if I had one beer with dinner? What if I had six and drove a car?"

This shows that abuse is dangerous to oneself and, potentially, to others.

The concept of drug dependence can also be introduced to children in an age-appropriate manner.

"Some people," you can tell your children, "take drugs to feel good. But if this is the only way they know how to make themselves feel good, then they will *depend* on the drugs. They will *need* them to feel good. Their lives will center around drugs, and they will care about nothing else.

You can also say that drugs sometimes stand in the way of learning about life. People depend on drugs to have fun and deal with stress but don't learn how to have fun or deal with stress *without* drugs. In that sense, drugs keep them weak. You can use an analogy to illustrate that drugs make things too easy: "It would be like my doing your schoolwork. That would make it easier for you, but you wouldn't learn anything." Or: "If I selected the clothing you wear every day, you would never learn to do that yourself."

The concept of tolerance—that you need more and more of certain drugs to attain the same effect—can be understood by children. A good way to illustrate this is to use the most recent thriller movie that the children have seen, one they went back to see several times:

"Do you remember the thrill you got the first time you saw *Friday the 13th* [or whatever happens to be the current thriller]? When you went back the second time, did you get the same thrill? How about the third time?

"Sometimes drugs are like thriller movies. You want that same feeling, so you keep going back for more. But you're never satisfied the way you were the first time. When this happens with drugs, it's called tolerance. People keep coming back for that same effect but find themselves disappointed unless they take larger doses.

"With thriller movies, sometimes kids watch for scenes that are more and more gruesome. One difference, however, is that drugs that are safe in small amounts may become harmful and dangerous in larger doses."

SPECIFIC DRUGS

Elementary schoolchildren are generally interested in an overview of the categories of drugs and, in simple terms, their effects. You might want to use the types of descriptions I presented in Chapter 2, explaining, for example, that stimulants speed up people and make them peppy, while depressants slow them down and allow them to relax.

In this discussion, highlight some of the special risks of each category of drugs and begin to talk about specific substances. It's not a matter of lecturing. You'll have to find appropriate moments for instruction in these matters.

In addition to discussing the obvious abused drugs, such as marijuana and cocaine, I believe it's very important to discuss tobacco. Tobacco is highly addictive, a serious health risk, and frequently one of the first substances used in a drug-using career. Caffeine is another drug worthy of special attention, because it often slips through the cracks. Some children drink coffee. Most children consume soft drinks without full awareness of the effects of caffeine.

Other drugs worthy of special notice are anabolic steroids, used by athletes to improve performance and by a subculture of males to look more muscular. Steroids are dangerous. One good way to approach this topic is in the context of the question "What price would you pay for success?"

In these discussions about drugs, alcohol merits *very* special attention because of its ubiquitous presence in our society. Children will see people under the influence of this drug and should be informed about its effects and dangers. As part of understanding the world in which they live, children should be informed about alcoholism.

Among the first dangerous drugs accessible to young children are inhalants. They should be discussed. Your children may have friends who try to encourage them to sniff the fumes of inhalants, such as airplane glue, in order to feel "drunk." Warn against inhaling fumes for recreational purposes. It is a very unhealthy and dangerous practice. It could even be fatal.

In discussing marijuana, a little historical perspective will help your child understand the confusion surrounding the dangers of this drug. Because the dangers were terribly exaggerated at one point in the past, there was a reaction by some people, who claimed that "pot" is harmless. But it is not. Let your children know that marijuana can cause serious health problems. Marijuana smoke is bad for the lungs. And let them know that many children, teenagers, and adults abuse marijuana to escape from their problems. Also make sure they realize that although marijuana is widely available, it still is illegal, and that, like alcohol, it can be hazardous if used before driving an automobile.

DRUG DANGERS

To keep your credibility, it's important not to exaggerate the dangers of drugs. You can acknowledge that many people use alcohol, and even illegal drugs (if they are willing to run the risk of getting arrested), carefully and without significant harm. They don't become addicted. They don't overdo it. But you also want to make sure that your children are well aware of the hazards and risks of drugs, and that they are not confused by some of the many myths. The following is material you may want to cover.

Addiction

Explain that *no one* thinks that they will become dependent on drugs when they first start using them. People assume that they will use drugs safely. However, people should pay attention, because some of them are wrong and will end up addicted. Young people should realize that they, too, could be surprised and develop a drug dependence.

One way that addiction sneaks up on people is when drugs are used to fend off "down" feelings. For example, stimulants give the body an immediate shot of energy for a short period of time, but eventually fizzle, causing the body to feel fatigued from overwork. Sometimes people take additional stimulants when the effects are disappearing so they won't get tired. Eventually, they are taking more and more drugs to avoid the down feeling. Similarly, some people try to mask the effects of a hangover by drinking more alcohol. Eventually they get hooked.

Children are often misinformed about alcoholism. Many don't realize it's a drug addiction. They don't know that countless children and teenagers are alcoholics and that someone can be an alcoholic without drinking every day.

In discussing addiction, if you or your spouse are hooked on cigarettes, short of breaking the habit, the next best action is to admit that you have made a terrible mistake. You're addicted. Say that you shouldn't have started smoking in the first place and that you regret what you've done. If you have made unsuccessful attempts to break the habit, tell this to your children.

Children need to know that drugs can be very harmful, even if they are not used frequently and even when a person is not addicted. Single episodes of drug abuse can lead to car crashes, unwanted pregnancies, or violent crimes, or to a person's doing something that they will really regret or that will cause them much distress. Probably the greatest source of harm from drug abuse by teenagers is that drug habits can keep them from learning to deal with life. They use drugs to deal with their problems and whatever causes them stress. They never learn to stand on their own two feet.

Drunk Driving

This should more generally be called driving while intoxicated, because safety can be compromised by other substances besides alcohol, including marijuana and legally prescribed medications.

It is hazardous to "drug and drive."

Children should be told never to accept a ride from someone who is intoxicated by alcohol or any other drug. They may need special training in how to refuse rides.

Alcohol is a factor in half of all highway deaths. It impairs judgment and slows reaction time. Because of the enormous danger of drunk driving, you should explain how alcohol works. It is absorbed into the bloodstream directly from the stomach without being digested, and it is slow to leave the body (most of it is eliminated by the liver). You can dispel the myth that a cold shower or a cup of coffee can sober people up. The only benefit is that it buys time and keeps them from getting on the road sooner.

As children get older, they should be warned that most people who drive under the influence do not realize that they are impaired—and sometimes they even argue that they drive better. They have a false sense of competence.

Illegal Drugs

Aside from the obvious legal risks, children should know that illegal substances present other hazards. For example, it is impossible for a purchaser to accurately determine the potency and purity of street drugs. Many of them contain adulterants. Some relatively mild drugs, such as marijuana, may be laced with more potent substances, such as PCP (angel dust).

Overdoses

Explain about the serious dangers—including the risk of death—posed by taking too much of certain drugs. This applies especially to inhalants, stimulants, and depressants, and to other drugs as well. Children should know that when two or more types of depressants are combined, the effect of each drug is multiplied, not added, and that this can be very dangerous. They also should be aware that the risk of overdose is greater as a person gets high and loses track of how much he or she has already consumed.

Immediate Effects

Research has indicated that young children are much more concerned with the immediate negative effects of drugs than the long-term effects. Still, talking about long-term risks is important, because it is part of helping children learn to think ahead to the future. But surely, for impact, it is especially important to discuss the more immediate effects of drugs. Thus, for preventing the use of tobacco, you might mention these negative effects:

·   Your hair and clothing smell bad.
·   You get bad breath.
·   Your teeth get stained.
·   You go crazy when you're stuck in nonsmoking buildings.
·   You can get into trouble if you are caught smoking in school.
·   It is an expensive habit.

This information will be of more concern to most children than facts about all of the serious health hazards.

What's Normal?

Many children have an exaggerated idea about the number of their peers who are actually using drugs. Consequently, they think of drug use as "normal." Sometimes they say that "everyone is using drugs" although this is not the case at all. You can use up-to-date statistics of the kind that frequently appear in the newspaper, or are available at libraries, to clarify the actual situation.

Now that we have discussed drugs, we can turn our attention to the other part of drug prevention and health promotion—building positive attitudes and teaching life skills. These skills and attitudes flourish in the type of empowering home atmosphere described in the previous chapter. Below are some specific activities you can do with your children to further empower them. You may want to use all the activities or choose only the ones that will be most useful in your own family. I think you'll find that this workbook helps keep you and your children on the right track.

LIFESTYLE: FEELING GOOD AND HAVING FUN

Children use drugs to feel good. Therefore part of drug prevention and health promotion is helping children feel good without drugs. This includes helping them find ways to engage in fun, exciting, and rewarding activities. It also includes boosting their self-esteem. Below are some activities that promote these goals.

Activity One: What I Like About You

Purpose: To increase the amount of affection that is expressed in the family and to increase self-esteem.

What to do: You and your children get together and discuss *only* what you really like and love about each other. The only requirement is honesty. You all have a homework assignment: to compliment each

114

other at least twice a day all week. At the end of the week, you talk about how it feels to give and receive compliments.

Activity Two: Role Models and Pride

Purpose: To increase self-esteem by identifying with a positive role model.

What to do: You and your children search for and read a book in which the main character is someone with whom your child can identify. For instance, the character could be someone struggling with a situation similar to your child's—perhaps having a kid brother, or going through a tough time in school. Or the character could live in your type of neighborhood or come from your religious, ethnic, or racial background. Discuss the problems the character faced and how they were overcome.

Activity Three: Kids Just Want to Have Fun

Purpose: To help expand your children's ability to create and enjoy pleasure. Children who know how to have a good time will not need to use drugs to prevent boredom.

What to do: You and your children have a discussion about fun. On paper, they list all the things they like to do and things they think they might like to do but haven't yet tried. You help them figure out how to do the activities on the list. Also, you help expand the list by making additional suggestions.

In expanding the list, think of broadening their interests. The idea is not to push your children against their will but to encourage new activities. If all their activities are quiet and solitary, suggest some adventurous ones that involve friends or family. Think about calm fun and exciting fun. Think about indoor and outdoor activities. Think about activities that involve creativity, such as music and art, and that involve imagination, such as reading or playing with dolls. If your child is very serious, buy a subscription to *Mad* magazine. Make sure physical activities are on the list. If they are not, talk about it. Make sure creative hobbies are considered, such as sewing, woodworking, and cooking. Consider after-school activities and various clubs, such as the Scouts, the YMCA, the YWCA, and 4-H.

If certain fun activities on the list are potentially dangerous, such as rock-climbing, discuss the risks and safety precautions that you know about. This is a good way to begin to discuss risk-taking. It's an important topic, because the urge to take risks can contribute to drug abuse.

Activity Four: Television World

Purpose: To discourage passive, excessive, and uncritical television viewing. The average American child watches five to six hours of television per day and will have spent about twice as many hours viewing television as in the classroom by the time he or she graduates from high school. This kind of passivity—sitting and expecting to be entertained—is a big reason that so many adolescents get bored and turn to drugs for fun and excitement.

What to do: Have your children keep a written record of what they watch on television all week. Discuss what types of shows they are viewing. Are they educational? Violent? Escapist? Scary? Sensationalist? Spectator sports? What television characters do they watch? Do they admire them or not? Why? Watch some shows together and discuss the quality of each show, the positive and negative aspects. Count the total hours spent viewing television during one week. If your children are watching anywhere near the average number of hours, have a discussion about cutting back. Raise the issue of doing more energetic and satisfying activities for recreation and relaxation. Try having the family go without television for either three days or a whole week. Observe how you spend your time. Discuss it.

Activity Five: What I Like About Myself

Purpose: To increase self-esteem and to show that feeling good about yourself includes allowing for imperfection, growth, and learning new skills.

What to do: Ask your children to name five things they like about their personalities. To help them, ask questions:

> "What qualities do you have that you like?" (Example: "I'm generous and loving, I'm smart, I have

116

a great sense of humor, I'm a good friend, I'm loyal.")

"What do you like about your body and physical self?" ("I have nice eyes and pretty hair, I dress in style, I'm physically strong, my weight is right, I'm good at basketball.")

"What things do you do that make you feel good about yourself?" ("I paint, act in school plays, dance, play the piano, play soccer, play with friends, get along with my sister.")

"Tell me something you did today that makes you proud of yourself. How about something you did yesterday? Something you plan to do tomorrow or soon?"

Sometimes a child will respond with frustration: "I can't think of anything I like about myself." If this happens, offer encouragement: "I know many good things about you. Try hard. I'm sure you can think of some."

If the difficulty persists, you can help by making suggestions yourself, but also take note. This is a self-esteem problem. Think about how you can give more love, compliments, support, and opportunities for success in order to promote greater self-esteem.

Part of promoting self-esteem is allowing for imperfection and planning for improvement. While working on lists of what they like about themselves, children sometimes spontaneously discuss problems. If they do, introduce another part of the exercise—writing a list of "what I want to improve about myself." The next activity in this workbook will help them achieve their goals.

Activity Six: Go for It

Purpose: To help your children learn to set short-term and long-term goals and make plans for attaining them.

What to do: Tell your children about some of your own goals and what you're doing about them. Explain that making plans and setting objectives are an important part of success. Ask them to write down their dreams and goals. Help them clarify realistic objectives.

Show how long-term goals can be broken down into short-term objectives. (Example: One boy wanted to be like his older brother, who played on the high-school basketball team. He could practice shooting baskets and other basic skills in elementary school. He could join a league. He could jog to get into shape. He could go to a basketball summer camp.) Help your children set up action plans for attaining their goals.

Activity Seven: Telling the Truth

Purpose: To help your children appreciate and accept themselves and their feelings, to encourage them to accept challenges, and to open up communication in the family.

What to do: Present the following incomplete sentences—and/or others you may consider meaningful for your children—and give them an opportunity to provide their own endings. You can do many of them at once or a few at a time, on different occasions. It's important to listen with unconditional love, as described in the previous chapter. Do not dispute or criticize what is said.

I feel good when I . . .
I feel hurt when I . . .
I find it hard to . . .
I like myself because . . .
A good decision I made this week was . . .
I feel sad when . . .
I feel scared when . . .
I feel frustrated when . . .
I feel loved when . . .
I feel left out when . . .
I feel best with our family when . . .
I feel best with my friends when . . .
I get angry when . . . .
What I most want to tell you, Mom and Dad, is . . .
I'm worried that . . .
My biggest gripe at school is . . .
My biggest gripe about my best friend is . . .
When I think about my schoolwork, I feel . . .

My one wish is . . .
My biggest goal is . . .
My strongest feeling about my brother [or sister] is . . .
I wish grownups wouldn't . . .
The last time I cried was . . .
If I could be doing anything else today, it would be . . .

STRESS AND KIDS

I remember smiling to myself when a ten-year-old girl told me, "I just had the worst day of my life." It was cute to hear those adult-sounding words from this girl. But I knew it wasn't funny and that stress was as real to her as it is to any adult. Children need to learn to plan their lives to prevent unnecessary stress. They also need to learn healthy ways of coping with unavoidable stress.

Children who feel good about themselves and can plan their time to include positive activities will experience less stress. But there's more to it. Some stress is good, such as the stress involved in learning something new, trying out for a school play, or playing in a little-league game. However, too much stress is harmful. It causes people to feel bad, sometimes even to become ill. Therefore, part of stress-management is picking appropriate challenges. Children have a lot to learn about stress. The following activities will give them a good start.

Activity One: Stress, the Pest

Purpose: To help your children understand the meaning of the concept, and to help them recognize their personal indicators of stress.

What to do: Ask them whether they have heard of "stress." They may have some ideas, such as "when things get crazy" or "when I'm under pressure." Explain that stress is the normal response of people to the demands of everyday life. We all have tough times. Even by first or second grade, a child can understand some of the harsh realities of life: Not everyone will like you. Not all days will be good ones. You will have positive and negative emotions.

Another important part of defining stress is to personalize it. Help your children learn to recognize stressful events by asking, "When do you feel stress?" If neecessary, make a few guesses: "When you have tests in school? When Grandma visits? When you go to Sunday school? When your sister and you fight?"

Fifth-grade children who were asked what makes them feel bad listed the following experiences most frequently:

- spending too little time with their parents
- parents arguing in front of them
- turning in their homework late
- having nothing to do
- having too little money to spend

In personalizing the meaning of stress, help your children learn to identify their own physical signs—"Where in your body do you feel stress?"—and their own reactions: "What do you do when you're under stress?" If they have trouble identifying the indicators of stress, list some: tight muscles, constricted breathing, whining, irritability, losing your temper, having a lump in your throat, feeling like crying, breathing fast, feeling really hot and sweaty, pounding heart, trembling, difficulty sleeping, sweaty hands, cold hands, feeling tired and weak, headache, upset stomach, feeling helpless. Explain that by recognizing the signs of stress, people can take better care of themselves.

Point out that some responses to stress are physiological and largely out of our control, such as sweating, but that other responses can be controlled. Some are better than others. Discuss the idea of good and bad responses to stress. Explain that we can do things to help ourselves relax or we can do things—such as overeating or taking drugs or throwing tantrums—that can only make us feel worse.

Activity Two: Stress-Busters

Purpose: To help your children become aware of positive options for coping with stress. These "stress-busters" are alternatives to using drugs to deal with stress.

What to do: Let your children brainstorm ideas about positive ways to deal with stress. You can add to their repertoire. If they have not listed the following ways, you can mention them:

- Distract yourself. Read a book or see a movie.
- Engage in physical exertion. Go for a walk or a swim.
- Uplift your mood. Listen to upbeat or relaxing music. Sing along or dance. Or use your imagination to think about nice things. (Nine-year-old Sara was stressed-out and bored while babysitting for her younger sister. I suggested that she use her imagination to think pleasant thoughts. She said she concentrated on her favorite things—rainbows, unicorns, and her dolls—and felt much better.)
- Accept your bad feelings and let them pass. Cry and look forward to brighter days.
- Make your body relax. Take six deep breaths or get someone to massage your neck, back, or feet, or wherever you feel tense. Take a nap. Take a warm bath.
- Energize your body. Take a cold shower. Splash water on your face. Go outside in the fresh air.
- Use problem solving. Figure out what's bothering you and do something about it.
- Get support. Talk about problems with a friend or your parents. Ask for help.
- Communicate feelings. If you are upset with someone, talk it over.
- Stop doing whatever is stressful. If you are run down and tired, stop pushing yourself. Relax instead. If you feel stressed-out from boredom or sluggish from watching too much television, then get active. Go get some exercise.

Activity Three: Barbara the Beaver

Purpose: To increase awareness of healthy and unhealthy ways to react to problems. If children know healthy ways of dealing with problems, they will be less likely to use alcohol, tobacco, or other drugs as "solutions."

What to do: Tell a fictional story, such as the one below, based on the story "Albert the Ant" by Jessica Horne. Four characters are stranded on a desert island. One panics, hides under some lumber, and screams in terror (Charlie the Chicken). One blames the other three and chases them around, paddle in hand, trying to swat them in the behind (Brian the Bulldog). One makes believe everything is okay, tans herself on the beach, and hides her head in the sand (Ellen the Ostrich). But the heroine, Barbara the Beaver (for girls), or the hero, Billy the Beaver (for boys), tells his animal friends to "chill out" and starts thinking about what to do. Then she industriously builds a raft with the wood and paddles them all to safety.

This story is a good example of the fact that sometimes you have to solve problems in order to feel good. It wouldn't have helped if Barbara the Beaver had drunk beer to forget that they were stranded on an island. Even if Barbara had found a good way to relax—for example, by taking a nap—it still wouldn't have helped them escape. She had to solve the problem in order to feel good. You can use Ellen the Ostrich to begin to discuss escapism—how people sometimes try to make themselves feel good but in so doing overlook important problems.

Ask your children about times when they, you, or anyone in the family may have behaved like the characters in the story. Suggest that they act like Barbara the Beaver all week long. Check in with them every day: "What happened to Barbara the Beaver today?"

Activity Four: Let's Solve a Problem

Purpose: To enhance problem-solving skills. Children who can solve problems can minimize stress and cope with life without using drugs.

What to do: Ask your children to identify a problem. For example, they can't afford to buy a particular toy or they are angry at a sibling about something, or they are being picked on by a kid in school.

Now guide your child through the problem-solving process. First pick the goal. Then identify available resources. Think of all the possible alternatives. List the pros and cons of each alternative. Choose the best ones. Make an action plan for success. (You may want to reread the section about problem-solving in Chapter 3.) Your discussion might go something like this:

Child: "There's a great toy I want to buy, but I can't afford it."
Parent: "Oh, I'm sorry to hear that. How much does it cost?"
Child: "Twenty dollars."
Parent: "How much do you have?"
Child: "About four dollars. But I'm spending that on a movie. "
Parent: "I see that this is a problem. Any ideas about how to solve it?"

Child: "I don't know. Can you just buy it for me?"

Parent: "That's one possibility. Let's look at all the other ones, too. First, what's your goal?"

Child: "To get the toy."

Parent: "How else could you get it?"

Child: "Like I said, you could buy it for me." (This kid has a sense of humor!)

Parent: "Seems like we covered that one already. What are your other ideas?"

Child: "I could get someone else to buy it for me. I could wait until Christmas."

Parent: "Yeah. Good. What else?"

Child: "I could save my allowance, but that would take a long time."

Parent: "Any other ideas?"

Child: "No."

Parent: "What about earning money?"

Child: "That's an idea. Do you have any jobs I could do?"

Parent: "I could offer you some, like working in the yard or washing the car."

Child: "But it takes so long to save money."

Parent: "Is the toy very important?"

Child: "Yeah. I really want it."

Parent: "Maybe you could do a better job of saving your money. Have you ever thought of that?"

Child: "That's a good idea."

Parent: "I'd help you with that."

As the discussion unfolded, the child recognized that he could try to get someone to buy the toy for him or he could save up for it. He decided to save his allowance, to reduce the amount of money he spent on junk food after school, and to wash the car to earn extra cash. That way, he figured he could buy the toy in three weeks.

Activity Five: Decision Making

Purpose: To show that decision-making is part of problem-solving and that making decisions usually involves weighing pros and cons and comparing immediate and long-term benefits. This prepares children for future decisions about drugs. Drugs feel good at the moment but can create problems in the long run.

What to do: Present imaginary bad decisions children sometimes make, such as the following:

Joan decided to watch television instead of doing her homework. She got in trouble with her teacher.

David ate so much Halloween candy that he couldn't eat dinner. He threw up.

Ginger ran away after she broke a window in the neighbors' house, but they saw her.

Talk about why these imaginary children decided to do what they did. Talk about other options they had. Talk about the pluses and minuses of each option. When Joan watched television instead of doing her homework, the plus was that she had fun. The minus was that she felt bad later about not doing her homework. Also, she got into trouble the next day and had to stay after school to catch up. If Joan had thought carefully about the future, including *all* the pluses and minuses of her options, she might have made a better decision.

Discuss the major steps in decision-making: (1) List the choices. (2) List the pros and cons of each. (3) Determine which is best at the present moment, which is best in the long run, and which is best overall. (4) Make a choice. (5) Do it and see how it goes.

Your children will realize that people don't always make the best choices. But if they carry out step 5 above and "see how it goes," they can benefit from their experiences and learn to make better decisions in the future.

Ask your children what decisions they need to be making these days. (It is important that you give them some freedom to make choices so that they can learn from their experiences.) Guide them through the decision-making process, using the steps listed above.

Activity Six: Taking Risks

Purpose: To explore the role of risk-taking in decision-making. When children use drugs, they are taking a risk. This exercise helps children think twice before taking risks and encourages them to look for positive ways to challenge themselves.

What to do: Write out a list of activities that have unpredictable outcomes, such as the following:

- Perform in a talent contest.
- Try out for the soccer team.
- Sneak a beer when Mom and Dad aren't home.
- Run for class president.
- Steal something from a store.

Ask your children what all of these activities have in common. Introduce the ideas of uncertainty and unpredictability. In the simplest terms, these activities may turn out okay or may turn out badly. You can't know for sure ahead of time. Explain that many decisions involve uncertainty. Give an example from your own life: "I quit a job with a pretty good salary in order to go back to school, because it didn't pay as much as I thought I could earn if I had more education. For a while, though, while I was in school, I had very little money. As it turned out ... "

This helps your children see that even you, a parent, have to make tough decisions and deal with uncertainty.

Explain that doing something without knowing for sure how it will turn out is taking a risk. Risks can be very exciting and therefore appealing, but only some of them are worth taking. A good way to make a decision about a risk is to list the pros and cons and also the best and worst possible outcomes. Consider how likely it is that it will turn out well or badly, and then decide whether the risk is worth taking.

Make the concept real with exciting examples: "Some risks are really dangerous. If you stole clothing from a department store, you'd have a bit of an adventure. You'd also have some new clothing. Those are positives. But you know you can get whatever clothing you need from us anyway. Then there are negatives. You might feel guilty. And if you got caught in the store, they would arrest you. You might not get caught, but the consequences of the worst possible outcome are very bad. In my opinion, it's a bad risk. There are better ways to find adventure.

"On the other hand, imagine auditioning for the school play. It's a risk, too. You might not get a part. If you didn't, you'd be disappointed, but it's not a very big deal. If you did get a part, it would be terrific fun. That would probably be a risk worth taking."

Discuss why people take risks. Some people attempt to excel, such as by running for class president. Some are looking for excitement, such as by climbing a mountain or using drugs to see if they can get away with it. Some people take risks to be popular, such as kids who take drugs to show their friends they're cool. Some guys do dangerous things to prove they're macho. Sometimes people take risks because of their convictions: "I'm going to say what I really think, even though I know my friends won't agree."

Finally, children can be asked to name good and bad risks they have taken recently or in the past.

Activity Seven: Loosening Up

Purpose: To empower children to relax. If they can relax themselves, they won't need drugs to relax.

What to do: Explain to your children that by learning to relax when they are tense, they can alter their moods. At first do this exercise all together. Then explain that they can do it alone, without your assistance, whenever they want.

Start by telling them to get into a very comfortable position on a chair. They can take off their shoes if they wish and loosen constricting clothing. Tell them to take a few deep breaths to relax and then imagine they are in the most wonderful place in the world. Guide them through the relaxation process. Start with the tips of the toes. Tell them to tighten this part of their body as much as they can, then to relax it. Go on to the rest of the foot, with the same instructions: "Tense the rest of your foot as much as you can. Hold it for a second or two. Now let it relax." Move to the ankles, then the lower leg, knees, thighs, midsection, buttocks, stomach, chest, shoulders, arms, neck, jaw, nose, eyes, ears, and top of the head. Tense and relax the muscles throughout the body. If any part starts to feel tense again, go back to it, tense it, and then let it relax.

When the whole body is relaxed, ask some questions: "How does it feel? Do you see what power you have to make yourself relax?"

Activity Eight: Stress at Home

Purpose: To improve communication and identify causes of stress at home. To learn problem-solving as it applies to home life.

What to do: Ask your children to help you make a list of sources of stress at home. Then discuss how to cope with stress by either responding better to the pressure or finding solutions. Make a plan, put it into action, and set a time to discuss what progress has been made.

In the Romanella family, the biggest source of stress was a mad rush for everyone to get off to work and school in the morning. They decided to shift their scheduling—to prepare school lunches and to lay out the next day's clothing before bedtime. They also all decided to get up fifteen minutes earlier so that they could have a more leisurely time together.

A couple of weeks later, they agreed that the scheduling changes had been successful, but that nobody liked waking up early. They went back to the old wake-up time and found that the mornings were still better than they had been. The plan was successful.

In the Thomas family, the problem was that Eric, a fourth-grader, didn't have a quiet place to study at home. He shared a room with his younger brother, and the only desk in the house was in the living room. When he studied in his bedroom or at the desk, Eric would hear the television blasting. The family decided to establish a quiet time in the house when no radio, stereo, or television would be on. Eric agreed to do his homework during that period.

SOCIAL INFLUENCE

One reason children use drugs is in response to the influence of others, most notably the media, adults, and peers. Children can be protected against the negative influence of the media by being aware of the downside of using drugs and by developing consumer awareness.

They can be protected against negative adult influence by getting a more complete understanding of what it means to be an adult and of the process of becoming an adult.

They can be protected against negative peer influence by having positive friendships and knowing how to resist peer pressure. The activities below provide a solid foundation for teaching "resistance" skills—the ability to go against negative social influence.

Adults have their problems, too. You often hear about children and peer pressure, but we should recognize that conformity is a problem for all age groups in this culture. Many adults drink, use drugs, and engage in many other activities just to be accepted by their peers.

Activity One: Media Drug Dealers

Purpose: To increase awareness of manipulation and social influence in sales pitches, and to increase consumer awareness.

What to do: After watching commercials for beer and wine with your children, discuss them in terms of the sales pitch. Also, have your children gather alcohol and tobacco advertisements from the print media. Identify each sales gimmick. Look at the key words and concepts associated with drugs: romance, glamor, fun, success. Consider the visual message: What does the picture show? More friends? A happy family? A good time? What are the subtle messages? Who is the target? Whites? African-Americans? Hispanics? Young people? Children? Parents? Men? Women? Blue-collar workers? White-collar workers?

It is interesting to observe that much of the drug advertising is geared to young people. Most people who smoke cigarettes or drink alcohol begin during their youth. That's when advertisers want to establish loyalty to their products. Also, as older smokers and drinkers break the habit or die, the industry seeks replacements. They need young people to be drug consumers. Children should realize that they are targets.

Examine advertising tactics: the bandwagon approach (everyone's doing it); snob appeal (join the in-crowd); promises (be sexy or popular or happy); the desire to feel glamorous (identify with stars who use the products).

Point out the bias in media advertising. Alcohol is always shown being used on festive occasions, such as birthdays, parties, and weddings. People are always enjoying themselves. Ask your children to think about how alcohol could also ruin or detract from such occasions.

Point out that alcohol commercials are often used for sports and entertainment programs, so that the products are associated with health and good times. Note, too, that the alcohol industry sponsors many athletic events, such as tennis tournaments and bicycle races, probably to attempt to counter the image of their products as unhealthy. Observe that in cigarette advertisements you sometimes don't find smoke, as if the stink wouldn't permeate a room.

Part of building consumer awareness is explaining that the motivation of advertisers is to sell products and make money. They want people to be consumers, to buy and use their products. They are not interested in your well-being, so you have to protect yourself.

The bright side of what is happening in the media is the recent upsurge of public-service announcements supporting children in resisting the temptation to use drugs. But these, too, use sales tactics. To do a balanced job of helping children gain consumer awareness, look at those tactics.

Activity Two: The Age Game

Purpose: Sometimes children smoke cigarettes, drink alcohol, or use other drugs because they are trying to act grown-up. This activity is to help your children find positive ways to grow up.

What to do: With your children, conduct a survey of local rules and laws in your community related to age. Find out when children have to pay full price for movie tickets. Find out how old you have to be to get a learner's permit to drive a car, get a driver's license, drop out of school, get a job, enlist in the military, buy alcohol, buy tobacco, and vote in an election. You can expand the activity to look at the elderly, particularly if the children are close to their grandparents. Find out what the age requirements are for Social Security benefits, retirement, and senior discounts. Discuss the merits and problems of these age issues.

Introduce the concept of maturity. Maturity comes from learning through experiences. Age allows for more experience but doesn't guarantee maturity.

You can discuss the transfer of power in this context. You are giving your children opportunities to be increasingly responsible so that they will be prepared to succeed as mature adults.

Be specific. Tell them what you are allowing them to do that is part of growing up. Give examples of increasing freedom, such as places they can go where they couldn't go before. Give examples of increasing responsibility, such as the household chores or babysitting. Discuss the freedom and responsibilities they will have in the future.

Activity Three: Peer Pressure

Purpose: To help your children understand peer influence and pressure, and the concept of individuality.

What to do: Tell a make-believe story, such as this one, about fitting in with a crowd and being influenced by others: "John is out with a group of friends. They all order Big Macs, and he wants a fish sandwich. It's hard for him not to do what everyone else does. Why? What do you think John's friends would think if he ordered a fish sandwich? What would they say?"

Discuss influence and subtle peer pressure. When does influence become pressure? Also, brainstorm related situations, such as kids all wearing the same brand of jeans or liking the same songs.

Give your children support to be different: "You don't need to do everything your friends do in order to keep your friends." Discuss the concept of individuality. Talk about what makes a person special. Pick specific people, friends, and relatives, and list their special qualities. Ask your children to list their own special qualities.

Activity Four: The Bully

Purpose: To identify and resist power plays.

What to do: Children learn early, from experience, what a bully is. Talk to them about their definition of a bully and their ideas about standing up to bullies. Talk about how physical violence and the threat of physical violence are often used to push people around. Introduce the concept of power plays, the ways that people try to control others. Children will recognize violence as a type of power play. Discuss other, more subtle types of power plays. Give examples such as these:

- "Do what I tell you to do, or you'll hurt my feelings."

- "Do what I tell you to do, or I won't be your friend."
- "Do what I tell you to do, or I'll call you names." ("You're chicken." "You're stupid.")
- "Everyone will laugh at you if you don't do what I say."
- "Cool kids do it."

The second part of this exercise is having a discussion about responding to power plays. Strong responses begin like this: "I'm going to do what I think is right." Or: "I'm going to do what I want to do."

The rest of the answer to the power plays above is: "I don't care about your threats, and I don't have to explain myself to you or defend my choice."

In other words, you are teaching your children to be assertive. They don't have to take a defensive position. They don't have to explain themselves. Example: "Why don't you want to try drugs?"

The answer is simple: "Because I don't want to." Or: "Because I don't feel like it."

"Well, give me some reasons."

"I don't have to give you reasons."

Children need to know that they don't have to explain themselves to pushy, aggressive people or to bullies.

Activity Five: Just Say No

Purpose: To teach assertiveness, especially as it applies to drugs.

What to do: Children who have been raised to be gentle, agreeable, and loving individuals may find themselves with a dilemma when faced with pushy friends who are pressuring them to take drugs or act in some other way against their own will. Children often confuse assertiveness (sticking up for themselves) with aggression (attacking others). Assertiveness is an important concept to understand and an important skill to develop for coping in our society.

In this activity, you playfully test your children's ability to resist pressure and help them build their resistance skills. Ask them: "What would you say if I told you to steal food from the supermarket?" They will probably say something like: "No, it's wrong."

Taking it from there, ask: "What would you say if I said you should do it anyway, because I'm telling you to do it?"

131

You can try other examples of power plays as well, such as asking: "What if I said: 'I insist'?"

"What if I said: 'I'm your parent—you should do what I tell you to do'?"

"What if I said: 'C'mon, be brave—don't be chicken'?"

This playfulness gives you an opportunity to talk about the difference between aggression and assertiveness. You can also tell your children how important it is that they not let other people control their behavior.

After you've had some fun with the argument about stealing, you can change the focus to drugs and assertiveness. Ask your children whether they understand about not using drugs. Do they know the dangers? If they know them, discuss situations that might occur in which a group of children are trying to talk them into drinking alcohol or smoking marijuana. Ask if they could be assertive and refuse an offer. Ask what they would say and how they would feel about it. If they are nervous about "saying no," you can validate their feelings by agreeing that it is difficult to be different from a crowd.

As a parent, this is an opportunity to promote the value of individuality, of being assertive despite pressure, even when a person very much wants to be accepted by friends. Explain that, in the long run, most people respect you more when you hold on to your convictions.

Because it is difficult to resist peer pressure, suggest the strategy of staying away from people who use drugs and the places where they use them.

Give some resistance strategies, such as using "strength in numbers." If drugs are present, find the other kids who aren't using drugs and stick with them.

Now raise the issue of power plays—situations in which drug users try to coerce their friends into joining them. Pamphlets published by the National Institute on Drug Abuse suggest these responses to peer pressure:

- "No, thanks."
- "I'm not interested."
- "No way."

One good idea is to practice these responses, over and over again. Some children have difficulty being this assertive. They find it easier to make excuses or to change the topic. That's fine if it works. But they may find themselves up against one of the classic power plays, in which the aggressor keeps the other person on the defensive:

Pushy child: "I don't get it. Why not smoke weed?"

Defensive child: "My mom would kill me if she ever found out."

Pushy child: "You don't have to tell her. She'll never know."

Defensive child: "I'd rather go to a movie."

Pushy child: "That's no fun. You're just chicken."

Defensive child: "I don't think it's safe."

Pushy child: "Oh, you're chicken."

Defensive child: "Let's talk about something else."

Pushy child: "Quit being so scared. Let's just do it."

Defensive child: "My parents said they wouldn't let me use the car if I ever smoked weed."

Pushy child: "Don't be a wimp. Quit making excuses."

The pushy child will go on and on unless the other child stops being defensive. An excellent way to stop the power play is to turn the tables:

"I told you where I stand, and I don't want to change my mind. Stop trying to bully me into something I don't want to do. Get off my back."

One option children should always remember is simply walking away.

I have found that children and parents can have fun role playing imaginary scenes with peer pressure. Invent a variety of situations, involving or not involving drugs, to help your children practice their assertiveness skills. Take turns "pushing" and "resisting." Here's one to start with. Tell your children this:

"Make believe you're part of a group of kids who want to climb a fence and swim in a reservoir at night. You want to convince me to come along. I think it's too dangerous. Try to talk me into it anyway."

Or try this one:

"I want to talk you into stealing a pocketknife at a drugstore. You know you shouldn't, but a group of us want you to do it with us."

HEALTHY LIFESTYLES

The prevention of drug problems is part and parcel of promoting health. You can't have one without the other. Therefore, this workbook starts with a section on drug information but also includes activities for improving self-esteem, having more fun, minimizing stress, coping with stress, and resisting the negative influence of parents, peers, and the media. An activity that ties it all together—a sort of "master activity"—is to prepare a healthy-lifestyle checklist with your children. The idea is to get them thinking about their own physical, social, and psychological well-being. It's an opportunity for them to appreciate their strengths, identify their weaknesses, and make plans for improvement.

After your children complete the following checklist, ask them which of their health habits are good and which ones are weak and in need of improvement. Follow up with problem-solving and then help them make an action plan for change. This is an activity that can be repeated from time to time.

Weight and Nutrition
Do I eat a balanced diet?
What do I usually have for breakfast? Lunch? Dinner?
Do I eat healthy snacks?
Do I eat too much junk food? If so, which kinds?
Do I have an accurate body image?
Do I have a positive body image?
Am I in my proper weight range?
Do I eat too much sugar?
Do I drink soft drinks with caffeine? How much? How do they affect me?

Rest And Sleep.
What is the right amount of sleep for me?
Do I go to bed at my bedtime?
What happens when I don't get enough sleep?
Do I rest when I'm tired?

Recreation
What are my favorite activities when I'm alone?

What more could I do alone that I haven't been doing?
What do I like to do with friends?
What more could I do with friends that I haven't been doing?
What are my television viewing habits? How may hours do I watch? What types of shows do I watch? Do I want to change my viewing habits?
What do I do for physical exercise?
Do I exercise every day?
What are my favorite hobbies? Do I want to start new ones?
Do I read? Listen to music? Play music?

Social Life
Am I happy with the friends I have?
Do I want new friends?
Do I want to do things with my friends that I've never tried before?
How well do I get along with my friends?
Can I go "against the crowd"?
Do I want to join any clubs, such as the 4-H or Scouts?
Do I tell my friends what I feel?
Are there after-school activities that I might want to do?

Attitude and Healthy Stress Level.
Do I have a positive outlook on life?
Do I have a sense of humor?
How do I deal with stress?
Do I plan my life so that I don't have too much stress?
What is my stress level (high, medium, or low) in school? With friends? At home?
Do I face my problems? Do I solve them?
Can I say what I feel?

Hygiene
Do I bathe every day?
Do I take care of my skin?
Do I take care of my hair?
Do I brush and floss my teeth several times every day?
Do I know how to protect myself and other family members from communicable illnesses?

Safety

Do I practice bicycle safety?

Do I wear my seat belt in the car?

Do I know what to do if I'm home alone?

Do I know where I should not go alone?

Do I know what to do in case of fire?

Do I know what to do with strangers on the street and at the front door?

Do I know about poisons, medicines, prescription drugs, and illegal drugs?

Do I take undue risks?

Family

Do we say what we feel?

Do we all pitch in around the house?

Do we know how to work out our differences?

Do we have fun together?

Children who grow up in an empowering home environment with a healthy lifestyle will enter adolescence with positive attitudes and basic life skills. They will be well-equipped to handle the important decisions about drugs and other health matters that they'll be facing. In later chapters you will read about the next step—empowering adolescents through education and dialogue. But first a chapter about a special health hazard—tobacco.

5
PREVENTING
TOBACCO PROBLEMS

"I hope my kids don't smoke cigarettes, but tobacco is the *least* of my worries."   *Parent of a child who does not smoke*

"I wish my child didn't smoke, but I'm glad it's *only* tobacco."
                                                   Parent of a child who smokes

Many parents treat tobacco lightly, focusing much more attention on alcohol and other psychoactive drugs. I believe that this is a serious error. Tobacco is an extreme health hazard and an important "gateway drug." That is, it serves as an entry point to a lifestyle that eventually, or perhaps concurrently, includes the use of alcohol and other drugs that have the potential for abuse. It's a stepping-stone toward dealing with life's problems and one's own mood by using chemical substances.

Because there is so much panic about psychoactive drugs in our culture, I deliberately wrote this book as a calming, rational influence. About one subject, however, I want to express alarm: tobacco. We are in the midst of a public-health crisis. Increasing numbers of children in the United States are smoking, and they are starting younger. We have been far too weak and meek in confronting tobacco, the drug that causes the most health harm and the biggest addiction problem in the country.

Tobacco is the direct cause of one in every six deaths in the United States. It causes more than 435,000 preventable deaths each year. Cigarette smokers are more than ten times as likely to die of lung cancer than non-smokers. Tobacco causes nine out of ten cases of lung cancer and nine out of ten cases of chronic lung disease. It is the main cause of chronic bronchitis, a serious lung infection, and emphysema, a crippling lung disease. Smoking doubles the chance of heart disease and is one of the three leading causes of heart attacks.[1]

Oral forms of tobacco cause cancers of the mouth and throat as well as gum disease. The craze of cigar-smoking which has extended to youth is also dangerous. Regular cigar smokers triple their risk of getting lung cancer and double the risk of stroke and heart-attack. Cancers of the mouth, larynx and esophagus are associated with cigars. Both pipe and cigar smoking are risk factors for pancreatic cancer, a disease which is almost always fatal.

What is sometimes lost in the maze of dramatic statistics about serious diseases is the equally important fact that all tobacco use is harmful, even if you do not die from it. As physician/author Tom Ferguson has stated: "Every cigarette you smoke harms your body."[2] The same statement can be made about incidents of smoking a pipe or cigar and about every chew of tobacco. Tobacco is harmful to the body. Tobacco smoke is also harmful to developing fetuses and to non-smokers.

More than three million adolescents currently smoke cigarettes. More than one million adolescents use smokeless tobacco, including almost 20 percent of male high-school students. Twenty years ago the average age at which people began smoking was sixteen. Today it is variously estimated at between twelve and fourteen.[3,4] Smoking amongst eighth-grade students rose 30 percent in a recent three-year period.[5] Of the three thousand Americans under the age of eighteen who begin smoking each day, one of three who continue to smoke in adulthood will die prematurely from smoking related illnesses. A recent study cited in *Newsweek*[6] stated that 23 percent of people ages fourteen to nineteen had smoked a cigar in the last year.

As parents, you should bear in mind that if you can keep your children from getting hooked on tobacco before they graduate from high school, they probably won't become smokers. But you had better start early on tobacco prevention, because the tobacco industry starts early in aiming its six-billion-dollar-a-year advertising and promotional programs at your children. Until recently they have used cartoon characters for the young ones and awarded prizes (gym bags, hats, t-shirts and other gear) that appeal to teen smokers. Your children are the target of their business minds as they attempt to replace smokers who die or quit with new and younger ones. *Advertisers know that nearly all first use of tobacco occurs before high-school graduation and that children are the chief source of new customers.* The tobacco industry makes more than $270 million annually in profits from selling cigarettes and chewing tobacco to minors,[7] although this is incidental to their main purpose, which is to recruit new, young customers.

As parents, you are up against promotional activities and advertising that have included sponsorship of sports events and public entertainment, outdoor billboards, point-of-purchase displays, and distribution of specialty items that appeal to young people. Half of the children who smoke own clothing or gear, such as gym bags, with cigarette logos, making them walking billboards.[8] Tobacco promotions have been rampant in the auto-racing industry. Tobacco companies have sponsored tennis events and advertise widely in stadiums and arenas.

What can tobacco do for you? What can you expect to get from smoking or chewing tobacco? Let's consider the perspective of an adolescent. Adolescents are experiencing a tumultuous period in life when they are supposed to establish their own independent identities. They are looking for answers to the questions: Who am I? What is the meaning of life? What is important to me? As they seek to set their own course, there is a period of uncertainty, experimentation, and vulnerability. They no longer take for granted everything their parents have taught them. They are looking for new answers. Tobacco advertisers have played on the vulnerability by portraying a positive image of smokers. They present images that appeal to adolescents trying to form an identity. They portray smokers as extremely attractive young men and women having a great time in outdoor and glamorous settings. The smokers are slender. They are engaged in healthy activities and are independent, which is what adolescents are striving to become. They are adventurous, a characteristic admired by adolescents. Advertisers try to capture the imaginations of adolescents and show them a way to improve their self-images. Smoking is presented as self-enhancing: It relaxes people, leads to fun and adventure in life, and makes you attractive—important to adolescents, who are maturing physically and thinking about sexual relationships. It is an exciting pastime, essential to popularity, and a way to bond with peers.

Tobacco advertising is a hotly contested political issue. Whatever the outcome of the political battles, the impact of advertising and the need for parents to deal with it will remain for the foreseeable future. If all tobacco advertising were to be banned immediately, we still would have to deal with the legacy of these images. We would probably also have to deal with teens who have an increased desire to engage in an activity that is "so bad it is banned." Even if advertisers were prohibited from taking direct aim at young people with cartoon characters and teen "gear" giveaways, they would still find subtle ways to appeal to the emotions and vulnerability of teens and adolescents. Furthermore, the recent sales pitches to children and adolescents has probably contributed to the increased glamorization of tobacco in Hollywood, as reflected in films with lead actors and actresses lighting up on screen. This, too, is part of the legacy of tobacco advertising. At this time, tobacco smoking and chewing is seen as attractive by a large sub-set of the adolescent population.

Advertising also fosters the perception that smoking is more common than it is, and therefore acceptable. On the average, children and adolescents think that the prevalence of smoking is two or three times higher than the actual rate. Those with the highest overestimates are more likely to become smokers than are those with the most accurate perceptions.[9]

SPECIAL ISSUES IN TOBACCO PREVENTION

The challenges faced in the prevention of tobacco dependence are very much like the challenges faced in the prevention of the abuse of other drugs, with a couple of key exceptions: (1) Because tobacco is a legal drug, openly used by adults, its use is perceived as less harmful and more "normal." (2) Because you, as a parent, are opposing a billion-dollar industry whose aim is to promote this drug, you have to be much stronger in countering the industry's legacy of false propaganda, which portrays tobacco both as safe and as image-enhancing.

Other than that, it is back to the basic principles of drug prevention as presented in previous chapters:

- Teach children about healthy living. Within this context, help them understand the potential harm from tobacco and teach them about the addiction process.

- Raise children who can meet their needs without drugs. Then, if they experiment with tobacco, they will not need this drug to regulate their mood or to give them a positive self-image.
- Create a family climate in which children feel they can talk with you about anything without fear. Then, if they are contemplating the use of tobacco or have experimented with it, you will be included in the discussion. You will be a positive resource.
- Give an unambiguous message about children not using drugs: Tobacco products are a serious health hazard and are not to be used. You can enforce such a rule with younger children. With older adolescents you need to increasingly rely on persuasion and reasoning.
- Maintain ongoing family discussions about alcohol, tobacco, and other drugs.
- Should your children experiment with drugs, you can express your strong feelings. It is important to say what you think. But avoid overreacting to drug experimentation. Overreaction locks children into a rebellious position, reduces the likelihood of dialogue, and adds to the desire to smoke.

WHAT IF YOU ARE A SMOKER?

What if you are a smoker? Parents worry about the perception of hypocrisy. Would it be hypocritical for a smoking parent to insist that a child not smoke? As I said earlier with regard to marijuana and other drugs: Regardless of what you do or have done with your own life, you are still responsible for promoting healthy behavior in your children. That's a primary responsibility, calling for a clear message that smoking is unhealthy and children should not smoke, even if you smoke and may be accused of hypocrisy. To increase your impact and credibility, I recommend that you also ask your pediatrician to talk with your children about the health risks of tobacco.

If you are addicted to nicotine and regret that you smoke, you can say this to your children. Let them understand what has happened to you and that you hope they can be spared the same fate. Obviously, the best thing for all involved is for you to overcome your own addiction. There are at least four good reasons for this: (1) being a good role model by showing your commitment to health; (2) eliminating second-hand smoke from your home environment; (3) improving your own health for your own sake; and (4) improving your own health for your children's sake. (You wouldn't be reading this book if you weren't clearly committed to being a good parent. If you stop smoking, you will decrease the likelihood of premature death and thereby increase your availability to your children.) As I said earlier, sometimes people cannot make difficult changes for themselves but can for their family. You could channel an urge to care for your children into something that would be positive for you personally. I don't make this recommendation lightly. Tobacco addiction is one of the toughest addictions to break. Breaking it could be one of the most difficult challenges you will ever face. Sometimes people try to stop and fail several times before they finally succeed.

If you are committed to continuing to smoke and willing to run the health risks, then you certainly lose some credibility with your children. I would urge you to take another look at your own decision-making process. Make sure that you are not rationalizing a health hazard—thinking, "Everyone has to die sometime"—and that you have not simply given up on your ability to quit. If so, I encourage you to make a new start at overcoming your addiction. Even if you have failed before, you can still quit now.

TOBACCO DANGERS

You don't have to convince most younger children about the dangers of tobacco. They probably think that tobacco is "a smelly, dirty habit that can cause cancer and other diseases." That is the starting point unless you, yourself, smoke or somehow deliver a different message. Therefore, as you educate children about the harmfulness of tobacco, you will be reinforcing their own preexisting negative perceptions. However, because of the aggressive advertising and promotion of tobacco, you have to be equally aggressive in countering the positive messages. You can support your case about the health hazards with information presented on the previous pages. With younger children, graphic pictures of some of the diseases caused by tobacco can have an impact. You don't want to cause nightmares, but you do want them to have a realistic view of the potential harm.

In addition to planned discussions with your children, you will find numerous opportunities to spontaneously discuss tobacco, such as when you are stuck in a smoky environment. In this setting, you can ask for your children's reaction to the tobacco smell and to breathing air filled with smoke. This could evolve into a discussion about potential harm to the lungs.

In day-to-day life, you can point out people smoking and, preferably through questioning, help your children see how unattractive it is. You can have them take note of people throwing cigarette butts out of car windows, and get their reactions. You can talk about smoking when you request a seat in the non-smoking area of a restaurant or get stuck in a smokers' room at a hotel. You can have them observe smokers hacking away with serious coughs, but still lighting up. (This could lead to a discussion of addiction.) As for tobacco chewers, ask your children how they react to seeing them spit tobacco juice on the sidewalk. On these occasions, you can also talk about the health risks of chewing tobacco.

One of the best ways to introduce a discussion of tobacco is by having your children note the enormous amount of advertising and promotion for cigarettes and chewing tobacco. This is a starting point to help them see through and debunk advertising.

HARM THAT SPEAKS TO KIDS

As children get older and consider the possibility of smoking, there are certain negative consequences that seem most persuasive against tobacco use. It is not the long-term health risk that worries most young people. Rather, they are much more concerned with the economic cost of smoking and the fact that smoking causes bad breath, stains teeth, and makes their hair and clothing smell bad.

Young people also are interested in such information as the results of a survey, conducted by the American Cancer Society, that showed that 78 percent of boys twelve to seventeen say they don't want to date someone who smokes. Among girls, 69 percent say they prefer to date someone who doesn't smoke. Another concern of some young people is diminished athletic performance. Smoking reduces the amount of oxygen that the bloodstream can deliver to the body. Most coaches forbid their athletes from smoking.[10]

143

So Why Do People Smoke?

With all the convincing evidence about the harmfulness of tobacco and the reality of bad smells and stained teeth, a smart child may ask: "So why do people still smoke or chew? Why don't they stop?" This line of questioning presents an opportunity to launch a full-scale discussion about the advertising and promotion of the tobacco industry. You can talk about how this industry attempts to make smoking seem desirable so that people will start using tobacco products. Later you can talk about how people get hooked on smoking and then can't stop.

People start smoking because they see it as meeting certain needs. Tobacco is portrayed in advertising as a way to be cool; a grown-up thing to do; an attractive, sexy, and glamorous activity; a way to have fun; a way to be comfortable with other people and a way to enhance self-image. The legacy of advertising is further reflected in popular cultural trends that make tobacco seem appealing to some people. People also start smoking because they are curious about the effects of tobacco, because they believe it will alter their mood, and sometimes because smoking is forbidden, and they want to rebel or defy their parents. When a large group of peers smoke for these or other reasons, others follow suit to fit in with the crowd.

Most young people see smoking as something temporary. They start out by experimenting. They are curious or looking for a little fun or excitement, and think of it as a short term activity. They know tobacco is addictive but think, "I can't get hurt—I'm just dabbling." Practically no one thinks they will get hooked. Most expect to stop sometime in the future. As they smoke more, they begin to discover that tobacco has a positive effect on their mood. We should be honest with this information, as with other drugs. Many people derive pleasure from tobacco. If they like the effect, they begin to seek it. Eventually, many of them are surprised to discover that they have become addicted. So when children ask why people smoke, we can tell them the truth about the good feeling. But we also should emphasize our conviction that the great harm from tobacco far outweighs the benefits, and that there are other, healthier, more positive ways to feel good.

Another reason people smoke despite the dangers is that they see it as normal and widespread. Research has shown that people who overestimate the numbers of smokers are more likely to start smoking. Accurate statistics may help prevent tobacco use. That is why, when answering your children's questions about why people smoke, you should take the opportunity to discuss statistics. You can get the latest statistics about teenage smoking from the American Cancer Society. Current estimates are that 16 percent of twelve- to eighteen-year-olds and 28 percent of high-school seniors smoke. In other words, most teenagers *do not* smoke.[11]

THE ADDICTION PROCESS

Because tobacco is legal and advertising is so flagrantly deceptive, the dangers of this drug are underestimated. So children dabble with tobacco, thinking they can't get hurt. As their tobacco use increases, they still think that they can somehow beat the odds, that they won't get hooked. They should be told that nobody starts chewing or smoking tobacco, or using any other drug, expecting to get addicted. Everyone believes that he or she can get the benefits without the harm. This belief is wrong—dead wrong.

Even when they become regular smokers, many teens think they will smoke for only a few years and then quit. But they should be warned that regular use soon results in addiction and that in many cases smoking persists throughout adulthood.

Young people need to know about the ravages of nicotine addiction. It is a huge problem: Each year twenty million people try to quit, and only three percent have long-term success. Even among those who have lost a lung because of cancer or had cardiovascular surgery, only about 50 percent maintain abstinence for more than a few weeks. It's no different for adolescents: Most adolescent who smoke a pack a day are addicted to nicotine and report that they want to quit but are unable to do so. They experience relapse rates and withdrawal symptoms similar to those reported by adults.[12]

MEDIA AWARENESS AND DEBUNKING ADVERTISING

One of the best ways to counter the aggressive advertising of the tobacco industry is by debunking the strategies of the advertisers. This builds a parent-child alliance to resist and oppose what some young people have come to call "the trickmasters." Adolescents do not want to be controlled by anyone. They should learn about the subtle and manipulative techniques employed by the tobacco industry to control their choices.

You can debunk advertising by helping your children develop media literacy, which means having the ability to see how messages are delivered and what the messages really represent. In doing this, you will help your children develop their critical thinking skills.

Help your children look for the sales pitch—how advertisers are trying to reel in customers. Look at the images of smokers (slim, attractive, sexy, athletic, rugged, popular individuals) and their lifestyle (full of fun, glamor, exciting activities, parties, and sexual possibilities). Ask your children what advertisers want them to think their lives will be like if they smoke. What are the implied implications of the images presented? Help your children notice that by sponsoring athletic events and music concerts, advertisers attempt to get people to associate good times and athletic skill with cigarettes.

Some parents may enjoy making a collage with their children about tobacco advertising. Ask your children to cut out print ads for tobacco products and paste them on a sheet of poster board. Together identify the sales pitch of each ad and write it down next to the ad. For example, a sales pitch might be: "You'll look great and have lots of friends if you smoke this particular brand of cigarettes." This activity increases your child's media literacy, and the poster can be hung on a wall at home.

Help your children identify distortions of the truth in ads. For example, a healthy, athletic lifestyle is portrayed as characteristic of cigarette smokers. This is precisely the opposite of reality. Help your children notice that the negative consequences of tobacco are ignored, or even denied, by these portrayals.

Another distortion is that cigarettes in print ads generally emit no smoke and are usually extremely small and inconspicuous. What is being sold is a lifestyle: good times, popularity, sex appeal. Cigarettes are portrayed as a way to achieve this lifestyle.

Help your children understand that *they* are the targets of advertisers. For example: Cartoon characters are meant to attract young kids. Promotional items are aimed at teens. Help your children think about the strategic placement of advertising: An enormous number of signs and displays promoting tobacco are concentrated in stores *near schools.*

Popular music, television, and especially films portray various images of the use of tobacco products, some of which may be positive. The artistic expression is not designed to sell products, but can certainly influence behavior. You can discuss the way tobacco and other products are presented in popular culture with your children. You might notice and want to discuss situations which seem to glamorize or make tobacco use look "cool." This could lead to a discussion about the way dangers tend to be minimized in popular culture, and the important issue of what makes something "cool." The younger your children are when you begin to have these discussions with them, the more chance that you will start and be able to remain "on the same page." Even if you have disagreement about what makes something "cool," a discussion will at least provoke thinking and dialogue.

CHILDREN WHO DO SMOKE

Much as we would like children to stay away from tobacco, the majority of young people try smoking. Current statistics show that two-thirds to three-quarters of eighteen-year-olds fall into the category of at least trying a couple of cigarettes. This means that you must have a strategy that includes an appropriate response if you discover your child has smoked or is tempted to.

Some excellent research has demonstrated that there are five stages in tobacco use.[13] Not all people move through all five stages. Someone can stop at any point along this continuum, and that is precisely what we, as parents, want to have happen with our children. We want to stop, or at least slow, the progression through these stages:

1. The stage of forming attitudes, beliefs, and expectations about what you get from smoking.
2. The stage of trying smoking, which means the first two or three times that cigarettes are used.
3. The stage of experimentation, which involves repeated but irregular use.
4. The stage of regular use, which means at least twice a week.
5. The stage of dependence.

We know that first use is usually motivated by curiosity and sometimes by a desire to fit in with a crowd.

We know that most experimentation takes place in high-risk social environments—with a best friend who smokes, or at parties.

We know that positive attitudes about the benefits of tobacco generally lead to regular use.

We also know that it takes an average of two to three years to go from first use to regular use of tobacco. Thus we have some time to work with our children. We should be very cautious about overreacting to first use. In the remaining part of this book, a model is presented for opening a dialogue with young people so that you can encourage them to talk honestly and think clearly about their own decisions. You also want to avoid a power struggle. All too often parents harshly punish their children in response to early drug use, thereby closing the dialogue. Children become sneakier and more rebellious, stop talking with their parents, and move closer to their perceived allies, their smoking or drug-using friends, who also become their chief source of information about drugs.

We need to realize that adolescence is a period of risk-taking and experimentation, and to expect that in a drug-oriented society, with a wealthy industry pushing its products, many young people will try tobacco. We must talk with our children about what has led them to try tobacco, what they may have liked about it, and what harm could result from its use. With younger children we can hold the line with a no-smoking rule. With older adolescents we do not want to set ourselves up as someone to rebel against. Instead, we should rely on the art of education and persuasion to promote healthy choices.

If your children tell you that they have smoked, or you smell cigarette smoke on them, or they have friends who smoke, it's long past time for a serious discussion. The following chapters will help you proceed with confidence.

ACTIVITIES FOR TOBACCO PREVENTION

In addition to the types of discussions proposed above, some activities that may help prevent your children from developing tobacco problems are listed below:

1. With your children, do some research about the dangers of smoking or chewing tobacco. Call or visit the American Heart Association, American Cancer Society, or American Lung Association. Ask for free literature. Go to the library and take out books on the subject. Speak with your family doctor about the dangers of tobacco.
2. Show your children the Surgeon General's warnings on tobacco products and discuss them.

   The four warnings rotated on all cigarette packages and in all cigarette advertisements state the following:

   SURGEON GENERAL'S WARNING: Smoking Causes Lung Cancer, Heart Disease, Emphysema, and May Complicate Pregnancy.

   SURGEON GENERAL'S WARNING: Quitting Smoking Now Greatly Reduces Serious Risks to Your Health.

   SURGEON GENERAL'S WARNING: Smoking by Pregnant Women May Result in Fetal Injury, Premature Birth and Low Birth Weight.

   SURGEON GENERAL'S WARNING: Cigarette Smoke Contains Carbon Monoxide.

   The three warnings rotated on all smokeless tobacco packages and advertising (except billboards) state the following:

   WARNING: This product may cause mouth cancer.

   WARNING: This product may cause gum disease and tooth loss.

   WARNING: This product is not a safe alternative to cigarettes.

3. Have your children ask adults why they smoke and whether they wish they could stop (more than 70 percent want to stop). Talk with your children about other ways these adults could meet their needs without tobacco.
4. Have your children ask non-smokers why they don't smoke. Discuss the reasons.
5. Have your children observe no-smoking and smoking sections in public places (airports, theaters, restaurants). Ask them which they prefer and why. Discuss the pollution issue and the discomfort of non-smokers in situations where non-smoking areas are unavail-

able. Discuss the discomfort of addicted smokers when they feel a need to smoke but it is restricted.

6. Present a peer-influence situation involving cigarettes (or chewing tobacco) and help your child learn to cope with it. For example: "Imagine that you are with your best friend at a party and everybody is smoking a cigarette. How would you feel? Would you smoke? What would your friends say if you smoked? How would you feel if you smoked? What would your friends say if you didn't smoke? How would you feel?" You can practice numerous variations of this, including situations in which one other friend resists or in which your child is being pressured to smoke. Also, you can discuss positive ways of resisting peer pressure without appearing afraid, including answering assertively ("I don't want to smoke") or walking away. This exercise reinforces the exercises in the previous chapter on resisting social influence.

7. With your child, design and make an anti-smoking commercial on a piece of poster board. Your child can draw the poster and/or cut photos from magazines for a collage.

With our knowledge of the health hazards of tobacco, there is no reason in the world that we should have so many young people smoking or chewing tobacco. It is a problem we should face squarely. This means raising healthy children who feel good about themselves, are physically active, want to take care of their bodies, know about the dangers of tobacco, and have the skills to resist peer influence. This means raising children who can meet their needs without drugs. This means creating a family climate in which parents and children talk openly about important life decisions. Your children should know that if they feel like smoking or have smoked, they can come to you for guidance and support. They will be given help, not punishment. This must all be accomplished in opposition to an industry with a history of spending enormous sums of money trying to make tobacco products appear attractive, especially to children and teenagers. You need to fight fire with fire to aggressively counter the advertising and promotion legacy of tobacco companies, starting at an early age, when you and your children agree that tobacco products are smelly drugs that are bad for your health.

The tobacco industry has the money and buys the media. But you have love and respect within your family. This is a struggle you can win. You want your children to get their information about tobacco from you, not the tobacco industry and not the legacy of "coolness" it has left behind. You want to make it clear that you are against smoking because it is a health hazard. With younger children you should enforce a no-smoking ban. With older teenagers you should not set yourself up as someone to rebel against. Rather, you master the art of using the power of persuasion and logic so that you can help them make their *own* wise decisions, which will protect them from getting hooked on tobacco. Many of the techniques in the following chapters will help with that. Finally, as you will see in the last chapter of this book, there are many things that parents can do by banding together in their own communities to reduce tobacco consumption.

If you are interested in learning further information about how to teach your children about the dangers of tobacco, please refer to my most recent book from Newmarket Press devoted to this serious subject.

PART II
TALKING WITH TEENS
To Prevent or Intervene
in Drug Abuse

6

OPENING THE DIALOGUE

"How can I find out whether my child is using drugs?" That's the question I'm asked most often at lectures and workshops by parents who want to know the signs and symptoms of drug use.

Many parents who ask this question are trying to decide whether to talk with their teenagers. I point out that such a discussion is necessary whether substances are being used or not. In fact, the ideal time for the discussion is *before* suspicions arise.

Sometimes parents who ask about the signs and symptoms of drug use are trying to decide whether to play detective by snooping through their child's room. I hope not. Such an action could destroy any trust that exists in the relationship. Before taking such drastic measures, it is important to try to establish open communication.

At lectures and workshops, I warn parents who ask about detecting drug use not to wait for "evidence" before taking action. I point out that the signs and symptoms are usually quite obscure when children first begin using drugs. Unless parents stumble upon a stash, catch their children in the act, or overhear a conversation, it is unlikely that they will know about the early stages of drug use. Signs and symptoms become evident only when there is already a serious drug problem. Therefore, parents should start drug discussions before the signs and symptoms become obvious. This is especially important when you consider research indicating that many parents are unaware of their children's drug use until long after it has begun.

Nevertheless, it is important to know the signs and symptoms of drug use, such as the following: sudden and inexplicable mood changes, withdrawal from the family, behavioral and academic problems at school, money disappearing at home, bloodshot eyes, changes in sleep patterns, the sudden appearance of new friends, and a variety of others. (See Chapter 2 for a more comprehensive listing.) Various combinations of these indicators could mean that a child is involved with drugs. Parents don't want to be naive and miss the warning signs. On the other hand, I warn parents against jumping to conclusions. The signs and symptoms described above can have a variety of other causes, including depression, stress, or family problems. Regardless of cause, once difficulties occur, your children need your help.

If your children are not deeply involved with drugs, the best way to find out whether they are using drugs at all is to create the type of relationship in which you can ask for the truth and get an honest answer. I know that some parents think it is silly to ask children about their drug use: "Sure. Ask and expect an honest answer? It won't work."

It is true that children often lie about their drug use, that the barriers to communication are sometimes enormous, and that sometimes families cannot break down these barriers. But that doesn't mean *you* can't have open and honest communication in *your* family. It certainly is not easy. You need a very special relationship with your children to get honest answers about drugs. But it can be done. And if you want maximum influence in protecting your children from drug abuse, it *must* be done. If you fail to establish a family climate that allows open and honest dialogue, then you won't play a significant role in your adolescent child's decisions about drugs. Your child's peer group will be the main source of information and discussion.

Open, honest discussions are absolutely essential in preventing drug abuse. It is through discussions that teenagers learn to make wise decisions. It is also through discussions that parents can find out what their children are thinking and help them expand their awareness. Though harder to establish after drug use has already commenced, drug discussions are still essential. Even when children are deeply involved with drugs, accustomed to lying, and scared to tell the truth, the path to preventing further harm from drugs is through discussions.

In this chapter, I introduce "the exchange-of-information process," a way for adolescents and their parents to have a disciplined exchange of views about emotionally charged issues such as the use of alcohol, tobacco, and other drugs.

This process is more than merely exchanging information. But when I first devised the concept about fifteen years ago and started using it in therapy, I wanted a name that put the focus squarely on the need for parents and teenagers to be *rational*. I was seeing families in which emotions had reached such an intense level that discussions were free-for-alls, devoid of any exchange of information whatsoever.

The exchange-of-information process has five parts:

- You suggest a discussion and your children agree to participate.
- You present your thoughts and feelings about drugs.
- Your children present their thoughts and feelings.
- You discuss each other's point of view.
- You reach an understanding and make agreements with each other.

The immediate goal of the exchange of information is that adolescents, assisted by their parents, set high standards of behavior and make wise decisions about alcohol, tobacco, and other drugs. The long-term goal is that they maintain these standards and learn to make wise decisions on their own, without the help of parents.

This chapter focuses on the first stage of the exchange. It tells how you can establish the sort of special relationship that allows adolescents to talk honestly about themselves. A warm and non-threatening family climate is required. Often a great deal of work is needed to improve the climate at home before it's possible to engage in a nuts-and-bolts discussion about drugs.

WHAT ABOUT SNEAKY, LYING KIDS?

How will you know whether your child is telling the truth? The best predictor of honesty is past experience. If there is a past history of honesty, especially if your child has been willing to tell you "difficult truths," then it is likely that he or she will do so now.

If there have been lies and contradictions in previous discussions, it is possible that there will be lies now. But that doesn't mean you shouldn't talk. Rather, it means that you have to work hard to create a different climate in the family. You have to make it feel safe for your children to tell you anything. You especially want them to feel that you will protect their self-esteem and treat their problems, setbacks, and insecurities with loving support. You want them to know that honesty is an important value in your family. If they are honest about difficult truths, you will help them learn from their experiences. You will not punish them for telling the truth. If you have been too harsh or overbearing in the past, you need to change and reassure your children that they will be safe talking with you now.

Children with serious drug or other problems sometimes become chronic liars. This poses a special but not insurmountable problem. Although the philosophy of the exchange of information is one of trust and honesty, it is important that you remain observant and pay attention to your intuition. You know your children. If your children are lying, you will begin to find contradictions in their statements. Your gut feeling will tell you that something is amiss. If reality doesn't match up with what you observe or sense, then you have to discuss the discrepancy. If, for example, there is no logical, coherent alternative explanation for the signs and symptoms of drug use, then you should suspect dishonesty and talk about it. If you get one excuse after another to explain problems, you should talk about this. Observation and intuition are your backup as you strive for ever-increasing honesty. Discussion of lies and contradictions is the way to attack the problem of dishonesty. The issue of honesty will be addressed further in the next chapter.

THE BENEFITS OF THE EXCHANGE-OF-INFORMATION PROCESS

The exchange-of-information process gives adolescents a significant voice in setting rules and standards for themselves. Part of the process is parents listening to their children. This worries some parents who are concerned that this sounds too democratic. They worry about loss of parental authority. Perhaps they imagine an arrogant thirteen-year-old son, hands on hips, telling his parents that he plans to use drugs: "We had our discussion. Now it's time for me to make my decision. I think it's okay to smoke weed, so I'm going to do it."

This is *not* how the exchange-of-information process actually works. By agreeing to respectfully listen to your children and to strive for mutual understanding, you do *not* surrender your authority.

Although the ideal goal is reaching agreement (yes, it really can be done), parents and teenagers don't always see eye to eye. You still have the final word. You maintain the ultimate power in setting limits and establishing rules, as well you should.

But, you may wonder, if parents are to decide in the end anyway, why have discussions? Why go through the motions? Isn't this just a way of manipulating children?

Definitely not. There are many good reasons for having discussions:

- They provide an opportunity for parents to learn what their children are thinking.
- They provide an opportunity for children to learn what their parents are thinking.
- They increase the chances for mutual understanding.
- They increase the chances of coming to agreements.
- They increase the chances that children will comply with parental rules and regulations.
- By having discussions, parents help their children think through their own decisions.
- By having discussions, parents help their children learn skills that are needed for thinking through decisions on their own.
- Discussions give teenagers a sense of responsibility and thereby contribute to their self-esteem.
- Discussions serve as an excellent way to learn about cooperative, loving relationships.

Agreement, Understanding, and Competence

Parents who use the exchange-of-information process are often amazed to find that good discussions vastly increase mutual understanding and can lead to agreements when none seemed possible. Adolescents benefit from the input of mature adults. Parents benefit by gaining an understanding of the problems and conditions of the era. Without such discussions, parents are too far removed from their children's lives.

When agreements are made, children who participated in a discussion feel a sense of ownership in the outcome and are likely to abide by the terms that they helped to establish.

Even when parents and children do not agree after a discussion, the probability that teenagers will comply with the parental "bottom line" is greatly increased, because they have been treated with respect during the exchange-of-information process. They were given an opportunity to express themselves. Their parents listened to them. They heard the point of view of their parents and the reasoning behind it. Under these circumstances, adolescents are more likely to abide by parental rules, even if they consider them unduly restrictive.

However, to ensure success with this process, parents *must* respectfully listen to their children. Some parents have discussions because they have been told that they should, but show no tolerance for opinions different from their own. They don't realize that listening with an open mind is an opportunity to better understand their children. Even if they aren't swayed by the input, they could at least acknowledge and address the concerns that are raised.

Most of us have had the experience of talking with someone who wasn't listening or with people who were planning what they would say next while we talked. We know how bad that feels. Children feel the same way when their parents don't listen or when they talk down to them.

A good indication of open-minded communication is having a willingness to budge from your starting position. Although parents maintain the ultimate authority, children must have input. If parents are doing most of the talking, something is wrong. If children are talking, but they never have any influence in the rules and decisions that are made, they will eventually doubt that their parents are really paying attention.

Self-Esteem, Good Reasoning, and Good Relationships

Another set of reasons for using the exchange-of-information process, and probably the strongest case for it, has *nothing* to do with setting limits or establishing authority. It has *everything* to do with good parenting—parenting that empowers children to grow up as healthy and competent human beings.

As you know, an important part of preventing drug abuse is helping children develop high self-esteem, good thinking skills, and the ability to form good relationships. During the adolescent period these goals have special meaning. Children are establishing their sense of identity. They are attempting to find answers to basic questions such as: Who am I? What do I believe is right or wrong? Where do I fit into this world? In their younger years, they relied on their parents' values. Now, nearing adulthood, they seek their own answers. At the same time, adolescents are also beginning to develop mature thinking skills—in particular, learning formal logic, the ability to consider all possibilities and all outcomes in complex situations.

Let's look at an example of how a teenager's convictions can be challenged by a group of peers. This example shows why it is so important to have a clear sense of identity:

Six teenagers were crammed into a small car, five of them smoking marijuana. Fifteen-year-old Sandra didn't want to participate. But her friends passed her the joint and encouraged her to smoke. Sandra's ultimate decision to decline the offer depended upon the strength of her own sense of identity. She was sure about her position, wasn't frightened of losing approval, and held firm in her position. A clear identity was an excellent defense against peer pressure.

Thinking skills are also important in wise decision-making. Let's look at how they can influence an adolescent's decision about drugs:

Fourteen-year-old Tim lived in a school district that had a serious drug problem. He had done some careful thinking about the issue. Many of his friends used drugs and told him how much they enjoyed it. Tim saw them feeling good but also noticed that some were high almost all the time and getting into trouble. The grades of some had declined dramatically. So, although he saw that his friends were having fun, he also observed the whole picture and decided that the potential dangers of drugs outweighed any interest he had in using them. His clear logic enabled him to make a good decision.

To prepare for encounters with the real world, teenagers such as these two need a compass in order to find their way and answers about how to conduct their lives. But these answers don't come automatically with age. They require experience, practice, and effort.

By engaging your children in the exchange-of-information process, you give them much-needed experience. You help them forge an identity and learn to think for themselves. You give them a chance to clarify their own opinions and values. When it comes to drugs, this is an opportunity for you to voice your disapproval of children using drugs. But the best thing you can do for adolescents is to help *them* learn to think clearly, make good decisions, and choose a healthy lifestyle.

Another benefit of the exchange-of-information process is that it promotes high self-esteem. Children feel good about themselves when they are respected and taken seriously. This translates into greater internal strength, a stronger sense of identity, and therefore greater resistance to peer pressure.

Finally, the exchange-of-information process also supports adolescents in another important developmental task—learning about mature relationships, both romantic ones and friendships. By engaging in dialogue at home, children learn communication and cooperation skills that apply to other meaningful relationships. They learn about mutual respect. Without question, the family can be the best place to learn about mutual respect and loving relationships.

But What About Parental Authority?

In spite of the apparent logic of the exchange-of-information process, some parents believe that it puts them in a weak position. Concerned about the decline of parental influence, they want a demonstration of parent power. They say, "We have to lay down the law." They want to spell out strict rules and severely punish transgressions. They believe that fear of punishment will keep children under control and therefore away from drugs. They are very concerned with obedience.

Authoritarian parents usually start their sentences with statements such as these:

- "When I was a kid..."
- "Under my father's roof, we always knew..."
- "We wouldn't have dared..."

Many of these parents fear they would lose authority if they involved their children in a discussion. Ironically, it usually works the other way around:

1. Parents set rules without involving their children
2. Children feel that they have been discounted and therefore rebel against the rules.
3. Parental authority declines because children have not been involved in the decision-making process.

In other words, the rules and limits imposed by parents without discussion are perceived by children as obstacles to their well-being. Teenagers disregard parental authority when they feel ignored or unloved or when they don't understand the rationale for rules they are told to obey.

Once, at a workshop, I was explaining the exchange-of-information process to parents when a father in the audience started talking about how he "ran things" in his home: "My children know the rules. I tell them what's right and what's wrong. They know they'd better behave."

I was concerned that he might have misunderstood me. I explained that I advocate parental authority and believe in rules and consequences for misbehavior. I added, however, that I believe it is wise to include teenagers in the process of establishing rules.

I also explained that there are many different types of power. Rules and punishment are one type. But a parental repertoire should include others, especially the power of education—that is, the power to influence children by teaching them to make wise decisions. I asked if he explained the reasoning behind his rules to his children.

"No," he answered. "I don't believe parents need to do that. We are the adults, after all. We know what's best."

I thought about two things. First, adults may know what's best, but somehow they must help their teenage children gain that insight. I also wondered whether this man's children were rebelling, a common reaction to an authoritarian style.

"How's it working?" I asked.

"Great," he said. "All these other parents worry about their children using drugs. I never worry. My kids do as they're told. It's the same way I was brought up. My kids know that if they break a rule they'll be severely, *and I mean severely*, punished."

A woman sitting in the audience couldn't stand it. "You sound just like my father. You're driving me crazy." Then she told her story:

"When I was a kid, I had a father like you. He was always laying down the law. I hated him. The stricter he got, the trickier I became. He wouldn't let me talk on the phone at night, so I climbed out the window and went to a pay phone.

"In fact, it was kind of a challenge. Whatever he said not to do, I did. He gave me ideas about things I never even dreamed about doing. He would boast about how great his kids were—just like you—while we were being real lunatics behind his back.

"I still hate him for it. He has mellowed over the years. Now I have my own children. But I felt unloved and so untrusted. I felt as though I had to fight for my independence. I made mistakes I never would have made otherwise. He made me learn the hard way. I never felt as though I had anyone to talk to.

"Maybe the worst thing was, he made me feel that I was a bad person."

The two parents debated one another. The man insisted that he loved his children. The woman said he didn't. If he did, she said, he would trust them. I believed that the man sincerely loved his children, but I also had a strong suspicion that they didn't *feel* loved.

Parents, such as this father, who rely on strict authority and punishment to prevent drug problems are usually well-intentioned. They take what appears to be powerful action but often discover later, sometimes much later, that their power is an illusion. They huff and puff while their children openly rebel against them or sneak around behind their backs. The children become contemptuous, secretive, and cunning. As the parents try to clamp down, their teenage children become more defiant.

Authoritarian parents have a one-dimensional sense of power. They see power as attempting to control the behavior of their children. They don't understand that this kind of power is not only ineffective but counter to the healthy development of adolescents, who are striving for independence.

To quote a knowledgeable friend of mine, "Parents should give away power before it is taken away." This brings us back to the central theme of this book, empowerment.

Parents who involve their children in discussions about rules and limits give away a certain measure of control. They surrender the right to arbitrarily set limits without input. Yet, this is appropriate. In fact, the more teenagers demonstrate responsible decision-making, the more they should be granted freedom and responsibility. This is inherent in the transfer of power that occurs throughout childhood. By the time children become young adults, they should be prepared for independence.

The exchange-of-information process promotes a gradual transfer of power from parent to child. In so doing, it maximizes parental influence by promoting the strongest power that parents possess, the power to influence by education. Children who feel safe with their parents will come to them for help and advice when they need it. They will use the guidance of their parents to make wise decisions.

CONTROL VERSUS TRUST: A TRADE-OFF

Helping a child grow means gradually giving a little more responsibility to a child than he or she has had before. By relinquishing control, parents extend trust to their child, who thereby gains self-esteem.

A mother allowed her teenage son, David, to attend a large party at school. He said there wouldn't be any drugs. She was concerned, however, that a small group of students might bring alcohol or marijuana. She was making a trade-off. She traded control (she could keep him at home under her observation) for trust (she was going to show confidence in his good judgment). David knew that he should stay away from drugs, and his mother trusted that he would do that.

Will David succeed with the freedom and responsibility that have been extended? The answer to this question depends upon what is meant by success. It is inconceivable that a child (or anyone) would never make mistakes. We all experimented and made mistakes in adolescence. If success means never making mistakes, then extending trust is doomed to failure. On the other hand, if it means doing one's best and learning from mistakes, then trust helps children develop competence. If you believe in children and help them learn from their experiences, they will have their ups and downs but ultimately do just fine.

David went to the party, was surprised to see that drugs were being used, but steered clear of them. His mother had given him freedom that he was able to handle successfully. David wasn't even tempted by the drugs. Had he been tempted, he and his mother had the sort of relationship in which they could have had an honest discussion.

DISCIPLINED PASSION

"What? No pounding fists? No threatening gestures? Where's the passion in the exchange-of-information process?"

These are questions asked by parents who hold strong convictions about drugs and are concerned that calmly talking with their children about drugs could be as boring as white bread.

On the contrary, success with this method requires passion. Because you care, you *should* have strong feelings and convictions about drugs. The exchange-of-information process gives you a rational and disciplined way to express your feelings, and a structure for thoughtful and loving discussion of issues that arouse your passion.

Feelings are discussed during the exchange, but in a disciplined manner. They are described in detail, not acted out. Intensity of feeling is expressed in words rather than gestures. The idea is not to intimidate children but to let them know what you are thinking and feeling, and to let you know what they are thinking and feeling.

Below are examples of two different ways that parents communicated their feelings in similar situations. The first is an undisciplined expression of emotion:

When Maria, age sixteen, came home an hour past curfew without calling, her father turned red in the face, yelled at her, and called her "an irresponsible girl." Without even responding, Maria ducked into her bedroom. But he threw open the door and angrily told her that she couldn't go out for two weeks. Then he left.

Another girl, Marsha, also came home past her curfew without calling. Her father was much more caring and disciplined about what he said. He explained that he had been scared that something bad might have happened. When Marsha said she was fine but had simply lost track of time, he said that he was angry and that she would have to be more careful in the future. Marsha apologized, said she could understand his point of view, and promised that she would do better next time. Her father was glad to hear that she understood but said she would have to wait two weeks for another opportunity to go out on a weekend night.

Both parents punished their daughters. Some people might not feel that punishment was necessary in the second example, because Marsha admitted her mistake. In any case, the communication was more effective. Marsha definitely heard what was said. She knew that her father had been worried. She understood that he was angry, and why. Marsha's father knew that his daughter had not deliberately defied the curfew but had been careless. He knew that she regretted her error. This type of caring and disciplined communication is what takes place during the exchange of information.

In addition to the communication of feelings, the exchange-of-information process allows for strong and passionate opinions. After all, we're talking about drugs, very powerful substances. Children would be shortchanged if their parents didn't communicate their opinions and convictions. This isn't to say that parents have all the answers. But they do have more experience and are responsible for the well-being of their children. In the exchange-of-information process, strong opinions are stated, described, discussed, and explained. They are not arbitrarily imposed. It's one thing to have strong convictions, but something else to impose them on others.

PREPARATION: A CLEAR POINT OF VIEW

An open and honest discussion with teenagers about alcohol, tobacco, and other drugs is an ambitious goal requiring a great deal of preparation. The first part of preparation is being sure of your own point of view. This means being informed about alcohol and other drugs. If you are confused or uninformed, you won't be able to help your children achieve clarity. You don't need to become a drug expert or learn street lingo. Basic drug knowledge—enough information to engage in the exchange—is included in Chapter 2 of this book.

Be careful of the pitfall of self-certainty, best summarized by the phrase "If I think it's so, then it must be so." Your point of view is based on three different elements. One part is facts. Another part is interpretation of facts. A third part is values. In preparing for discussions about drugs, it's important to learn to differentiate among the three.

Failure to differentiate results in confusion. In a counseling session, I heard this exchange between a parent and child that illustrates the confusion of facts and opinions. The topic was marijuana. First, some facts: Marijuana is an illegal drug that creates a mild euphoria among users. Now the dialogue, with my comments in parentheses:

Parent: "Marijuana is illegal."
Child: "Yeah, I know."
(As you see, they agree on the facts.)
Parent: "It's a very bad drug. I don't want you using it. Do you understand?"
(Here we see an opinion, that marijuana is "a very bad drug," presented without any factual back-up.)
Child: "It's not any worse than the martinis you drink."
(The child is responding tit for tat.)
Parent: "Anyone who smokes marijuana would have to be crazy."
(An opinion is presented as a fact.)
Child: "I don't agree. I know kids at school who smoke, and they aren't crazy."
Parent: "Well, it's illegal."
Child: "So is speeding on the freeway. You do *that* all the time. Are you crazy?"

In this dialogue, the parent and child agreed about the illegality of the substance. But when the parent began presenting opinions as if they were facts, the child became oppositional and was prepared to argue against *anything* that was said.

Opinions about what is good and bad are almost always subject to debate. The same is true with right and wrong. In a good discussion, people have their opinions, perhaps strong ones, but don't state them as facts. However, they are capable of explaining why they hold a particular opinion. They can say, in their own words: "This is what I know is a fact.... This is my opinion about the facts.... "

Even though opinions and values are subjective, they are still an important consideration in drug discussions and agreements. This is well illustrated by a statement that a father made to his son during a counseling session:

"I'm strongly opposed to teenagers' drinking alcohol at parties. I know that alcohol helps people relax. But if you use it to relax, you won't learn to deal with people. The alcohol will cover your nervousness at parties. In my opinion, it's important to muck your way through tense feelings, to learn how to connect with other kids, and to enjoy being around them without using drugs. I think it's not a good idea to go to parties where kids are drinking. If someone does bring alcohol to a party, I want you to abstain."

PREPARATION: BEING PERSONAL

The effectiveness of the exchange-of-information process is based on honesty and openness. It is a two-way affair. Parents who want their adolescent children to talk openly about themselves should be prepared to do likewise. Your children will probably be curious about your own history with drugs. Your point of view will certainly reflect your life experiences.

In a counseling session, a father who was a police patrol officer expressed his strong feelings about alcohol at parties to his daughter. He told her that he didn't want her going to parties where alcohol was served. He recognized that his own viewpoint was skewed by his experiences as a police officer:

"You know, because of my work I'm particularly sensitive about legal issues. And because you're a minor, you shouldn't drink alcohol. But the toughest thing for me is that I see firsthand the most horrible results of drunk driving. I know I'm probably supersensitive because of my work experiences. But that's part of who I am. I want you to be able to go to parties but not to those with drugs and alcohol. I want to be able to relax when you go out. I couldn't relax if you were at a party where drugs were present."

Though his daughter wanted more freedom, the father's ability to articulate the *personal* basis for his point of view helped the two of them understand each other and reach an agreement.

In the course of a discussion about drugs, it's very likely that teenagers will ask you about your own habits and experiences, past and present. You're a role model. There's no escaping it. Parents who haven't resolved their own drug problems—and there are millions of them in this country—will have diminished effectiveness with their children. Sometimes the realization of this negative influence on children serves to motivate parents to get much-needed help for themselves.

You don't have to have a flawless background to be a good influence on your children. If you've had drug problems, it's important only that you've solved them or are in the process of solving them and that you can explain your experiences. Such candor is appreciated. The more you open up, the easier it will be for your children to talk honestly.

Some parents think that to be effective with their children they themselves should be drug-free. They believe they will have to give up their glass of wine with dinner and cocktails over the weekend if they are to ask their children to refrain from indulging. These parents need to realize that there's a difference between a mature adult using drugs and a teenager using them. Furthermore, adults who use legal drugs *responsibly* provide an excellent role model for future behavior.

PREPARATION: WHAT IF YOU DON'T LIKE WHAT YOU HEAR?

Once your own ideas are clear, another part of preparation is thinking ahead to what your children may say. You may not like what you hear. Your children may be thinking thoughts, or doing things, that will make you uncomfortable. Even if they aren't, they still may test your sincerity by saying that they are. How will you respond if you hear something discomforting? Some parents panic about the safety of their children. Others feel insecure about themselves ("I've failed"), which may be translated into resentment and insecurity about their children ("They have failed me"). Will you be tempted to end the discussion and slip into the mode of control power?

I gained insight into this tendency during a workshop I conducted for parents and teenagers at a hotel a few years ago. I asked some of the teenagers in the audience to volunteer to come to the microphone. Then I asked them whether they could talk openly about drugs with their parents.

I had done this before. Occasionally one or two teens would say they could talk with their parents, but the majority would say they couldn't. Then I would ask the ones who couldn't talk why this was so. Usually they feared punishment or a lecture of some sort.

On this particular occasion, eight teenagers were on the stage with me, *all saying they could talk openly with their parents.* If they could talk with their parents, I wondered, why was I invited to discuss family-communication problems? Something was wrong. I probed a little, first asking one teenager:

"Are you sure you can talk openly about drugs?"

"Yes. "

"How about you?" I asked another.

"Yes."

"You?"

"Yes."

I was getting nowhere. "Can you talk about sex?"

An echo of yeses reverberated. It appeared that these kids had good communication with their parents. It was a rare audience. I began to wonder whether I was in the right conference room. But then I figured it out:

"What if you smoked weed? Could you tell your mom?"

"No way! Are you kidding?"

Aha. These kids could talk with their parents about anything, even sex and drugs, as long as they said exactly what their parents wanted to hear. Communication would break down if they said something that their parents didn't want to hear.

The exchange-of-information process will not work if parents overreact. To be successful, it's essential that you accept your child's opinions or actions as the *starting point* for discussion. At times the temptation will be to revert to strict authority, harsh criticism, and punishment. That will mean converting to the ever-so-easy mode of "control power." It will probably mean the end of honest and open discussion, too. Momentary control may be gained, but the chance of a significant learning experience will be reduced. In the teenage years, the best educational experiences always involve dialogue.

In preparing for what you may hear, I think it helps to be aware of a certain paradox. I suggest that you imagine the worst possible scenario about a child. Maybe you will think about a teenage daughter admitting to regular use of cocaine. Pretty terrible, but let's make it worse. Suppose this girl is also pregnant.

171

This scenario could get anyone's heart beating rapidly. If you can respond to this situation *without panic*, in spite of inner turmoil, then your teenagers will be able to talk to you. The ideal response would be something like this, said with affection:

"I love you. I'm on your side. I'm glad you could tell me what has happened. Solving this problem won't be easy, but together we can figure it out."

In other words, if children are certain that you won't panic, that the roof won't cave in on them, then they will feel free to talk. If the lines of communication are open, they will have the benefit of your mature input into their decision-making process. When this happens, you decrease the likelihood that the disaster described above, or any other terrible problem, will occur.

A cool, calm, and collected parental response to hearing something painful will go a long way toward increasing understanding. Such calmness requires discipline but pays great dividends.

THE SHY CHILD

At drug workshops some parents have said that their children are introverted and very shy about talking about themselves. They doubt that the exchange-of-information process would work with them.

My response surprises these parents. I say that their children *especially* need the exchange. If they cannot articulate their feelings, then they are holding them inside and growing up without feedback and input from others. These children are isolated, alone. They need support to deal with drug pressures and temptations. They need parents who will help them open up and overcome their emotional barriers.

This doesn't mean the hammer approach. Intimidation won't work. It means parents empathizing with their children about how hard it is for them to express themselves, yet saying that they must learn to overcome their shyness. It is only by bringing their inner thoughts and feelings into "public" view that children can benefit from guidance and support.

Shy children will not open up suddenly. They need encouragement but also patience and, most of all, a feeling of safety. As they reveal their inner thoughts, parents should be accepting and supportive.

If a child is severely withdrawn, the family may need to seek professional help.

THE METHOD: CAN WE TALK?

The exchange-of-information process borrows from an old line of comedienne Joan Rivers. The first step is to ask, "Can we talk?" This is a simple but important way to initiate a dialogue with your child.

In the exchange-of-information process, "Can we talk?" is a serious question. Without consent, it's pointless to proceed.

A discussion should be proposed in a relaxed, non-threatening way, with enthusiasm rather than anxiety, possibly after the topic of drugs arises spontaneously or simply as an issue worthy of discussion. You can calmly say, "I'd like us to talk about drugs. What do you think?"

If you're the parent of an eleven-year-old or older child and you haven't previously broached the subject of drugs, you might start by expressing your own desire to "get with it":

"I know that lots of kids begin to drink and use drugs at a young age. Let's talk. I want to know your thoughts and feelings, and I want to tell you mine. How does that sound?"

A child's response to this proposition will be influenced by previous history. An enthusiastic "Yes, let's talk" would be unusual. If your child does agree, you can proceed to the next step, the discussion itself.

One possible response to a proposed discussion is: "No way. I'm not going to talk with you." If this happens, the most important issue is the family climate, not drugs. The question becomes: What can be done to improve the climate so that discussions can take place?

Another common response to the question "Can we talk?" is an unconvincing "Yeah, yeah, sure. Go ahead." The not-so-hidden message is "Get it over with. Give me your usual lecture. Set the rules as usual. I'll pretend I'm listening."

Eager parents take this "Yeah, yeah, sure" literally and begin the discussion. It's a mistake, because the child has not really agreed to talk. The best response is: "It doesn't sound as though you sincerely *want* to talk. You're not at all convincing."

This will probably elicit another "Oh, just go ahead," with an implied "Get it over with." But this "Go ahead" is no more convincing than the initial one. The parent again should resist the temptation to proceed: "It *really* doesn't sound as if you're ready for a discussion. It sounds more like you want to go through the motions and get it over with. I don't want to have a discussion until I'm sure you want to talk. I want to talk *with* you, not *at* you."

If your child says "No way" about a discussion or persists with an insincere "Yeah, yeah, sure," then you have to work on improving communications before you can discuss drugs.

Behind every "No, I won't talk" is an unspoken reason. To open the dialogue, the obstacles must be revealed and addressed. This means probing for problems. Sometimes it's a simple misunderstanding, sometimes just a minor reluctance to proceed. But be prepared. Asking about obstacles to a dialogue about drugs is an invitation to be criticized.

This is the hard part of opening the dialogue. If you ask your children to honestly say what is keeping them from talking, you must be willing to hear their criticism and to make some changes. Sometimes you even have to courageously invite and encourage criticism:

"Why is it that you can't talk about drugs with me? I'm willing to hear your feelings and your criticism. I'll take them seriously. I know you have to feel safe to talk. If I've done anything to keep you from opening up with me, I want to hear about it."

It takes a major-league commitment to invite criticism. But the alternative—a poor one—is a closed relationship and diminished influence about drugs and other important decisions.

Some parents worry that accepting criticism from their children means admitting mistakes and therefore losing authority. While it does sometimes mean admitting mistakes, such an admission is a positive step. It shows that you are listening to your children. Also, you set a good example: You want your children to admit mistakes too, so that they can learn from their experiences.

SIX OBJECTIONS TO TALKING

When parents ask their children why they can't talk freely about drugs, six major reasons are usually given: anger about an intrusion into their personal business, anger about not being trusted, suspicion about this sudden interest in dialogue, doubt that they will be understood, fear that they will be punished, and fear that they will be given a lecture. These reasons are listed below, along with a commentary on each and a suggested response.

Objection: "It's none of your business. It's up to me to make my own decisions about drugs. I don't need to explain myself to you."

Commentary: You can support the notion that your adolescent child should be making wise decisions and explain that this is precisely why you want to talk. In the past, when your child was younger, you would have simply laid down a rule. Also, you can clarify your intent: Your child does not need to explain himself or herself to you. Rather you want a dialogue. Finally, it makes sense to acknowledge that you cannot control your child's behavior, but you should disagree with the assertion that a decision about drugs is "none of your business."

Response: "You know, I agree that when all is said and done, it's your decision about using drugs. I can't, and shouldn't, try to control you. But I disagree that it is none of my business. I'm your parent, and love you very much. I have a big stake in your success and want to do my job as a parent well. All through the years, as you make more and more of your own decisions, I want to be having discussions with you. I want to support you in making good choices. I would be irresponsible if I sat on the sidelines. Anyway, I think you might be surprised: You might even find my input helpful."

Objection: "What's the matter? Don't you trust me? I'm probably the only kid in my class who doesn't use drugs. You should see the other kids. But with my luck, I'm the one who has a mom who accuses me. I don't even drink alcohol. You're being ridiculous. I wish you'd leave me alone."

Commentary: Children who are not accustomed to open-ended discussions about personal matters may assume that their parents are suspicious about them. Parents need to make clear the purpose of the discussion and offer reassurance that they are not suspicious (if they aren't). If there is reason to suspect drug use, you should be honest about that, too, yet express an openness about hearing differently.

Response: "It's important that we be able to talk about things like drugs in this family. I'm not accusing you. I'm glad that you don't use drugs and that you're doing so well without my input. But there are drugs all around. It must be hard if you're one of the few kids who don't use them. I think these are tough times to be a teenager. I want to be on your side. In order for me to do that we need to talk with each other. Even if you were using drugs, I'd still be on your side."

Objection: "Why the sudden interest in talking? You never seemed interested in what I was thinking before. Did you read a self-help book or something? No way I'm going to talk with you."

Commentary: This is an understandable response in a family in which personal issues have not been discussed very much. Under these circumstances, it helps to begin with a little self-criticism.

Response: "You know, with all the news about young people using drugs, I think I've been kind of hiding my head in the sand and shirking my responsibilities by not discussing drugs with you sooner. Not that I suspect you're using them or anything, but simply because I know that drugs are available, and I want our home to be a place where you can talk about everything. I want us to face this issue together. And by the way, you're right. I did read a self-help book. I want to be the best possible parent I can be. I want this to be the beginning of a positive change. We need to start talking with each other."

Objection: "Don't be silly. I don't want to talk with you. You'd be the last ones I'd talk with. Times have changed since you were a teenager. You wouldn't understand."

Commentary: Times certainly do change. The concern about misunderstanding is probably sincere. But the whole idea of good communication is to break down barriers and reach mutual understanding. This point needs to be stressed.

Response: "I'm sorry you see us as the last ones you'd want to talk with, because if things were all right in our family, we really would be the first. I know we're from a different generation. I know times have changed. That's why we want to have a dialogue. We want to be able to understand the changes. If we don't talk with you, we'll be out of touch. And, you know, we do have *some* knowledge and experience. We want to share it with you."

Objection: "Yeah, sure, talk with you and get punished. Forget it. Even if I told you why I *don't* want to talk, you'd punish me."

Commentary: If punishment has been the mode in the family, then your children most certainly will expect the same in the future. Even if it hasn't been the mode, they may fear it. You need to reassure them that you want mutual understanding and won't be punitive. Punishment would not lead to the type of result desired from the exchange-of-information. You should provide amnesty (or forgiveness) for what has happened to date, even if your child has used drugs. Remember: Amnesty doesn't preclude stating a strong point of view and establishing high standards of behavior henceforth.

Response: "I promise that I won't punish you for what you say or what you've done. I know that at times I've lost my temper when you've told me something I didn't want to hear. This time I'll listen to you. I'll take what you say seriously and use more self-control. I want us to be able to talk."

Objection: "I know what you'll do if we talk. You'll lecture me just like you always do. You'll tell me that when you were a kid you never did things like kids do nowadays. Then, if I argue, you'll interrupt me and turn stone-cold."

Commentary: If you've been preachy in your discussions to date, small wonder your children anticipate more of the same. Remember, the exchange-of-information process is based on dialogue. You need to listen attentively without interrupting. Give your opinions instead of lecturing and explain the *reasoning* behind your opinions.

Response: "You're right. I've been preachy at times. It's been a mistake. This time I'll try to share my opinions with you, but I won't lecture. And I'll listen to what you think and feel. Things are going to be different, because I want us to have good discussions. Most of all, you can be sure that I won't panic and throw down some big punishment." (Some parents worry that making this commitment leaves them powerless if they discover their child is harmfully involved with drugs. This underestimates their ability to influence their children through reasoned discussions.)

It Takes Time

The transition from a closed family to one with open communication takes time. One of the most effective and least-used communication methods is backing off and giving space.

When a teenager is wavering, he or she may be thinking, "I don't know whether I really want to talk with you yet." This is an opportune moment for backing off.

An effective reply is: "Why don't you think about it a while, and we'll discuss it again in a couple of days."

Sometimes people need time to think in privacy. The whole idea that a parent is willing to *really* listen and won't dish out heavy duty punishment might take a while to sink into the consciousness of a teenager who expects a parental lecture followed by parental control. The willingness to back off shows that you are going to be respectful.

Patience is a virtue in the exchange of information. Usually that patience is rewarded. Sometimes the discussion will take place right away. In most cases, children will at least begin talking about their hesitations within the first week. Even if dealing with drugs is put on the shelf temporarily, improving the family climate is the most important first step toward parents' having a powerful educational influence on their children. It may take time to build up trust. But it will be time well spent.

Meanwhile you are sure about one thing: Because you love your children, you will persevere in your efforts to open the dialogue about drugs. You would be doing them a disservice if you did anything less. You will continue to work to establish a dialogue until it happens.

When You Find Cigarette Papers in Your Child's Dresser

After explaining the exchange-of-information process to parents, I like to use role-playing techniques to demonstrate it. This is the situation I often present at workshops:

You have done your son's laundry and are putting his underwear into his dresser. You are *not* snooping. To your great surprise, you stumble upon cigarette papers. You know that they can be used to roll "joints." You've never talked about drugs with your child. That evening, after dinner, you ask your son whether the two of you can have a personal talk. He stays behind. You want to open a dialogue about drugs. How do you do it?

When I first started using this exercise in workshops, I let parents do the role-playing with each other, one parent playing the role of a parent and another one playing the role of a son. But I noticed that, most of the time, the one who played the parent scared the daylights out of the one who played the son, usually by bringing up the issue of the cigarette papers very abruptly. So nowadays I usually ask a parent to play son, but I play the parent.

Realizing that there are a variety of ways to successfully open a dialogue about drugs, I play my part differently depending upon the audience. If the parents in a particular audience tend to be alarmists, I ignore the discovery of the cigarette papers. By doing this I emphasize that the issue is opening the dialogue, not building a case based on evidence. I figure that if drugs have never been discussed in this imaginary family, I can start a discussion on the ground floor without mentioning the cigarette papers. The drawback of this tactic is that it leaves me, the parent, with a secret, and perhaps also a burning desire to discuss it.

At other times in this role-playing, I take a different approach and discuss the cigarette papers. Below is the transcript of such an interaction I had with a parent who played the role of a difficult teenager. After I asked, "Can we talk?" this is what happened between my "son" and me:

Me: "You know, I was putting away your laundry today, when I stumbled upon cigarette papers in your drawer. I really wasn't snooping. I was just . . . "

Teenager (played by a parent): "You what? You were snooping in my room! Damn it, I can't have any privacy. This house is awful. You had no business looking through my things."

Me: "I wasn't looking through your things. I never do that. I was putting away your laundry. That's all."

Teenager: "You creep. You snoop."

Me: "Please, don't get nasty and call me names. I wasn't snooping, and I'm not accusing you of anything. But you're fourteen years old, and we've never really had a talk about drugs. I think we should be talking, and it's my mistake that we haven't. Whatever you're doing, using them or not, we need to talk and understand each other.

Teenager: "Well, I don't want to talk with you. Not after you were looking through my dresser."

Me: "Truly, I wasn't snooping. But I can see that you're upset and not ready to talk right now. I'm going to wait a couple of days before bringing it up again. But I do want us to be able to talk."

As you can see, in the role-playing I was self-critical about not discussing drugs sooner. Self-criticism is a powerful tool in developing a positive family climate. It is disarming. When parents are honestly critical of themselves, children feel safer. They feel that they can be more open and admit their own mistakes.

I gave my "child" a few days to "calm down." We then continued the role-playing.

Me: "Son, I want us to talk openly about drugs. You know it's really hard for me to bring up the topic, and I'm sure it's hard for you to talk about it with me. But I want us to have good communication. I love you a lot."

Teenager: "Go ahead, get it over with. Let me hear your lecture."

Me: "I don't want to lecture you. I'm sorry if that's what you expect. I want us each to talk."

Teenager: "Yeah, sure. I'll tell you what I think, and you'll punish me."

Me: "I promise I won't."

Teenager: "You say that now. Maybe you won't do anything right away. But who knows? A week or two later, when you're mad about something, you'll probably throw it back in my face."

Me: "If I've done that before, I'm sorry. I promise I won't do it now. I want us to reach some understandings. I'll tell you what I honestly think. But I'll also be respectful of your opinions."

Teenager: "That'll be a change."

Me: "Yeah, it will. But it's the kind of change I want to make."

Teenager: "Well, I've tried weed. It's no big deal."

Me: "I'm glad you could tell me that. I want to keep on talking, so that we can understand each other."

In playing my role, it was difficult hearing that my son had smoked marijuana. I regretted I had waited so long to talk with him. But I knew that we were making progress. We began talking. We opened the dialogue. And I believed that through our discussions I could have a positive influence.

Opening the dialogue about drugs with adolescent children is a big challenge. If your children find it difficult to talk with you about sensitive topics, then this problem temporarily takes precedence over the drug issue. Creating a family climate in which your children can talk openly is crucial, with regard to not only drugs but all other emotionally charged issues as well. Time spent in opening the dialogue is time well spent. Open, honest dialogue probably won't happen overnight, but the benefits last a lifetime. Once the dialogue is open, the next two tasks in the exchange-of-information process are listening to each other and making family agreements. The following chapters tell how to do that.

7
LISTENING TO EACH OTHER

You could cut the tension in the room with a knife. Mrs. Robbins, home from a workshop on drugs, started a discussion with her son, Mark, who seemed reluctant to talk. He complained that she overreacted to everything. She promised to stay calm but knew it wouldn't be easy, because Mark's reluctance made her suspect that he might have something to hide.

"I think," Mark said, "that kids using drugs is no big deal. Lots of kids smoke weed. And I think the reaction of adults to cocaine is *way* overblown."

Mrs. Robbins was close to panic. She had promised restraint and now wondered whether that had been a mistake. She sat there quietly as Mark continued.

"But Mom, I'm not interested in drugs. It's just not my thing."

Suddenly Mrs. Robbins was almost ecstatic, but not quite. She needed reassurance. "Really?" she asked.

"Mom, don't you trust me?"

She thought for a moment. She knew the various signs and symptoms of possible drug use. Mark had shown none of them. He had a history of responsible behavior. He hadn't lied to her about anything.

"Yes, I do trust you," she told Mark.

"Then let's drop it already. I want to go do my homework."

Mrs. Robbins knew that many parents would kill to have their kids eager to do homework. So she happily dropped the topic.

Mark had told the truth. He had never used drugs and had no interest in them. But by allowing the conversation to end as it did, Mrs. Robbins missed an important opportunity for a discussion. She could have trusted her son, as he requested, but still talked with him and helped him become more fully informed and better prepared for future decisions about drugs.

That same evening, a few houses away, Mr. and Mrs. Jordan, who also had attended the drug workshop, had a discussion with their daughter, Lisa.

"Sure I smoke weed," she told her parents. "What's the big deal?"

Her confession started a long and serious discussion. Lisa explained why she smoked. "Everything's more fun when you're high. I like it. Anyway, it's the same as you guys having a couple of beers at night."

The Jordans listened to their daughter and then very reasonably explained their thoughts and feelings. They emphasized the health risks, the risks of addiction, and the possible legal consequences.

The discussion dragged on for almost two hours. Mr. and Mrs. Jordan wanted "success," but not based on a rule they couldn't possibly enforce (Lisa could smoke marijuana secretly). They wanted "success" based on education. They wanted Lisa to understand the potential harm of using drugs and, on that basis, to agree to stop.

After their very lengthy discussion, Lisa finally said that she would not smoke marijuana anymore. Her parents beamed with satisfaction, thinking that they had successfully confronted a very tough issue without making threats. They didn't realize that Lisa had grown tired of the endless debate. They hadn't attempted to impose harsh rules, but their desire for immediate success had led them into a long and embattled competition of words. Lisa felt that the discussion wouldn't end until she agreed with their point of view. So she promised to give up marijuana but never really intended to hold to that promise.

As you can see, there are many potential pitfalls in discussions about drugs. Mrs. Robbins missed an opportunity to help prepare her son for future decisions. Mr. and Mrs. Jordan overpowered their daughter with words.

This chapter will help you avoid these and other pitfalls. In the preceding chapter, the first stage of the exchange-of-information process—opening the dialogue—was presented. Once it's open, it's time for the discussion to begin. In this chapter, the focus is on parents and children explaining and clarifying their points of view. The emphasis is on promoting openness, so that your children can speak freely. The emphasis is also on using communication skills to help your children expand their awareness.

BEGIN WITH YOUR THOUGHTS AND FEELINGS

Someone has to go first in this discussion. Ask your children what they prefer. Probably they'll want you to start, just to get a feel for your position.

Much of what you say will be personal, based on your own values and experiences. My recommendation is to start with a statement that demonstrates open-mindedness about drugs and shows your love. Continue by sharing some of your beliefs and opinions. Keep your opening statement brief, bearing in mind that this is only the beginning of a dialogue and the first of many discussions. You don't have to say everything.

Most children will have heard "drugs are terrible" statements from radio and television public-service announcements and possibly school anti-drug programs. They may have heard "drugs are wonderful" statements from friends, siblings, and other sources.

In your opening remarks, I recommend more neutral "drugs are available" and "drugs are powerful" statements. In this context, you can say that you want to be on your child's side in facing this drug-filled world.

One father put it this way:

"I know that anyone who wants to get alcohol and other drugs can get them, even kids. Because drugs are such powerful substances, I think it's important that we talk about them. I want to support you.

"Drugs change the way people feel and behave. They can make people feel good or make them feel bad. People take drugs to feel good, but as you may know, they can cause serious problems, too."

I like this beginning. This parent avoided pharmacological statements. He knew there was plenty of time for that later.

Some children, however, may be curious about drug pharmacology and ask questions. If this happens, Chapter 2 provides the basic information you will need in order to answer such questions.

Now talk about yourself—your opinions, your attitudes, and if you want, your experiences. You may want to talk about people you and your children know who have been adversely affected by drugs. You may want to discuss the way your own opinions have changed over the years. Self-disclosure is a complicated issue. When you open up about your own history with drugs, you increase the chances that your teenage children will talk openly, especially if you are willing to be self-critical. You also open a can of worms. If you have used drugs, combative teens can say, "Aha! You did it, so I can do it, too." If you haven't used drugs, they can say, "You've never used them, so you don't know what you're talking about." I believe, therefore, that disclosure of your own drug use can be helpful when there is an existing spirit of openness. It can be used to promote further openness. However, it should not be viewed either as a key factor in establishing a "gold standard" (if you look "good") or as an example of what is wrong with drugs (if you look "bad"). Also, if there is a great deal of tension, guardedness, and hostility in the family, this problem should be addressed first, before your own drug history becomes the focus and gets you off track.

If you do have a problem with alcohol or other drugs, it has probably been detected. Hopefully, you are working on it yourself. You can talk honestly about how drugs have adversely affected you and say that you hope your children can be spared this pain and suffering. If you're not working on it, don't expect that your discussion about drugs will carry much clout with your children.

In this stage of the exchange-of-information process, one task is to begin to discuss your beliefs about teenagers and drugs. As you speak, make a distinction between facts and opinions. You might say, for example: "My opinion about teenagers' drinking alcohol is ... I base this opinion on these facts ... I base it on these observations ... I base it on these experiences ... "

Be brief. Say a little and give your child a chance to talk. Most of all, right from the beginning, it is important to avoid what I call "conversation-stoppers." These are threats or extreme statements that cast aspersions on anyone who may think or behave in a certain way. These statements abruptly end discussions:

- "Anyone who does drugs has to be crazy." (There goes mutual respect. If a child has experimented even once, he or she has been put down and may simply clam up.)

- "Anyone who thinks about doing drugs is irresponsible." (This silences the child who has even thought about it.)
- "No one in this family would ever even consider using drugs." (A child may wonder, "What am I, chopped liver?")
- "If I ever find out one that of my kids has used drugs, I'll turn him over to the police." (Testing a threat like this would be a worthy challenge for a teenager working on a sense of independent identity.)

YOUR POSITION ON DRUG USE

This stage of the exchange is not the time to set rules. In this part of the discussion, you are sharing thoughts and feelings. The rules and agreements are established during the final stage of the dialogue, after everyone has had an opportunity to speak.

My recommendation to parents of younger teenagers is to assert the position that drugs are not for children because of the potential health hazards. I personally believe that, as a society, we should send a no-drug-use message. Even if many teenagers experiment without harm, too many of them are harmed. I see no reason to accept the inevitability of drug use by children. It's inevitable only if we fail to set a high standard.

You may have different ideas about the unequivocal "say no" attitude. A convincing argument can be made that certain older teenagers have the ability to control their use of alcohol or other drugs and could use these substances without substantial harm, even though it is illegal. Literally millions of adults smoke pot without significant harm, and that, too, is illegal. Many of these adults have not developed a dependence and are willing to take the risk of breaking the law. It is possible, therefore, that some older, more mature teenagers could do the same and that some parents would approve. These are personal decisions involving risks that you and your children may be willing to take.

I trust that you're aware of the dangers of drugs. I'm not going to try to scare you away from your position. This doesn't mean—as I'm afraid some readers may misunderstand—that I encourage drug use, only that I can't tell people what to do with their own children. However, I do *not* recommend allowing drug use, and I urge you, if you permit it, to closely and carefully monitor what happens, in order to make certain that no self-deception about possible harm takes place.

Because most parents share my point of view that children should not use drugs, this chapter and the next are written from this perspective. If you accept drug use by older teenagers, you can use the same principles of communication and negotiation, but you will have to extrapolate the specific applications.

At this point it would be wise to account for the possibility that a teenager may already be using drugs or at least considering the possibility. I would say:

"It may be you are thinking about using drugs or already using them. All I am saying now is my own point of view. If you are thinking about using or are already using drugs, we still need to talk. I won't panic about what you say and will hear you out. It is important that we share our points of view, even if we disagree."

I would present my point of view in terms such as these:

"The reason I don't think children or teenagers should use alcohol or other drugs is that this is a time for you to learn to get high on life, without drugs. It's a time to learn how to cope with stress and how to solve problems, without drugs. It's a time to learn how to make good relationships, without drugs. But if you get high on drugs, they can keep you from developing your own inner strength.

"Anyway, drugs are powerful substances and can be harmful. As you know, even adults make poor decisions about drug use and can't control themselves. I think the risks are greater for young people. Also, drugs are illegal. I don't want you to break the law. That's my point of view."

I would save the issues of addiction, peer pressure, and lack of life experience for later, once the flow of the discussion is going.

STOP TO LISTEN

Now that you've started the discussion, it's time for your children to talk. Ask them what they think. For a dialogue to occur, the atmosphere has to remain loving and supportive. You want your children to feel safe. Like anyone else, they won't talk openly about personal matters if they feel threatened.

If I had only three words to say about good dialogue, they would be *listen to understand*—that is, listen without defensiveness or distortion. When emotions are aroused, this is sometimes easier said than done. However, try to avoid interrupting and the temptation to pick apart, rather than to understand, what your children say.

Concentrate on listening. Try to avoid distortions. In an extreme example, a teenager asked to have her curfew extended past midnight because of a very special party. Her father said, "You're telling me that you want me to say it's okay for you to use drugs and have sex. Well, I won't say that." This father was listening to his own assumptions and not to the words of his daughter.

One helpful listening technique is simple—pause and take a moment to think about what you have heard before responding. This prevents interruptions and reduces defensiveness.

Another excellent technique for good listening is to paraphrase what someone has said: "Let me see whether I understand you. It sounds as though you feel . . . " When paraphrasing, you don't agree, disagree, or interpret. You just validate your understanding.

WHAT YOUR CHILDREN THINK ABOUT DRUGS

Some younger adolescents with little or no interest in drugs may not know where to begin when asked, "What do you think about drugs?" They may answer with a question of their own, "What do you mean by that?"

A parent could answer, "I mean: What's your opinion? Do you know about them? Are they available in your school? Do you know people who use them? Have you thought about using them? Do they scare you? Do they interest you? These are the sorts of things I mean."

Even the most frightening statistics about drugs show that a large percentage of teenagers do not use them. Your children may say, and be telling the truth, "I think drugs are stupid. I wouldn't touch them with a ten-foot pole."

Even if your child says this, *it's still important to talk*. Remember that the discussion isn't simply for your reassurance. The idea is to help expand the thinking of your children. Calling drugs stupid is an interesting remark but reveals very little about underlying thoughts. You can ask your children why they think that drugs are stupid. Perhaps point out the positive uses of some drugs—aspirin and penicillin, for example. Ask them whether they know that some people take drugs to "feel good." You can mention the responsible way that some adults drink alcohol.

It might appear that this is encouraging drug use. On the contrary, these are facts that do not have to be hidden. Children will eventually see the positive side of drugs. Full disclosure gives you credibility. Children can deal with the truth, especially at this point, when they're not even inclined toward drug use. Now is a good time to catch their attention. Your candor puts you in good standing for future discussions. Later, when they may be more interested in experimenting, they will think, "I can trust my parents to be honest and open-minded."

At this point, your children may ask, "So why shouldn't I take drugs?" This would be an opportunity to help them see that the dangers and risks outweigh the benefits. Remember, the idea is to get them thinking. If this thinking doesn't occur, a child who calls drugs "stupid" at one stage, without thinking, may call them "super" a short time later, also without thinking.

Here are some questions you could ask:

- "Do you know kids who use drugs in your school?"
- "How has it affected them? How do you think it will affect them later?"
- "Have you used drugs?"
- "Have you ever been offered drugs?"
- (If so) "What did you say? Were you tempted?"
- (If not) "What would you say if you were offered drugs?"
- "What if your friends really pushed you to try them? What if they said, 'Don't be so chicken—it's a lot of fun, and we're all doing it'?"

The intent of these questions is to help expand your children's consciousness. For you, it's an opportunity to assess their knowledge of the topic and their ability to respond to pressure. If it appears that your children may have difficulty resisting peer pressure, you can review Chapter 4 and help them learn the skill of assertiveness.

If your children are not interested in using drugs, it will be easy to reach a no-drug-use agreement.

Much of the rest of this chapter is about discussions with children who have used or are considering the use of drugs. Even if your children do not fit this description, you'll probably find the communication techniques of value for discussions of other topics and possibly for future discussions about drugs.

THE BIG LIE

With the exchange-of-information process, you can be direct and ask your children whether they've ever used drugs.

Of course, any former drug-abuser worth his salt will surely tell you that he frequently lied to his parents. "My parents were so stupid," an addicted teenager once told me. "They used to drive me to parties where we did a ton of drugs. They had no idea what was going on. If they'd asked, I would have lied."

"So," you may wonder, "how can I know whether to trust a child, and what's the use of asking if I'll never get an honest answer anyway?"

Many former addicts and parents of addicts, drawing on their own experiences, say that people who use drugs can't be trusted. They recommend an inquisition of teenage children, extending to room searches and urinalyses.

People who have endured serious drug problems may not be aware of something very important: Many people have *excellent* family relationships and *will* be honest about drugs. Many children who think about using drugs or have experimented with them are not pathological liars. They may even be frightening themselves with their drug use or with their temptation to use drugs and may therefore welcome an opportunity to talk.

Certainly, you don't want to be naive about drug use by your kids. However, if they are harmfully involved with drugs, there are signs that give it away. Keep your ears and eyes wide open. These are the best safeguards against unawareness. Stay alert to the signs and symptoms discussed in Chapter 2, keeping in mind, though, that these indicators can also be caused by other problems.

You should be concerned, for example, if your child's performance in school begins to decline, or if he or she is suddenly in possession of large sums of money, shows less motivation to succeed, has less interest in extracurricular activities, is increasingly absent or tardy in school, or has unexplained mood changes. If several of these events occur, you would be unwise to accept a simple "I'm not using drugs" assertion. These are signs that something is wrong. Whether it's drug-related or not, it demands your attention.

On the other hand, you don't have to accuse your child of anything. If signs of some sort of a problem are clear, don't look away from it. The question shifts: "If you're not using drugs, then how do you explain what's happening? What is the problem? What are *your* solutions? When can we expect changes? How can I be helpful?"

The other effective deterrent against overlooking a drug problem is a good sense of intuition. Parents with keen intuition detect cues that may indicate dishonesty. It would be going too far to say they should assume that they are right, that their child is definitely lying. The best way of handling intuition is *not to assume you are right, but also not to assume you are wrong*. In other words, if something doesn't seem right, ask about it. For example, one father said: "It seems like a long time since I saw your report card. When did you bring one home last? It also seems as though you don't do as much homework anymore. What's happening at school?"

"Why are you so suspicious?" was the reply.

"I just have a feeling that something is wrong."

"Well, you should trust me."

"I want to be able to trust you. Let's talk some more, so that I can be reassured."

Note that the parent doesn't back down. He says he wants to trust and is open to trusting. He simply says he needs to talk further in order to be reassured. The feed-it-back approach, discussed later in this chapter, is excellent for exposing problems, such as when a child says drugs haven't affected his or her school performance, yet grades have fallen dramatically.

When there are compelling reasons to believe that problems do exist, parents should persist in seeking an explanation of what is happening. They should not stop until the problem is identified or they are convinced that everything is okay.

But you can't forget another possibility: Your child might be telling you the truth. For every parent who naively accepts a drug-using teenager's denial of drug use, there is another parent who unfairly accuses a child and drags him or her in for a urinalysis or places him or her in some sort of hospital program unnecessarily.

REACTING TO WHAT YOU HEAR

As you and your child engage in dialogue, you'll certainly have reactions, probably strong ones, especially if you hear hints or a confession of drug use, or serious consideration of that option.

Let's say the alarm goes off. You have heard information that makes you squirm—perhaps that your child has smoked marijuana or taken acid (LSD).

At this moment you might question your solemn pledge to remain calm and supportive. Isn't it time to get tough? You may think that your child needs a lecture about the good old days, punishment to teach him a lesson, and a threat to keep him in line. The lure of "Rambo parenting" will be strong. With one overpowering attack, everything can be fixed—at least so goes the fantasy. Here's the scene, straight from the movie:

"After all we've done for you," the Rambo parent says, "how could you do this to us? How can you look at yourself in the mirror? Your behavior is disgusting. You're grounded for a month, and you can't hang out with your friends anymore. They're a bad influence. If I ever hear of anything like this again, I'll tan your hide."

"Thank you," the child responds. "You have saved me from the blight of drug addiction."

The fantasy is a quick fix. But the real outcome, as you know, would be bitter feelings, the end of the discussion, and possibly increased rebelliousness. When the dialogue ends, so does the educational influence of parents.

In real life, you know that you need patience. You certainly will be concerned, perhaps frightened. But if you push the panic button, it's not likely that you'll be able to help your child get a grip on things.

If you feel like a failure because your child is using drugs, my warning is to be careful not to turn that feeling into a self-fulfilling prophecy. Don't allow yourself to fail by panicking. Remember, this is your first attempt to talk openly. You can still have a dialogue, become a strong influence, and solve any problems that may exist.

Using "I" Messages

Begin first by expressing your feelings about what you have heard. An important part of the exchange-of-information process is being able to honestly express emotions in a disciplined way. This is accomplished through the use of "I" and "my" messages, as discussed in Chapter 3 in the section on fill-in-the-blank sentences. These are statements of personal feelings. They are not judgments about your children, especially not "you" statements, as in "You are an irresponsible kid." Clearly, "you" statements would end the dialogue.

"I" and "my" statements start with clauses such as these:

- "I'm concerned about ... "
- "My fears are ... "
- "I get alarmed when I hear that ... "

An example of an "I" statement is the following: "When I hear that you have smoked marijuana, I get scared that you could get arrested."

The immediate reaction of your child may be: "Don't worry. I know what I'm doing."

Rather than getting into a power struggle, consider your statements at this early stage of the dialogue as planting seeds. You are simply expressing your feelings. There will be plenty of opportunities to express them again later. Don't try to bulldoze your way through. You could say:

"We clearly see things differently. But I am concerned, and I wanted you to know it."

One of the skills that teenagers often need to learn is to identify and express their feelings. If you can handle your own feelings well in these discussions, you will help your children by providing important feedback, showing that you care, and modeling positive ways to communicate feelings.

Gathering More Information

If alcohol or other drugs have been used, you need more information in order to make a good assessment. As you gather information, you will also be helping your children look at important issues about their own drug use. You will be helping them make a self-assessment.

What, when, how, where? If your children have used drugs, it is important to discuss the experience. You will want to know: Which drugs have been used? How often were they used? How much was used on each occasion? How did it feel? What happened when drugs were used? In what setting were they used? Was it at home? School? Parties? Friends' houses? Was it on schooldays? Weekends? Before school? During school? In the evening?

The reasons for drug use. You will want to know why drugs were used. What was the motivation? What needs were met by the drugs? Was the purpose to have fun? To alleviate boredom? To escape pain? To conform in a social situation? There may be multiple reasons for drug use and different explanations on different occasions.

Drug Effects. You will be interested in the impact of drug use. How have drugs affected your child? Has harm occurred?

What happened at the time drugs were used? Potential problems include fights, driving under the influence, and unplanned sexual activity.

You will also want to consider long-term effects. Potential problems include damaged friendships, strained family relationships, problems in school, and legal problems.

It's also possible that the teenager used alcohol or other drugs the way some mature adults do, without any significant damage. Though reassuring, this doesn't preclude the possibility of problems in the future. What is the potential for harm?

Your child's attitude. Another important assessment is your child's attitude about drugs. Is it rebellious? Is it "I do it and I'm proud"? Is it "I do it and I'm frightened about what I'm doing"? Is it "I do it because everyone else does it"? Find out whether your child wants to continue using drugs or stop using them.

Your child's knowledge and self-awareness. Another important part of the assessment is understanding your child's awareness and knowledge about his or her drug use. You will want to know what your child knows and doesn't know about drugs—what he or she has thought about with regard to dangers and consequences, and hasn't thought about.

Before the current discussion, had he or she considered the immediate and long-term dangers of drug use or thought about the effects of his or her own drug use? Is he or she aware of why he or she is using drugs? Is he or she self-critical?

In other words, you not only want to know why your child uses drugs, but you want to know whether he or she is aware of why. You want to know the effects of the drug use, but you also want to know whether he or she is aware of them.

The current status of drug use. Has drug use stopped? Is it increasing? Decreasing? Stable? When was the last time? If use is continuing, at what level and under what circumstances?

A crucial question in evaluating the current status of drug use is harm. Are drugs being used dangerously? Is harm already occurring? Is it imminent?

In evaluating the status of drug use, figure out where your child stands on the drug-use continuum, described in Chapter 2. Is it experimental use? Seeking the mood? Harmful, regular use? Dependence?

Too Much, Too Soon

Once the dialogue commences, children vary in their readiness to openly disclose personal details. With so much information needed for a good assessment, you will be eager to get the facts. In your eagerness, you can get too pushy or overbearing. Sometimes the result is an onslaught of questions, one after the other—"pumping for information":

• When was the first time?

- Who were you with?
- Who got the drugs?
- What was it like?
- When else did you use drugs?
- Where are you getting the drugs?
- Which of your friends use drugs?

All these questions will be of interest, but asking them one after another will probably create resistance. Remember, the discussion is just beginning. If you try to find out everything right away, you may find yourself locked into a power struggle. You'll be trying to extract information, and your child will be trying to withhold it. Think of this initial discussion as the beginning of a long-term process requiring patience.

Defense Mechanisms

If teenagers do have a problem with drugs, several forces, discussed below, work against their recognizing it: feelings of invincibility, the defense mechanism of denial, the defense mechanism of externalization, and erroneous information. In a dialogue, in order to reach an understanding you may have to reckon with any or all of these forces.

Teenagers typically have false *feelings of invincibility* that extend to many types of behavior: "Nothing can happen to me. I won't get pregnant from unprotected sex. I won't get AIDS. I won't get hooked on drugs. I know what I'm doing."

With the defense mechanism of *denial*, drug-users say: "Drugs aren't a problem. They don't affect me. I can stop whenever I want to." (Sometimes this assertion is true. Sometimes it's a denial of reality.)

Still another characteristic defense used by teenagers is *externalization*. They blame everyone and everything except themselves for their drug use, and they take no personal responsibility for their own behavior: "I only use drugs because school is so bad and this city is so boring." It's as if drugs have been imposed on them by outside forces. If the world would change for the better, their drug use would cease of its own accord.

197

Erroneous information about drugs and their effects is another factor preventing teenagers from accurately assessing their drug use. Teenagers may, for example, assert that there are no dangers in smoking marijuana. They may also have mistaken notions of what a drug problem looks like. In their minds, the only real alcoholics are people lying in the street drunk. They don't recognize subtler forms of abuse and addiction.

Another misconception is about what is "normal." Many teenagers enormously overestimate the number of their peers using drugs and therefore see their own use as "normal."

Because of all these factors, you may find that your child is unaware of the extent of his or her drug use, the factors that motivate it, and the consequences and risks of his or her actions. Your child may be making contradictory statements and misleading either you, himself or herself, or both of you.

The Rebuttal Cycle

With all these obstacles to an objective assessment of the problem, many parents feel the urge to make an aggressive challenge, either by asking accusatory questions or by rebutting what their children say. Unfortunately, this causes the discussion to degenerate into a no-win argument, with the children getting defensive. It goes something like this:

"You said there weren't any drugs at the party, but now you're telling me that Stephanie was there. You've told me that Stephanie uses drugs. You're contradicting yourself. You're lying."

The message here is: "I don't trust you. We're in a competition. I'm going to try to prove you wrong."

The rebuttal cycle is a serious pitfall. Parents get hooked into it when they are too eager to disprove their children's point of view They tear down what their children say instead of helping to broaden and expand their thinking.

Children will answer a rebuttal with a counter-rebuttal of their own. When engaged in the rebuttal cycle, no one listens seriously to anyone else:

Child: "There's nothing wrong with weed."
Parent: "But it's illegal."

Child: "Driving over the speed limit is illegal, and you do that."

Parent: "I'm a grown-up, and you're a child. I have some prerogatives that you don't have. I don't want you breaking any laws."

Child: "Oh, a double standard. Anyway, all the kids in school use drugs."

Parent: "I doubt that Melissa and her friends use drugs."

Child: "Yeah, but they're nerds."

In this "discussion" (really an argument), the parent is seriously concerned about the child's seeming disregard for the law and what appears to be an inaccurate assessment of the extent of drug use among peers. But by falling into the rebuttal cycle, the parent fails to get any serious attention. As you will see later in this chapter, there are better ways to communicate without trying to "win" in a contest for dominance.

POSITIVE WAYS TO GET MORE INFORMATION

In making an assessment, you want more information but don't want your child to feel that he or she is on trial or under investigation. You're not trying to expose wrongdoing. You're trying to increase communication and understanding.

Open-Ended Questions

One underused strategy for gathering information without cross-examination is to invite openness and self-disclosure by asking open-ended questions. These are questions that allow people to answer on their own terms, in contrast with closed questions, which allow only limited responses.

To illustrate, consider the difference between these approaches in gathering information from a child who has smoked marijuana.

Closed questions: "Did you enjoy it?" (yes or no) "Who gave you the drugs?" (name the person) "Will you ever do it again?" (yes or no).

The open-ended approach goes like this: "How did it feel? What was it like? What are your thoughts about smoking in the future?"

These open-ended questions encourage the child to think and talk. With the open-ended approach, you could even say: "You know that

I'm very curious about what's happening with you and drugs, but I don't want to start bombarding you with questions. Could you tell me what's going on?"

Don't give up if you get an "Oh, nothing" response. Encourage further discussion: "What do you mean by 'Oh, nothing'? I'd like to know more."

Or you can ask a few closed questions such as "Where were you? Who were you with?" before switching to open-ended ones.

Lighten Up

During this early part of the dialogue, as you are gathering information, you should be developing sensitivity about the amount of questioning that is appropriate with your own child and when you need to lighten up or back off. Remember, nobody likes to be put through the Spanish Inquisition, especially teenagers, who are forming their independent identities.

If at any point your child indicates that he or she can't talk more or feels too pressured, show that you're not going to be pushy. Sometimes it helps to say something encouraging, such as: "I know it's hard for you to talk about this subject. But I think it's important. Please hang in there with me."

As it becomes clear to your child that you're not going to send in the cavalry, as he or she feels more comfortable about opening up, information will gradually be disclosed. Later you can ask more detailed and specific questions. Your child will answer if he or she feels safe.

A teenager may protest: "You're asking a lot of questions. I thought we were going to have a discussion. I wish you wouldn't pry."

You can remind your son or daughter of the purpose of the discussion: "Let me explain why I'm asking these questions. I want to help you think through what's happening with drugs. It's my responsibility as a parent to help you learn to make wise choices. That's why I'm asking. But if it feels like a lot of questions too soon, I'm willing to back off. We can talk again later."

"But," your child protests, "why are you so up-tight?"

It's an important question. If you are up-tight, you won't be helping matters. In that case, your child has given you important criticism. If you're not up-tight but only concerned, make that clear.

If your child still feels reluctant to talk, ask about the guarantees he or she needs in order to feel safe. (Refer back to the previous chapter for how to do this.)

If, for some reason, your consistent and patient effort to maintain a dialogue hasn't been successful, you can suggest alternatives. Again, it's important to insist on discussion:

"These are tough times for kids. Everyone is entitled to support, to someone to talk with. If you can't talk with me, I'm willing to set up an appointment with a professional [or a clergyman]. But I can't look away from this. I'm disappointed that we're stuck, but maybe a psychologist can help us get started. Or maybe you would want to talk with him or her alone. One way or the other, I want you to have the support you deserve."

The Columbo Style

When drug-abusers are asked about their drug use, some of them lie by omission, not by giving false information but by withholding important details. To a lesser extent, even people who dabble in drugs sometimes distort the truth.

"Okay, I confess," Michael tells his father. "I'm gonna come clean with you. I drank alcohol." He has also smoked marijuana and tried cocaine but doesn't offer this information.

Because of distortions like these, to get an accurate assessment of the situation you need to ask specific questions about which drugs have been used, how much of them, and how often. This is a delicate process. You don't want to start cross-examining, yet you want to he informed. The tone of these questions should be supportive, not confrontational. I think of the television character Columbo. You sort of scratch your head and ask some questions to get a few more details. Instead of saying to your child, "I don't believe that you've told me everything" or "Stop lying," you communicate interest and support.

Ask direct questions, but be intuitive about how rapidly to proceed. Start like this:

"Have you tried any other drugs?"

"I told you once before I smoked weed."

"Anything else?"

"Just because I smoked weed doesn't mean I've used any other drugs."

"I know that, but I'd like to know whether you've used anything else. What about cocaine? Have you tried it?

"Well, yeah, I tried it once."

"Is that all?"

"No, actually a few times."

"How many times?"

"Three."

"Is that all?"

"Yes."

"Are you sure?"

"Yes."

"How about crack?"

The questioning would continue with other drugs.

In therapy sessions with seriously addicted clients, one quickly learns about the importance of this type of questioning. I remember a high-school student telling me that he had had only one vodka all week.

A tumbler?

No way. It was a bottle.

Thought-Provoking Questions

As information unfolds, you will begin to have thoughts you want to share with your children. You may want to challenge misinformation or provide a different perspective about something that was said.

Before you offer your perspective, consider taking the approach of asking thought-provoking questions. This means asking whether a child has ever considered the flip side, the opposite, of what he or she is saying.

I was talking with a sixteen-year-old girl who was smoking marijuana and drinking alcohol on a regular basis. Her drug use was clearly creating problems for her in school and at home, yet she was boldly proclaiming the merits of drugs. She focused on how great she felt when she was high.

I rained on her parade by changing the focus with a couple of thought-provoking questions:

"Is there another side to this? Do you ever worry about your drug use?"

Taken aback, she admitted she had worried, then added, "But I don't dwell on it."

"It's unpleasant to think about, isn't it?" I asked.

"Yeah," she said.

"But not thinking about it doesn't make it go away, does it?"

"No. I guess I need to deal with it," she said.

And I agreed.

Because thought-provoking questions are so effective, I've listed a few that I frequently use in talking with teenagers:

- Is there another side to this?
- Do you worry about your drug use?
- Do you feel that your drug use may be out of control?
- Have you thought about the potential dangers?
- Do you see any risks?
- Do you have any concerns?

Thought-provoking questions are also a good opening for you to express your own thoughts and feelings. For example, I asked Marsha, age sixteen, if she was worried about her drinking. She said no. Then I said: "I guess you're not worried about how much alcohol you're drinking, but when you tell me that you have been drunk several times in the last couple of months, it concerns me." This is a way to state your concerns rather than to get argumentative.

Directed Questioning and Labeling

You want to understand your child's drug use and help him or her understand it. Certain questions not only help you gather information but also broaden your child's thinking. These are called "directed questions," because they increase awareness by pursuing a direct line of reasoning. As your child answers directed questions, certain information and patterns of behavior become apparent. You can ask whether your child notices the patterns or you can point them out yourself.

Many times children do not know *why* they are using drugs. They may not have thought about it. Their own reasons may be hidden from themselves. Directed questioning is particularly helpful in uncovering motivation.

"Okay," I said in a counseling session, "you don't know why you use drugs. Let's take a look at *when* you use them and see whether we can figure out why."

"I just do drugs when I feel like it. No special reason."

"Well then, let's look at when you've been feeling like it. When was the last time?"

"Saturday night."

"Where were you? What were you doing?"

"I was at Ken's house. We were bored."

"So at least one time when you used drugs, you were feeling bored."

"Yeah. So what?"

"Well, I don't know. Let's keep looking at this. Maybe we'll find a pattern."

"And maybe not."

"That's possible. Let's see."

"Okay."

"When was the next-to-last time you used drugs?"

"It was the weekend before. I had nothing to do."

"Kind of bored then, too?"

"I guess so."

"What do you think? Maybe one reason you use drugs is that you get bored and want something fun to do."

This dialogue shows a pattern of drug use for fun or to avoid boredom. Similar questioning of the same child uncovered other reasons for drug use at other times.

With directed questioning about motivation, it's important to search for root causes and not to stop with vague generalizations. Betty told her parents that she used drugs "to feel good." At first they thought she meant that she was using them for a "trip," to alter her consciousness. But as they asked more questions, it became clear that she was smoking marijuana and using cocaine to self-medicate against depression. She was having problems in school and didn't know how to cope with them, so she used drugs to escape the pain. That's what she meant by "to feel good."

As children explain the context of their drug use, you can identify the underlying motivation:

- "I wanted to see what cocaine was like. I wanted to try it." (experimentation)
- "At parties everyone does drugs." (peer pressure, conformity)
- "When you guys [Mom and Dad] fight, I get high." (to cope, to kill pain)
- "I drink on dates." (for fun and possibly to deal with stress)
- "I take pills before exams." (to deal with stress)

Sometimes the motivation is subtle. A young boy who says he smokes marijuana because he "likes it" may appear to be enjoying the sensation of being high. But another question reveals a different motivation:

"What is it you like best about it?"

"I can brag to my friends. I'm the only kid in my class who has smoked weed."

Besides revealing important information about patterns of drug use, directed questions are also useful in uncovering contradictions in thinking. This is a special type of directed questioning, called "the feed-it-back approach."

The Feed-It-Back Approach

As information begins to unfold, you will probably see gaps in your child's knowledge and contradictions in his or her reasoning that you want to discuss—for example, saying that he or she has not been harmed by drugs when it appears that there is evidence to the contrary.

The feed-it-back approach is a way to gradually help children see the contradictions in their own thinking. It helps them overcome denial mechanisms and other obstacles that could interfere with objectivity. Through careful questioning about feelings and experiences, hard facts are brought into the open. Parents "feed back" what they hear through simple comments about the hard facts.

The Swiss psychologist Jean Piaget once said that every time you teach a child something, you deprive him of the opportunity of figuring it out for himself. This maxim has special relevance for

205

younger teenagers, who are determined to take charge of their own lives and to reach their own conclusions.

The feed-it-back approach is an excellent teaching method to help children see all the facts clearly and arrive at their own conclusions. With skillful and tactful questioning, you can help them gain valuable knowledge about themselves with a minimal amount of explaining.

Even with this non-threatening approach, most children will not immediately acknowledge contradictions in their thinking. The feed-it-back approach is not a quick solution. It is an educational method for the long haul, a way to plant some seeds of wisdom, to begin to gradually crack defenses. Often you have to discuss the same material several times until the child can clearly see the facts.

The feed-it-back approach is best illustrated by actual transcripts. Below are examples of using the method to explore the assertion that "drug use hasn't affected me," to explore the assertion that "I can stop anytime," and to determine whether a child is dependent on drugs. As you read the dialogue, remember that the tone of voice of the parent is always warm and supportive, not confrontational.

The feed-it-back approach is applied here to the question: "How have drugs affected you?"

Parent: "How has smoking weed affected you?"
Child: "It makes me feel good."
Parent: "I know it does. Tell me more. How has it affected your life in other ways?"
Child: "I feel good more often."
Parent: "Have there been any negative effects?"
Child: "No."
Parent: "Well, let's look at this together. When did you start smoking marijuana?"
Child: "About a year ago."
Parent: "What were your grades back then?"
Child: "A's and B's."
Parent: "What are they now?"
Child: "C's and D's."
Parent: "It sounds as though the drug may be having an effect in school. What do you think?"

Child: "Yeah, it makes me feel better when I go to school."

Parent: "I know that. But it sounds as though maybe your school-work has suffered and the smoking is part of the problem. Maybe I'm wrong. Do you have any other ideas about why your grades have fallen?"

Child: "No, not really. I hate school."

Parent: "I'm sorry school feels so bad to you. I'd like to talk with you about that, to see if we can figure out some solutions. But smoking weed is probably part of it. It sounds as if it could be. Anyway, why don't we drop it for now?"

Child: "Okay. Fine with me "

The facts speak for themselves. The child has revealed a potential problem. The parent isn't avoiding the problem but maneuvering to reduce defensiveness. If the parent tries to hammer it home, he or she will only meet resistance. It is a wise move to back off. Soon another discussion of the same issue can bring these thoughts back to the attention of the child.

The feed-it-back approach is applied here to the question: "Could you stop using drugs if you wanted to?"

Mother: "It sounds as though you use drugs whenever you feel bad. I wonder whether you're becoming dependent on them."

Child: "I can stop whenever I want to."

Mother: "Have you ever tried?"

Child: "Yeah."

Mother: "Tell me, what happened?"

Child: "I didn't smoke for a couple of weeks."

Mother: "How was it?"

Child: "Fine. No problem."

Mother: "Good. Then what happened?"

Child: "My teachers started hassling me."

Mother: "Then what? Did you smoke again?"

Child: "Yeah, because my teachers were hassling me."

Mother: "Well, I'm pleased you could stop for a couple of weeks. But I'm concerned that you started again when you were feeling bad. I guess drugs help you deal with stress."

Child: "Well, my teachers were hassling me."

Mother: "I believe you. But I'm not sure the solution is to get high. And I'm concerned that you smoke weed when the going gets rough. Are there any other times you stopped using drugs?"

Child: "Yeah, there was another time."

Mother: "When was that?

Child: "Uh, about six months ago."

Mother: "How long did you stop?"

Child: "About a month."

Mother: "What happened?"

Child: "Well, I started again when you and Dad were fighting about the divorce stuff. It was really depressing."

Mother: "I know, those were tough times for all of us. I'm sorry it was so hard for you. But you know, I seem to be hearing two things here. One is that you must be concerned about your drug use, because you've attempted to stop it at least twice. The other is that you can stay off drugs as long as nothing is really bothering you. But when the going gets rough, you start using them again. Drugs kill the pain. But, you know, there are better ways to deal with problems."

Child: "What are they?"

Mother: "To figure things out, to deal with problems without getting high, and even to learn to prevent problems."

Child: "I know. You've told me that before."

Mother: "I guess it's a thought to keep in mind."

Child: "Maybe you're right."

Mother: "Do you want to talk about it a little?"

Child: "Yes, okay."

The feed-it-back approach can also be applied to the issue of whether a child is dependent on drugs. As you will see, this issue is related to the one discussed above—the ability to discontinue drug use.

Child: "It's not a problem. I'm not dependent."

Parent: "But you say that you smoke weed when things bother you at home or in school."

Child: "Yeah."

Parent: "Does this solve your problems?"

Child: "Well, I feel a whole lot better."

Parent: "I know that drugs help you feel better, but I'm concerned that they just help you escape from difficult situations. Do you know what I mean?"

Child: "I need to escape. I *have* to live at home. I'm still a kid. I *have* to go to school. I'm too young to drop out."

Parent: "But there is an alternative."

Child: "What's that?"

Parent: "We could talk things out at home. If you're upset, I'd like us to deal with the problem so that you don't feel bad. I don't want home to feel so bad that you need drugs to escape from feeling rotten."

Child: "What about school?"

Parent: "Look, I'll be honest. I didn't exactly love school, either. But there are ways to make it feel better. I'm concerned that you're getting into a habit of running away from things."

Child: "But I like drugs. They don't harm me."

Parent: "I don't deny that you like them. I don't deny that they lessen the pain. But I don't think they're a long-term solution. We all face lots of things in life that are unpleasant. If we take drugs to deal with them, we have an even more serious problem."

Child: "Well, I don't take drugs *every* time I feel bad."

Parent: "I'm glad to hear that. But I still think the number of times you *do* take drugs is worth thinking about, isn't it?"

Child: "Yeah, I guess so."

In this dialogue the parent almost lapsed into lecturing by discussing the long-term risks, but the comments were relatively brief, so this can still qualify as the feed-it-back approach. The parent helped the child take a look at a pattern of using drugs to try to escape from life's stresses and problems.

ANSWERING THE TOUGH ONES

No matter how skilled you are in helping children make their own discoveries, you will certainly have issues to raise with them, eye-openers that they may not have considered. As always in the exchange-of-information process, you want to state your point of view not as the ultimate truth but as the way you see things. Your tone should be respectful and supportive. Often you will find yourself going back and forth between expressing concerns, asking questions, making observations, and stating opinions.

Below I have listed some of the major areas of disagreement that arise in discussions with teenagers, along with suggestions on how to respond.

Everyone's Doing It

Many teenagers defend their own drug use by saying, "All kids are using drugs." Research has indicated that children tend to overestimate the number of their peers who use drugs.[1]

You could say, "I think you know it's not true that *all* kids use drugs. I believe fewer of them use drugs than you think. Why don't we check some statistics together?"

If your child is not interested in statistics, you can still say, "I guess that's one fact we have different opinions about."

Then there's the matter of conformity: "Even if many of your peers are drinking and taking drugs, that doesn't mean that you must do it, and it doesn't mean that it's no big deal."

You can discuss the merits of having an independent opinion, making one's own choices, and being willing to be different from the crowd. This is of special value to teenagers, who are at a stage in life when they are trying to define their own identity.

I'm Just a Teenager

"Hey, I'm a teenager and this is a time in life to have fun and party."

Unfortunately this is an increasingly common statement. In my view, it reflects an impoverished idea about what it means to have fun (you rely on alcohol and other drugs) and to "party" (you socialize under the influence of alcohol and other drugs). What about other types of fun? What about socializing and enjoying people without being high or "wasted"?

The "I'm a teenager" statement—or its alternative, "I'm a kid"— also seems to imply that adolescence is the same as childhood, and that it is a time reserved exclusively for play. Responsibility begins only when one becomes an adult. This distressing way of thinking is one reason I believe we should be challenging teenagers in school, giving them responsibilities at home and in the community, and holding them accountable. Otherwise, they will tend to view adolescence as an extension of childhood, and themselves as oversized children.

One way to counter the "I'm a teenager, and I want to party" mind-set is by having discussions about what it means to "party," how to have fun and excitement without drugs, and why responsibility is important during the teen years. With regard to responsibility, adolescents need to understand that they should be laying a solid foundation for adulthood by achieving success in school and learning how to deal skillfully with life's stresses and challenges. You can encourage them to think ahead a few years to when they will be supporting themselves in the work world and probably living on their own. I also think it is accurate to say that they will be in a lot better position to have fun as adults if they prepare themselves for the work world during the teen years.

It's Not My Responsibility

In discussions about drugs, many teenagers externalize their motivations for drug use, denying any and all responsibility for their own behavior:

- "I smoke weed because there's nothing fun to do in town." (Not because I'm bored and don't know how to find fun or make my own excitement.)
- "I drink because my mom is always hassling me." (Not because I try to escape from dealing with her and working out problems at home.)
- "I smoke weed because school is so boring." (Not because I can't cope with school—can't concentrate, or get the sorts of grades I want.)
- "I drink beer because everyone does." (Not because I am choosing to conform.)

When statements such as these are made, you can introduce the concept of externalization—blaming the world—and explain to your children that they aren't taking responsibility for their own behavior. You can show that they blame other people and other life experiences for their own choices. This can be done without invalidating their explanations. It's possible to accept their underlying feelings without agreeing that this entirely accounts for, or explains, their drug use.

A mother said the following to her thirteen-year-old daughter: "You say you smoke weed because there's nothing fun to do. I don't doubt that you feel bored, but I don't agree with you that there's nothing else to do that would be fun. I think that you could find fun things to do or even invent them. That's my opinion. I'd be happy to help you plan activities. I think it's important to learn to be able to entertain, amuse, and excite yourself. I'd like to see you do that."

A father said this to his fourteen-year-old son: "I notice that you say you use drugs because of your mother and me and because of school. It's as if you're impling we *make* you take drugs. I know you're having problems with us. But it's been *your* choice to deal with these tensions by using drugs. I think there are better solutions. Let's talk about some of them."

Drugs Are Harmless

"Marijuana is safe. Alcohol is harmless."

You should disagree. All drugs have their risks:

"I disagree with you. I'd be happy to gather some scientific studies, and we can look at the research together. I'm not saying that everyone has problems with these drugs, but I know there are dangers and risks from all of them."

Many teenagers who are harmfully involved with drugs do not realize the damage that has been done. They say, "Drugs haven't hurt me."

One good way to settle the difference of opinion is to refer to the discussion of the drug-use continuum in Chapter 2. Ask your children to determine where they would place themselves on the continuum, and why. Explain where you would place them, and why. The dangers of specific drugs are also discussed in Chapter 2.

I'll Never Get Hooked

Many children are unaware of the realistic danger of becoming dependent on drugs. Or, if they are aware, they feel that *they* could never fall victim to it. Teenage invulnerability is most evident in terms of sexual behavior. Teens who intellectually understand how a woman becomes pregnant somehow believe that they are immune to that possibility, that they can engage in risk-free sexual activity. The same tendency can be seen with drugs. They believe, quite simply, "It can't happen to me. I can control my drug use."

The best response is the straightforward truth: "Yes, it's true that many people can control their drug use. Only a certain percentage have problems with drugs. But there is no special reason to believe that you're immune to the risk. And the risk of becoming dependent is greater for young people, who have had only limited life experiences, than it is for adults."

Another important point to make is that nobody ever starts using drugs expecting that they will become addicted. If people thought they would get addicted and suffer the tragic consequences, they wouldn't start in the first place. Everyone thinks that he or she can handle drugs, including the people who end up with serious problems.

Mistaken Notions of Drug Abuse

As I mentioned earlier, many teens visualize the harm from drugs in extreme terms, featuring skid-row bums and heroin "shooting galleries." If they don't crave drugs, they may not understand that they may nevertheless have a drug problem. They are unaware of the subtler forms of drug abuse.

You can talk about drug abuse as distinct from drug dependence. For example, point out that people can be seriously harmed by even the occasional use of drugs, such as when they drink (or use other drugs) and drive, or when they get involved in unwanted pregnancies. People sometimes do dangerous things while using hallucinogens and can experience psychotic breaks.

Drugs can also become part of a lifestyle that leads to behavioral and academic problems in school, problems at home, problems with friends, and problems with the law. Sometimes problems caused by drugs have more to do with what does *not* happen than what does happen. By this I mean that young people use drugs as a crutch and *fail to learn how to deal with life*.

Teenagers need help in gaining a broad understanding of drug abuse. They also should be made aware that drug dependence sneaks up on people. Everything may be fine at the moment, but they could be headed for trouble.

Drugs as Crutches

Many adolescents don't grasp the full significance of their drug use. Their limited viewpoint is reflected in statements that begin, "I only use drugs when . . . " or "I just use drugs for . . . "

- "I just do drugs for fun. Everything feels better when I'm high. It's no problem."
- "I only do drugs when my teachers hassle me or you guys [parents] yell at me. Drugs relax me. It's easier to deal with school and you guys when I'm high."
- "I only do drugs when I'm depressed. They cheer me up. They make me feel good."

It would be a mistake to discount these motivations Drugs can make a person feel good. They can help with coping. They can relieve tension and stress. You can validate this point of view, but you should also help them see the risks and, especially, help expand their thinking about the future.

"So," you say, "drugs cheer you up when you feel down. How long does it last? When the drugs wear off, how do you feel? Don't you want more drugs because you still feel bad? It seems to me that it doesn't ever really *solve* the problem.

"I understand that you enjoy everything more when you are high, but I see some serious risks. If you always seek this sort of high, you'll be disappointed much of the time, when you're not high. You might end up being high all the time, and then you'd miss some of the other satisfactions of life, such as school success and eventually work achievement, not to mention a great relationship with a boyfriend or girlfriend. You can't succeed in school and be high. You can't work out a relationship if you're always high.

"If you start using drugs to accomplish these goals, they can become a crutch. You'll depend on them to create the feelings and won't learn other ways to do it. You might think, "So what?" But

214

there's a catch here. Our bodies grow accustomed to the substances, and we need more and more of them for the same feelings. In fact, we can get so accustomed to drugs, develop such a tolerance, that we need a huge amount just to feel normal. Drugs may seem fine at the moment, but over the long haul they can create serious problems. This isn't to say that everyone who uses drugs has problems. But when you say that you use drugs *only* for fun, it worries me that you're not seeing the bigger picture."

One parent made this statement to a teenage son who used drugs to calm down before going on dates: "I don't think it's a good idea to get high to relax yourself for dates. There's nothing wrong with being nervous. We all have to go through that. It's part of growing up."

Making Your Assessment

After engaging in a thorough dialogue about drugs, you and your child will know all the facts and potential dangers. You each will have shared your values and opinions and the reasons behind them. It's time to make an assessment.

One important question to resolve is whether your child is using drugs or not. If not, it is important to keep the discussion going, because decisions can change, and you do not want to wait for a crisis to resume talking. If drugs are being used, an important question is: What harm, if any, has occurred already or is likely to occur? Answers to these questions influence the types of agreements and rules that you will want to establish, as well as your strategy for negotiating.

If drug use is already causing harm or putting your child at high risk for harm, you'll probably want to take quicker and stronger action. If use is at a low level, you have the option of being more gradual in your intervention. You can pay more attention to your educational role—that is, helping your child learn to make good decisions. In some cases, it pays to be patient.

It is also possible—although some people consider it unspeakable—for some older teenagers to use certain drugs *without* significant harm. As much as it may seem desirable to oversimplify and say to older teenagers, "Never, never use drugs—they always cause

215

harm," and as much as this would be more comforting and acceptable to those who are worried about the drug problem in this country, we must be intellectually honest. Although drug use certainly is not ideal for developing minds and bodies, some teenagers can use drugs, even regularly, without advancing to dependence and without harming themselves. (Of course, they are always risking legal consequences.)

This doesn't mean that drug use should be accepted. There's no good reason to take unnecessary health risks. But the truth is that some teenagers can use drugs without injury. Unfortunately, many drug *abusers*, children and adults alike, *mistakenly* assume that they are indulging without harm.

Risk Factors

If drugs are being used and harm hasn't occurred, there are some important risk factors to consider.

Children who are deficient in basic life skills and using drugs to compensate for the deficiency are at higher risk for dependence than others. For example, if they have difficulty coping with stress—for instance, in school or social encounters—and use drugs to deal with their anxiety, they may start to depend on drugs on a regular basis.

Other risks occur without dependence or even regular use. Some involve recklessness, such as drinking and driving, or drinking (or using drugs) and unplanned sexual activity. Some involve the choice of drugs. For example, it is risky to experiment with highly addictive substances such as cocaine or crystal methamphetamine (crystal, speed).

Another risk factor is a family history of alcoholism or drug abuse. From a statistical point of view, families with this kind of history need to be more alert to potentially harmful drug use by children.

YOUR CHILDREN'S OWN ASSESSMENT

If your children are using drugs, part of your assessment is seeing how *they* assess the situation.

Are they aware of the risks and dangers? What stage of drug use do *they* think they are in? It is likely that you and your children will have some differences of opinion. Thought-provoking questions and the feed-it-back approach are helpful in reconciling differences. But drug users, young and old, are often defensive in looking at their behavior. They say, "No big deal."

This hooks many parents into an aggressive war of words, an attempt to talk their children into believing that they have a problem. Lots of luck! Teenagers smile and say, "Why are you so up-tight? Take some Valium and call me in the morning."

LOVING CONFRONTATION: ADDRESSING THE ISSUE OF HARM

Loving confrontation is a way to address the issue of harm, and potential harm, from drug use, without locking horns with your children. With information gained from discussions and observations, you begin by stating your opinion about the seriousness of the problem with love and concern, as this mother did:

"I believe that you're hurting yourself. I love you, and I'm very worried about this. I've noticed that you're not doing your homework and your grades are falling, and that you're not coming home on time for curfew.

"You seem very moody. You often seem tired. I've also noticed that you have a persistent cough. I'm concerned about you."

After making the observations, you ask some questions: "Have you been aware of this? What do you think? How do you explain it? How do you feel? Are you concerned?"

Your child may give the classic answer: "I don't care."

"What about school?" you ask.

"I don't care. School is boring."

It's usually a case of denial. I try to cut through this defense mechanism with a statement like this: "I don't believe that you don't care. I know that deep inside you must. It's hard to feel good about yourself when you're failing, even if you think the teachers are unfair and school is boring. I suspect that you probably don't *want* to care, and sometimes you feel so frustrated that you don't care, but I believe that it does matter to you."

Drug users in the denial stage will insist that everything is okay. But you can challenge this assertion with more loving confrontation: "Regardless of what you say, I see a problem, and I believe it's related to drugs. If you can explain it otherwise, that's fine. I would like to know how you explain it. But I love you too much to look away from this, to allow this type of self-destructive behavior to continue. We need to keep talking."

If harm has not yet occurred but your child appears to be at high risk, you can use loving confrontation to explain the risks you see. Here are a few examples:

- "I love you very much, and I'm concerned about what's happening with you and drugs. I know that you are shy in social situations. You've told me you're using drugs to go out on dates and be with your friends. I think this is a very dangerous practice. It's how drug problems develop—when people use substances to deal with stress in life."
- "I'm worried about something I've noticed. I know that you've been upset about the divorce, but you haven't been talking with me or anyone. I'm concerned that since the divorce you seem to be using drugs to deal with how you feel. This is a serious matter. I don't want you to become dependent on drugs to deal with problems. I want to help you learn how to cope with stress without relying on drugs."
- "I'm concerned about your use of drugs. You know that we have a history of alcohol problems in this family. For whatever reasons, children of alcoholics seem to be more prone to dependence on drugs or alcohol. I don't want you to suffer with drugs the way I have with alcohol. You may feel that everything is okay, but given our family history, I'm worried about you."

If your child continues to deny the harm from his or her drug use, it may be tempting to send in the national guard. But remember, as I said earlier, that you are dealing with an adolescent. The more you try to dictate behavior, the more likely it is that you will generate the opposite response—defiance and rebellion. Furthermore, a show of force puts an end to discussion. So when you and your child disagree about the dangers of drugs, it shouldn't mean that you stop talking. It means that you *keep* talking. You might want to suggest involving other people in the dialogue, such as clergy, professional counselors, trusted relatives, or friends. Allowing for a difference of opinion does not mean that you surrender parental power. Also, knowing that your child is using drugs will influence related decisions about curfews, privileges, use of the family car, allowance, and other matters.

We've now discussed the skill of loving confrontation, which you can use to respectfully challenge the point of view of your children. Don't forget, however, that they might have some challenges of their own, and good ones, too. You need to listen with respect.

The beauty of a good dialogue is that it promotes learning and understanding. With the exchange-of-information process, new insights bring family members into closer agreement about issues that may have separated them in the past.

The discussion of drugs—and related matters such as curfews, the family car, and parties—begins with everyone listening to one another's point of view. Then it is time to negotiate and make agreements. That's the topic of the next chapter.

8
MAKING VALID AGREEMENTS

"Yeah, sure," a father says to me in a workshop. "I'll make an agreement with my son. I've made hundreds of them, and he has never done anything he said he would do. I've tried this agreement stuff. It doesn't work."

Clearly, this father did not have *valid* agreements with his son—not if he made so many of them without success.

Valid agreements are fully understood by everyone involved. They are made in good faith—that is, with the intention of following through. They are based on mutual respect and careful thought and consideration.

Every day children make millions of *invalid* agreements with their parents: "Sure, I'll do my homework. Sure, I'll be home by eleven o'clock. Sure, I won't use drugs. Now leave me alone [so that I can go and do whatever I want to do]."

Children know that invalid agreements are a handy way to silence their nagging parents.

Sometimes invalid agreements are made unintentionally. Children may quickly say that they'll do what their parents want, believing at the moment that they will keep the agreement but never fully committing themselves to do so. They attempt to do as they have promised, but their efforts lack resolve and ultimately fail. It's an unthinking knee-jerk response to pressure rather than dishonesty.

This chapter is about parents and children making valid agreements with each other—how to make them, how to keep them, and what to do when they are broken. We begin the discussion with some general principles and then get specific about drug-related issues.

PERCEPTIONS AND STANDARDS

After a parent-child dialogue, it's time to compare perceptions, to identify areas of agreement and disagreement, to attempt to reconcile differences and come to terms.

An important parent-child issue is establishing reasonable standards of behavior—for example, concerning bedtime, curfew, drug use, and household chores. A good discussion always results in greater understanding of the facts and usually narrows the gap between differing points of view. After a discussion, remaining differences can be openly acknowledged, later to be negotiated and resolved.

Here's the way a discussion about housework was summed up by one parent:

"Let's compare our opinions. Tell me if I'm wrong. It seems that we both agree that we should all carry a share of household responsibilities. I think that you should continue to be responsible for your room, take out the garbage, feed the dog, and empty the dishwasher. You feel that this is too much to ask and that it should be up to you to choose your own standards for your bedroom. You think that someone else should handle Quey [the dog]. You've done it for so long that now you think it's someone else's turn. Is that right?"

"Yes, that's a good summary."

Once the differences are clarified, parents will either make compromises and concessions or insist on the final word.

Parents and children sometimes have very different ideas about the current situation—about how well the children have been meeting their responsibilities, whatever they may be. A father claims that his sixteen-year-old daughter has been missing her curfew, but she insists that she has not. In situations such as these, it usually doesn't make sense to argue. A good way to reconcile differences is to "watch together" and keep track.

The father says, "Let's not argue. Let's agree to watch the next few weeks and keep track of when you're late and when you're on time for your curfew. Okay?"

Agreeing to watch not only increases objectivity but also encourages "best behavior."

When negotiating about issues such as curfew, use of the family car, attendance at certain parties, dating rules, sex, eating habits, homework, grades, housework, choice of friends, and drug use, the more you and your children think alike, the easier it will be to make agreements. The longer you and you children have been having open discussions, the greater the likelihood of agreement. But you can't always agree on everything.

In a negotiation between equals, people try to meet each other halfway. Although parent-child negotiation should be based on mutual respect, it is not between equals. Parents have the ultimate authority. Still, the goal of parenting is to empower children. With the transfer of power, you extend trust by giving children increasing freedom as they get older and an ever-increasing influence in decision-making. You want them to have experiences that they can handle, to help them learn responsibility and control. You want them eventually to be fully independent and capable of making their own decisions without your help. Fewer and fewer rules are needed.

With older teenagers, it doesn't make sense to be unbending, to think that you can set down all the rules and limits on your own terms without making concessions. By the time they are sixteen or seventeen, your children should be making most of their own decisions, and they should have had enough learning experiences to make wise ones. This is the ideal although not always the reality.

If you have been slow to transfer power, it's time to get moving. Soon your children will be on their own. You don't want to send them into "the cruel world" unprepared for what they will face, having had only limited learning opportunities and experiences under your supervision.

When you and your teenagers have differences of opinion, some of your rules or standards of behavior may be non-negotiable:

"We disagree. We see things differently. This is something I feel strongly about. I ask that you do as I tell you."

In other words, you ask for an agreement based on respect for your authority. If necessary, you may have to ask for an agreement based on your power, as in: "Do as I say, or the consequences will be . . . "

All through the process of transferring power to your children, you make rules and set limits that serve at least three purposes: (1) establishing a high standard of behavior; (2) protecting your children from danger; (3) helping them to develop self-control. That is, you set limits so that they will learn to set their own.

During childhood, and especially during the intensely emotional period of adolescence, it's important that children understand the reasons behind your authority and use of power. Your purpose is not to dominate and certainly not to make their lives miserable. Rather it is to protect them and help them learn to cope successfully.

When asking for compliance with rules, it's important to make it clear that you're on their side. You want them to be able to stay out as late as is healthy. You don't want to unnecessarily limit their social life. You want them to have the car. You just want to make sure that they are prepared to handle these responsibilities. You look forward to backing off and letting them take over for themselves.

It's very important to make yourself clear, because the purpose of authority is often misunderstood, as in the following case:

Mrs. Schneider told her sixteen-year-old daughter, Judy, to he home by 11:30 on Saturday night. She had a great deal of confidence and trust in Judy, but this was her first date with a boy who had a driver's license. Mrs. Schneider wanted to set limits that she thought would help her daughter deal with this older boy. Later, when Judy had more dating experience and knew what to expect, Mrs. Schneider would extend the curfew. Her logic was sound. Her limits were fair. But she didn't explain her thinking process to Judy, who was terribly disappointed by the curfew and wanted to stay out later. Judy thought that the curfew meant that her mother didn't trust her.

Some children, angered by what they consider to be unreasonable limits, become rebellious. Judy happened to be a responsible daughter and didn't do that. But the damage in this case was that she believed that her mother was working against her. Mrs. Schneider didn't come across to Judy as supportive, which was unfortunate, because she really was highly supportive.

Many children, like Judy, fail to understand the purpose of rules and agreements. These misunderstandings can be prevented by providing greater clarity about their purpose (to protect them) and their intent (to eventually give them more freedom).

REACHING A COMPROMISE

When you and your teenager disagree, before you reach the non-negotiable issues there are a wide range of cooperative possibilities for compromise. Some are listed below, along with examples of each.

1. You can lay out the conditions and reassurance you need in order to give permission for certain activities:
   - "I want to give you the car, even though it makes me a little nervous. What I need to feel comfortable with this arrangement is your guarantee that you won't drink or use any drugs."
   - "I'll give you the later curfew you wanted if you'll agree to call me at eleven o'clock and tell me where you are and how things are going. Then I'll be reassured that you're safe and can go to sleep without being upset. I don't see phone calls as a long-term solution, maybe just for a few weeks."
2. You can give permission for certain activities (for example, going on a date, using the family car, or visiting particular friends) with an agreement to talk openly afterward about what happened. Then you have an opportunity to evaluate the experience and to determine which coping skills your child may need to develop:
   - "I'll let you go away for this weekend if you'll agree to talk about what happened in some detail, so that we can see whether it was a good idea and what to do about situations like these in the future."
   - "I'll allow you to have a later curfew on this special occasion if you agree to honestly discuss what happens when you keep these late hours, so that we can see whether it poses any special problems."
3. You can explain the type of evidence from the past or the future that would lead to greater freedom:
   - "Let's talk about how you've handled peer pressure to try drugs, and I'll consider letting you cruise down Speedway Boulevard and letting you hang out behind McDonald's, even though I know that some of the other kids who cruise have used drugs."
   - "Do a good job of coming home on time with this curfew, and after a couple of months of success we can extend it."

In many situations, if you are willing to be flexible, you can find a workable compromise. If you cannot, you must hold the line. And if you have listened to them, explained your logic, and made it clear that you *eventually* want them to have more freedom, then usually children will agree to your terms without a battle.

If your terms are not accepted, then you must rely on your power as a parent. The effectiveness of this strategy depends on how many "chips" you hold. That is, you need to be giving something of value that would make your teenager comply if you threatened to take it away. For example: "If you stay at parties with drugs and don't leave, I won't let you use the car," or "You'll lose your allowance," or "I won't pay for your auto insurance."

If you reach this point, don't get hooked into a power struggle. Make it clear that you value cooperation: "I wish we could reach an amicable agreement. But under the circumstances, I must insist."

There is an art to maintaining parental authority with grace. When you have to establish a "bottom line" that your children find objectionable, tell them that you are sorry they are disappointed, that you don't like disappointing them, but that you find it necessary. If possible, make it clear how things could change with time.

Making Valid Agreements

After the give-and-take of discussion, agreements are made. They can be based on shared understanding ("We see things the same way"), respect for parental authority ("I ask that you agree to my terms"), or parental power ("Agree to my terms, or the consequences will be . . . ").

A good, valid agreement is crystal-clear, understood by all, and accepted by all. Your children may not be thrilled with some of the terms you set, but that doesn't keep them from agreeing in good faith to comply. By the same token, you don't want to establish unnecessary limitations.

Agreements that are not fully understood and not truly accepted will probably be broken and should be considered *invalid*. Intuition is your protection against invalid agreements:

"It doesn't sound to me as though you really have decided to stop using drugs. It sounds as though maybe you're just saying so to get me off your back. Do you really intend to stop? I don't want you to make an agreement unless you plan to keep it."

Even with the response "Yeah, I'll keep the agreement," you have to listen carefully and perhaps ask your child to be more convincing.

Also, you have to be alert to situations in which your child agrees to your terms but without carefully thinking it through. To this you might say:

"I appreciate your willingness to agree to my request that you stop using drugs. But you agreed so quickly that I want to make sure you have thought it through fully. I'm certain that opportunities for drug use will present themselves. Are you determined that you will resist these temptations?"

You don't want to be a doubting Thomas, but on the other hand, you have to recognize that you're not negotiating with peers. You're talking with your children, who may be feeling intimidated. This makes it more difficult to establish valid agreements. Also, you yourself may be tempted to believe anything, because it would relieve your own anxiety. Therefore, it makes good sense to fully use your intuition and establish valid agreements, even if this slows down the process.

Once a valid agreement is made, the expectation should be that all involved will uphold their ends of it. So, when your seventeen-year-old daughter says that she'll come home by her midnight curfew, if the agreement is valid you don't have to wait up for her. That would be indicating mistrust. To do so is to invite childish behavior. However, it makes sense to establish evaluation points: "Let's talk about this after a couple of weeks to see how the curfew is working."

Broken Agreements

Another important aspect of making rules and agreements is establishing consequences for broken agreements.

If there is a history of broken agreements, you need to make consequences clear from the beginning. For example: "If you don't do your household chores, you won't get your allowance."

If there is no history of broken agreements, then you don't have to lay out consequences. The starting assumption is that everyone will do as agreed. There's no need to assume failure.

When agreements *are* broken, a non-punitive educational approach will usually get things back on track.

Step One: Begin with a reasonable statement: "You were supposed to be home by eleven o'clock, and I noticed that you were half an hour late. What happened?"

Then listen to the explanation. If it was a deliberate violation, determine whether your agreement was valid—that is, whether it was understood and accepted in good faith. If not, you both need to talk again and establish an agreement with validity:

"Do you think the curfew is reasonable? If not, say so. I'm not saying I'll necessarily change it, but if it's bothering you, we need to have more discussion."

If the agreement was broken because of an error in judgment or because your child forgot, ask what will be done differently to avoid repeating the problem in the future. Then say that you are serious about the curfew and want to make certain that your child is. Ask for assurance that this won't happen again and listen to determine whether the agreement is valid.

You may uncover problems such as "I wanted to come home, but my friends were teasing me about my early curfew." This shows that you have to help your child learn the necessary skills to keep the agreement. In this example, the child needs to learn how to stand up to peer pressure.

By the end of Step One, you want to feel assured that the agreement will be kept.

Step Two: If the agreement is broken again, discuss it again, reminding your child that this is the second time: "Once again you were late for your curfew. I'm very concerned about this. You have to start keeping our agreements. What happened? We need to get to the bottom of this."

Depending on the importance of the broken agreement and the history of the child, this step may be repeated another time if the agreement is broken again.

Step Three: This is the same as Step Two, except that at the end you discuss consequences: "This needs to stop, or the consequences for breaking the agreement will be ... "

Step Four: This is when you follow through with the consequences. You might say: "You will stay home for a weekend to think about what has been happening with curfew. Then we'll talk, and we'll see whether we can make workable agreements during the next week. I want you to be able to go out on weekends. I don't like grounding you, but I need to see improvements."

The goal of all these measures is to promote clear thinking and responsible behavior. You should always bring the discussion back to building good judgment by explaining the reasons for a rule or an agreement and the reasons for setting consequences for misbehavior.

If antagonism has reached a very high level, teenagers sometimes go for broke: "I don't care what you do to me. I'm gonna do what I want to do, anyway." This serious problem is discussed in the following chapter.

What you want to avoid in all these discussions is losing self-control and starting to rant and rave. I've seen this over and over again.

The children misbehave. The parents lose their tempers. The children then back off, donning a self-righteous smirk and wait in silence for the storm of words to blow over. They've gained a certain measure of control by staying calm while their parents got hysterical. To an outsider, it looks like child against child—the parents have lost their status.

Halfhearted Effort

Broken agreements come in many forms, from blatant disregard of a commitment to a sloppy, halfhearted effort at compliance.

Fifteen-year-old Tom did his chores around the house only sporadically. His parents resented the inconsistency but held back their feelings because they always hoped for improvement.

Halfhearted compliance such as this poses special problems. Parents tend to tolerate it longer than blatant disregard. Eventually, however, they get angry. Then, on the day they plan to talk about their feelings, their children do as they are told for a short period of time.

My suggestion is to treat a halfhearted effort as you would any broken agreement, using the several steps outlined above. For example:

"I've noticed that you haven't been meeting your curfew *regularly* [or "doing your chores," or "cleaning your room"]. Our agreement was that you would do it regularly. You agreed to come home on time for curfew, and I expect you to be on time, always, without my reminders. What's been happening?"

"Oh, I'm sorry, I forget."

"What do we need to do to make sure you remember? After all, I expect you to keep our agreements consistently."

The discussion then continues, following the same progression it would take with any broken agreement.

PRINCIPLES FOR MAKING VALID AGREEMENTS ABOUT DRUGS

Many books offer oversimplified advice about drug use or potential use, as if all parents and children were the same, as if all families had the same experiences, and as if the same strategies would be appropriate in every situation and with children of every age.

The gospel of prevention books is: no drug use, ever—set a rule, enforce it, and punish infractions. I wish it were so simple, but, determining the best strategy for preventing or minimizing abuse is a complex matter. It depends upon a careful assessment of a number of factors, including your child's age and maturity, and your child-rearing history. It also depends on whether drugs are currently being used, and, if so, at what level and with what amount of harm or potential harm.

As a parent, you have many ways to prevent drug abuse. First and foremost is to establish agreements based on a shared understanding. Another way is to make agreements based on respect for your authority as a parent. If needed, you can make agreements based on the threat of punishment. If all this fails, you can use a method called "watching closely" (discussed later in this chapter) or take more drastic measures to intervene (described in the following chapter).

In assessing a situation and taking action, I suggest a few guiding principles:

1. Make it clear that you oppose drug use.
2. Remember, the goal is not only to prevent harm but also to help your children learn to make wise decisions on their own.
3. Bear in mind that older teenagers are in a transition to adulthood. They will soon be adults who must make their own decisions.

4. Recognize pragmatic factors. Most parents have enough power and control to stop drug use by pre-teenagers and young teenagers. However, it is impossible to prevent determined teenagers from acquiring drugs. As your children become older, you have less control over what they do and must rely on other types of influence.
5. When children are using drugs and harm is occurring or is imminent, it's important to draw the line and make a strong stand.
6. When the risk of harm is less immediate, you can use more subtle, long-range strategies to assert your influence.

A Word About "Responsible" Drug Use by Children

As I have repeated throughout this book, my strong recommendation to parents is that you say, "The use of alcohol and other drugs is not for children."

I put it in these terms, rather than the alternative: "Only adults can use alcohol and other drugs." This statement seems to suggest that taking drugs is the "grown-up" thing to do.

In recent years, many parents and professionals have accepted the inevitability of drug experimentation by children. They say, "It's a rite of passage of adolescence. We must accept it, learn to deal with it, and minimize the damage."

Although the use of alcohol and other drugs is certainly a common occurrence, it should be noted that a large percentage of teenagers do not use drugs at all. I believe that even more would abstain if we set a clear "no-use" standard and believed in our ability as adults to inspire adherence to this standard.

A consequence of accepting drug use by children has been the practice among some parents and professionals of teaching "responsible use." Since children will take drugs anyway, they say, we must teach them to be responsible users who do not abuse drugs.

The problem with this argument is that it seems to legitimize drug use by children. I believe that instead of teaching them how to use drugs responsibly, our efforts would be better invested in teaching them how to meet their needs without drugs and how to resist peer pressure. If children are already using drugs, efforts should be made to help them stop, or at least to minimize or prevent harm.

It would be inaccurate to state that *all* drug use by teenagers automatically causes harm. However, there are significant risks. In view of this, the goal should be *no drug use*. Only in those situations when use by older teenagers cannot be stopped does it make sense to settle for the lesser goal of preventing a harmful level of use.

Adult Decisions

The "no-use" rule for children has to be seen in the context of a cultural standard that allows adults to legally use some drugs, such as alcohol, nicotine, and legally prescribed mood-altering substances, including tranquilizers. Millions of adults use legal or illegal substances, many without impairing their health and with a willingness to risk the legal consequences.

At some point a child will become an adult and can make his or her own choices. Although we arbitrarily assign ages for certain "adult" behaviors, such as driving a motor vehicle, voting, and drinking alcohol, there is no magical moment when a child becomes an adult.

Adolescence is the transition period to adulthood. In terms of drug use, some adolescents are ready to make adult decisions before others. Determining the readiness of an individual for mature decision-making is an important issue and often a source of dispute between parent and teenager.

Depending on age and maturity, there are differences in how to approach making agreements about drugs with your children. For the sake of explanation, I will somewhat arbitrarily divide the discussion about making agreements into two parts: making agreements with children and younger teenagers (up to age fourteen) and making agreements with older teenagers and young adults (fifteen and up). This is not to suggest that all fifteen-year-olds are capable of mature decision-making. As you know, other factors enter into the equation.

We begin with a discussion about making valid agreements with children and younger teenagers.

MAKING VALID AGREEMENTS WITH CHILDREN AND YOUNGER TEENAGERS (FOURTEEN AND UNDER) WHO ARE NOT USING DRUGS

If your children are not using drugs, it may be due to lack of interest or lack of access. In any case, it is important to make it clear that drugs are not for children and that "no-use" is a family rule.

If obedience in your family has been based on punishment for misbehavior, then your children should be told about the consequences of using drugs. At the same time, it's wise to phase out the threat of punishment and begin to incorporate other ways of promoting good behavior. Encourage your children to think for themselves and to make wise decisions without your supervision, so that as they get older they will become increasingly responsible.

The most important agreement to make with children who have not used drugs is that they will talk with you if they begin to consider the possibility. Above all, you want honesty and dialogue:

"I'm pleased you're not using drugs. If you ever get interested in them, I would like you to talk with me right away. Will you do that?"

You might add: "Sometimes people impulsively do things without much forethought. Personally I think it's a bad idea to start using alcohol or other drugs that way. But if this does happen, I want you to agree to talk with me afterward. This isn't to say that I think it's okay for you to use drugs. I would be disappointed if you did. But I want us to be able to talk, regardless. Okay?"

Most teenagers who are not using drugs will be willing to agree to these terms. If yours are reluctant to agree to talk in the future about drug use or the temptation to use drugs, the challenge is to figure out why this is so.

From the diagnostic point of view, this reluctance means that your children have agreed to talk *now* because they know you will approve of what they are doing—that is, *not* using drugs. However, you don't have the sort of home atmosphere that allows for complete honesty and openness. Your children won't talk if they are doing something, such as using drugs, that will not meet with your approval. If this is the case in your family, I suggest that you backtrack and work on establishing a climate of honesty in which your children feel that they can talk with you about *anything*.

If your children have already tried drugs and stopped using them, you will have discussed the experiences and the motivation that led to the experimentation in the early stages of the exchange-of-information process. Now you will want to set up the same agreement about being honest in the future as you would with children who have never used drugs. You will also want to be certain that your children have the ability to resist future temptation.

Sometimes children think that they have stopped experimenting, because they haven't sought out drugs, but they have not actually decided to reject drugs should they become available.

The key to finding out whether a decision to stop using drugs has been made is to ask, "What if alcohol, marijuana, or some other drug were *put into your hand*? Would you use it?"

MAKING VALID AGREEMENTS WITH CHILDREN (FOURTEEN AND UNDER) WHO ARE USING DRUGS

If your children are using drugs—so far without harm—and want to continue to do so, or if they plan to use drugs for the first time, you can explain the potential risks and, together with them, discuss this book and other books with drug information.

Ideally, they will agree to stop using drugs. If not, summarize the differences between their analysis and yours, and then establish the rules. For example: "You think smoking weed is harmless, and I see it as risky behavior, especially for someone as young as you. You could be right. It is possible that you could use drugs infrequently, as you say you do, without substantial harm. But I believe that it is not likely, and I'm unwilling to allow it. I want you to agree not to use drugs."

Another possibility is that your children understand the risks but are willing to take them. To this you might say: "We each agree that drug use is potentially dangerous. We also agree that it involves substantial legal risks. You're willing to take these risks. I don't want to allow it. That's the difference in our thinking. I want you to agree to refrain from taking drugs."

If drug use has already caused harm, you will have uncovered it in the dialogue. You might say: "You don't think that drugs are part of a problem, but I do. I see that your grades have fallen and that you haven't been doing a good job at home with your chores. I won't allow you to continue using drugs. I want you to agree to stop."

You can state the proposed agreement in a gentle yet firm way. You want a valid agreement based on respect, and an important goal is to promote good, clear-headed thinking. Even though you have the ultimate job of setting a standard, it's important that the discussion remain respectful. After a respectful discussion, many younger teenagers will agree to comply with your rules, even if they disagree with your point of view.

As a last resort, a hard line is usually effective with the fourteen-and-under age group. If they intend to use drugs, then you will stop their allowance, restrict their social life and after-school activities, and take other necessary actions. As always, the intent is not to hurt them but to protect them from engaging in a risky activity. Children should not be using drugs. Inform them of the consequences of continued drug use and then follow through.

Some children will agree to stop but won't mean it. You need to use your intuition to watch for phony, invalid agreements designed to end discussions. Listen to the tone of voice to detect sincerity. Listen for an angry "giving-in" tone or for a quick "Yeah, yeah, sure" tone, either of which could indicate an invalid agreement. If you doubt sincerity, say so in a nice way: "It doesn't sound as though you *really* are agreeing to this. I don't want you to say you'll stop until you intend to follow through. Of course, I'll be delighted if you assure me that you mean it. But I want honesty in our relationship. If you haven't really decided to stop using drugs, then we need to keep the discussion going."

The dialogue *must* continue until drug use ceases, no matter how long it takes and regardless of what consequences you need to impose. You may need to insist upon seeking professional help.

MAKING VALID AGREEMENTS WITH OLDER TEENAGERS (FIFTEEN AND UP) WHO ARE NOT USING DRUGS

Most parents want their older teenage children to remain drug-free. This age group has easy access to drugs. So, if they haven't been using them, they probably are not interested *at this time*. It's still important to establish a clear "no-use" expectation and to make an agreement to maintain an ongoing dialogue.

The way to communicate a "no-use" expectation is highly individualized. Thinking about your child-rearing practices will help in assessing where you stand in the transfer of power and in determining the types of agreements you want.

If you have given increasing freedom and responsibility over the years, and the transfer of power is on schedule, by age fifteen or sixteen mature teenagers should be ready to make their own wise decisions, even about drugs. All they need is guidance. It would be regressive to set rules and make threats when they are capable of making good decisions without them.

If the transfer of power is behind schedule, older teens need rules to guide their behavior. And if they behave properly only because they are scared of punishment, they need to know the consequences of misbehavior. But it is also important to work toward phasing out this method of control. Soon they will be young adults without parents around to supervise them.

If you've been overly permissive, allowing too much freedom, and your teenagers have been unable to develop self-control in various aspects of their lives (for example, truancy, refusal to do homework, getting into trouble in school, violating the law, breaking rules), then you need to regain control and establish limits. Accustomed to freedom, your children will probably resist your efforts to set limits, but one way or another, they need you to exercise control. Once you succeed in establishing limits, they will be relieved that you helped them settle down. They will be on firmer ground in the future if they ever consider using drugs. Then you can gradually give back freedom as they demonstrate the ability to behave responsibly.

If you've been too much the authoritarian, setting so many rules and restrictions that your children have rebelled, it's advisable to back off, pick only a few rules that *are* enforceable, and make the tone of the communication less threatening. Before establishing new rules, you have to improve the relationship.

MAKING VALID AGREEMENTS WITH OLDER TEENAGERS (FIFTEEN AND UP) WHO ARE USING DRUGS

When older teenagers are using drugs occasionally or regularly, it's likely that they and their parents will have differences of opinion about the risks and effects, and disagree about future use. The exchange-of-information process can help in assessing the effects of drug use and the potential dangers, both of which are important considerations in making agreements.

Some parents say, "If you're going to use drugs, then at least do it at home." The idea is that, in the safety of the home, the child will be protected from the temptation to drive while "under the influence" or to engage in other high-risk types of behavior. This approach is laden with problems. One is that it legitimizes the use of alcohol and other drugs. The message is, "Go ahead." Another problem is that once the child is comfortable using drugs at home, it becomes much more likely that he or she will take their drug use outside the home to social situations with friends. Sometimes the child will start inviting friends to his or her home to get high, and the problems multiply.

In deciding what to do about drug use, start with a thorough assessment of harm and potential harm. Look at such factors as the choice of drugs, the types of drugs that are combined, the frequency and quantity of drugs used, the settings where drugs are used, and the types of high-risk behavior that may coincide with drug use. Usually, tobacco, alcohol, and marijuana are the first drugs sampled, and the dangers associated with these drugs are less immediate. Your actions and your level of patience will certainly be influenced by your initial assessment of harm.

First you can use your educational influence to promote a decision to stop taking drugs. Sometimes an initial discussion may be unsuccessful, but as you continue the dialogue, your child may eventually agree to stop.

When drug use has been infrequent and harm doesn't seem imminent, the educational approach has advantages over simply punishing teenagers and trying to control their behavior. Although it takes longer and causes more discomfort—because you temporarily have to tolerate the use of drugs—family communication remains intact, and the possible outcome is that they will learn their lessons well and be prepared to make good decisions in adult life.

If an ongoing dialogue fails, you still have the option of setting a rule about no further drug use, based on either respect for your authority or, if necessary, the threat of punishment.

In families in which punishment has been the primary means to control behavior, a quick jolt of punishment sometimes effectively persuades a teenager to give up drugs.

One risk with any form of punishment is that it may increase the determination of a rebellious teenager to defy authority. And even if drug use is halted, this may be short-lived, because it is done out of fear. As he or she begins to feel more powerful or more rebellious, drug use may start again.

Because older teenagers are bigger, stronger, sometimes earning their own money, and in possession of a driver's license, they are much less likely to buckle under to the pressure of punishment than younger ones. They have more resources of their own and therefore greater independence. With this age group, you sometimes need to use different strategies for making agreements.

WATCHING CLOSELY

If dialogue and rules don't work in getting a "no-use" agreement from older teenagers, and punishment either is ruled out or hasn't worked, I recommend an educational process that I call "watching closely." The basic idea is to refrain from strong-arm tactics in exchange for an agreement that your children will behave responsibly in all important realms of their life (in school, with friends, with family) and will continue to talk with you about the impact of their drug use. If their functioning declines, they will have an opportunity to see it as they experience the natural and logical consequences of their behavior. They also can be held accountable for what they are doing.

Below is the four-part process of watching closely:

1. Express your perception of the problems and the risks of drug use.
2. Set high standards of behavior.
3. Maintain an ongoing vigil, together with your teenagers, over what is happening in their lives in regard to the agreed-upon

high standards of behavior. (That's why I call it "watching closely.")

4. Hold teenagers accountable for their behavior.

Watching closely is effective in promoting self-scrutiny. With this approach, older teenagers have an opportunity to really see how drugs are affecting them.

Intense supervision is important. If they do not meet the standards of behavior you set and cannot keep the agreements that they make, handle it respectfully, in a disciplined and constructive way, as you would any broken agreement. Guide them through the same process you would use if drugs were not involved. This gives them an opportunity to get back on track. If they don't improve, make connections between drugs and their misbehavior:

"You don't seem to be able to handle both drugs and your responsibilities. I think that you need to stop using drugs. What do you think?"

At this point, ask for a drug-free agreement or a more dedicated commitment to high standards of behavior. Explain that if they still don't meet their responsibilities after trying again, a whole set of natural and logical consequences will come to pass. Always provide an explanation to promote understanding of the problem.

For example, they may get suspended from school, fail classes, get into trouble with the law, or lose friends. They may lose privileges of family life such as allowance, late curfew, or use of the family car. These natural and logical consequences would be discussed in the context of drug use and a drug-using lifestyle. They are not punishments for using drugs, except school suspensions or legal problems which result directly from drug use. Rather, they are natural and logical consequences of irresponsible behavior. "Watching closely" allows young people to see the impact of what they are doing with their lives while using drugs.

Watching Closely: Too Liberal?

Is the idea of watching closely too liberal? Is it saying that drug use by older teenagers is acceptable? These are valid concerns, but the answer is no.

239

You can't physically stop drug use. Teenagers can get drugs in school or in other places where you can't be watching them. The parent-as-police-officer mode doesn't work with this age group. Education and dialogue are your most powerful influences.

Watching closely keeps your teenage children thinking and allows them to understand the risks and effects of what they're doing. The goal is to stop drug use, or at least to minimize harm and keep the use from increasing. The desired outcome is that they will monitor their own behavior. Such awareness helps prevent or minimize problems.

"Isn't this just teaching children responsible use of drugs," you may wonder, "the very thing that you've said is not a good idea?"

In a sense, it is, but only with older teenagers, not children, and only as a strategic move. It is based on the objective fact that the method of threats and punishment doesn't usually work and isn't always advisable with older teenagers. In many cases it is wiser to keep the dialogue open and sacrifice possible short-term gains for long-term influence.

In a way, this is saying that you want responsible drug use. However, it is more like this: If you as a parent can't effectively stop drug use, no matter what you do, then, yes, try to keep it responsible. Try to prevent or minimize harm, but don't get caught in a power struggle that completely takes away your power. Get your children to watch their own behavior, instead of having them spend all their time and energy pushing you away and being defensive.

Most teenagers who use drugs are not significantly harmed. Many of them outgrow it by their late teens or early twenties, when they are freer of peer pressure and have successfully assumed adult roles. However, if drug use clearly is harmful or is becoming harmful, *they will have an opportunity to see it themselves* if they are watching closely. You will then be in the strong position of having open channels of communication. You have time to talk with them before dependence occurs. You can be the calm voice clarifying problems, not the antagonist.

Watching closely is based on three often-forgotten facts: (1) Teenagers do not *want* to harm themselves. Like everyone else, they have a survival and growth instinct. (2) Older teenagers have the potential to think with mature logic. Given an opportunity to clearly understand self-destructive behavior, they can see what is happening and make changes. (3) As older teenagers approach adulthood, they begin to realize that they will soon have to fend for themselves. They will need to get jobs to put a roof over their head and food on the table. The pressure of this reality promotes increasingly mature decision-making.

Sometimes, however, it's too late for watching closely. If drug use has already reached the level of serious abuse or dependence, reasonable discussions are almost impossible. More drastic measures are needed to attempt to break through the denial and jolt the drug user into reality.

Watching Closely: No Harm, Lower Risk

The process of watching closely varies according to the level of harm or potential harm in different situations. It is especially difficult to persuade older teenagers that drugs are potentially dangerous if they have been using them without evident harm and they have well-developed life skills that put them at less risk of dependence. They are getting the pleasure of drugs without suffering the negative consequences. This is what you could say:

"As you know, I'm opposed to your using drugs. I see it as potentially hazardous to your health. I'm also worried about the legal risks. I know that I can't stop you, but I do expect you to do well in school, be responsible at home, maintain good relationships with friends and other people, and stay healthy. I think that using drugs may interfere with this. Let's watch closely and see what happens. I assume that if you see drug-related problems, you'll use good judgment and stop. Right? Will you agree to behave well at home, in school, and with friends? Will you agree to keep watching what happens and talking about it?"

At this time, set rules for your own protection:

"I'm not going to go crazy or get into a big fight and a power struggle with you. However, I'll protect my rights. For example, if you have drugs in our home, that puts me in legal jeopardy. I won't allow that. If you drive under the influence of alcohol or other drugs, that too puts me in jeopardy, and other people as well. You must agree not to use the family car on days when you use drugs. If I even

241

suspect that you're using alcohol or other drugs and driving, I won't let you use the car for a *long* time.

"I hope that setting these rules doesn't mean you'll sneak behind my back. I hope my honesty with you now will encourage your honesty and willingness to talk with me. If we lose trust, then we will really have problems."

This appeal to preserving a good relationship often is enough to convince most children to keep talking.

Maintain the dialogue and have ongoing discussions: "How are you doing in school? With friends? How's your health? How are you doing at home?" If harm begins to occur, use the feed-it-back approach to point it out. For example: "It looks as though your grades have been falling. Have you noticed this? What do you think?"

By watching closely, you trade quick intervention for good thinking. With this method, your children will be able to see the harm that drugs cause and stop before trouble escalates. Also, with the passing of time and nothing to rebel against, teenagers sometimes lose interest in drugs. But some older teenagers will continue to use drugs without significant harm.

Watching Closely: No Harm, High Risk

If drugs have not yet caused harm, but you see a potential for high risk, say something like this:

"I won't stand idly by while I see your drug use continuing. I love you too much to ignore it. I'm going to keep talking about what's happening. I want you to stop using drugs. But I know that I can't follow you around and that you don't intend to stop.

"You say that drugs haven't caused you any harm yet. I'm afraid that they will. I think that you've been using drugs to deal with stress. I realize that your grades are still fine, you are behaving well at home, and you're doing all your homework. But sooner or later, if you don't learn other ways to prevent stress or deal with it, I'm worried that you'll have a very serious problem. I hope you'll follow my recommendation to get professional help in learning how to deal with stress. I'll help you myself, to the extent that I can. I hope you will do what I think is right, which is to stop using drugs.

"In the meantime, let's see what happens. I'll expect you to keep up your grades, come home in time for curfew, maintain good relationships at home and with your friends, and do all your chores."

Watching Closely When You See Harm

The stakes are much higher when harm is already occurring. The critical distinction at this point is whether your child has crossed into dependence. If this has happened or is about to happen, the ability to reason is lost. The logical faculties are no longer fully functional. Watching closely won't help.

However, before dependence occurs, numerous problems should be evident. Under these circumstances I recommend an accelerated version of "watching closely." You want your child to recognize the harm quickly, before it escalates. If this fails, more drastic measures are needed:

"I see without question that drugs are harming you. Your grades have fallen. You're in trouble in school. You consistently ignore curfew.

"This is very, very serious. I love you too much to look away, to allow this type of destructive behavior to continue. It's urgent that you stop using drugs. They are harming your life and this family. I'm willing to arrange for professional help. You've got to face this problem. Something must be done. Do you agree? Will you stop using drugs?"

If he or she won't agree, lay out your expectations once again: "I expect that you will not drink and drive or use drugs and drive, that you will get enough sleep and start to take care of your health, that you will bring up your grades and come home on time for curfew, and that your behavior will start to improve *immediately*."

Some children will be relieved by your strong stance and accept the offer of help. Others will say that they can bounce back in school and that they will behave better. You can cut them a little slack, providing an opportunity to improve quickly within a time limit:

"Look, I believe that you have an earnest desire to fix things. I think that you need professional help, and I'm willing to provide for it. I'm not at the point of trying to drag you into someone's office. Maybe you'll prove me wrong—you'll stop using drugs and get your life back in order. I hope you do. But there's too much evidence of harm for me to wait long. I'm going to check in with you every week for one month to see how things are going. We need some big changes. Will you agree to make them?"

If your teenager won't agree immediately, back off and let him or her think about it for a couple of days. If there is still no commitment to making changes, it's time for more drastic measures (outlined in the following chapter). If there is a commitment to making changes, explain the consequences of not following through and then watch closely what happens:

"If you don't come home on time for curfew, I won't let you go out on weekends." (If that is unenforceable and your child will go out anyway, say, "I won't give you your allowance," or "I won't pay for your car insurance," or "I won't let you use the family car.")

As problems escalate, the warnings get more severe:

"If the situation deteriorates to the point of your being in trouble with the law, I won't hire an attorney. You'll be on your own. I won't bail you out. If you drop out of school, you'll have to get a job, and keep it, in order to continue living here at home. I may charge you rent or ask you to leave, depending on what it's like living with you."

If parents don't "rescue" their children—bail them out of trouble—drug abuse creates its own problems and brings matters to a head. You don't have to take your children to the police—although sometimes that's a good strategy—or tell their teachers. Problems in school, and eventually with the law, will surface of their own accord.

A teenager may ultimately see the need for professional help. Of course, it is important that parents impose consequences for misbehavior at home. However, there is some advantage to *not* being the one who turns him or her in to authorities such as teachers or the police, unless absolutely necessary. Otherwise, you will look like the bad guy. He or she may say, "I have a problem, and it's my parents." If consequences occur in school or with the law, and you are not involved, a child will see that drugs are causing harm. Forced to face the real problem—use of drugs—he or she can't shift the blame to you.

Sometimes it seems as though you need the patience and discipline of a saint to guide your child through a calm reasoning process when you are frightened about the outcome. However, children who are empowered to think can usually see what is happening. Their logical powers click and they recognize potential or existing problems *before* the harm is too serious.

If drug use already borders on dependence, or if your child has serious underlying problems, it's possible that this vigilance will not succeed. If drug use escalates, your child has clearly indicated to you by his or her behavior—and, more important, to himself or herself—that something more drastic must be done.

WALKING THE TIGHTROPE

I speak with experience when I talk about the difficulty of watching something very scary but holding back just a little to see whether long-term benefits will outweigh short-term gains.

I was counseling a sweet but very confused seventeen-year-old girl, Laura, and her parents. She was struggling with her use of marijuana and alcohol, and was barely passing in school. Her parents were upper-middle-class and had given her a car of her own. From time to time they would punish her for one transgression or another by not letting her use the car. The punishment was ineffective. It didn't stop Laura from doing everything she wanted to do. She always managed to find a friend's car to drive.

Soon after the initial session, her parents and I learned that Laura was drinking and driving. "Don't worry," she said, "I'm a safe driver, even when I drink." Her parents took away her car privileges for a week, until she said she would stop drinking and driving.

But that was no problem for Laura. When I met with her separately, she told me that she had managed to drink and drive a friend's car that week. Also, she lied to her parents about drinking, so that they would "get off her back."

Furthermore, Laura was angry that her parents had used the car as punishment.

"Don't you think it's unfair?" she asked.

"What?" I replied.

"That they punish me by taking away the car."

"I wouldn't say unfair," I answered, "so much as ineffective. It didn't really make a difference, did it?"

"No, not really," she answered.

"I want to be completely honest with you," I said to Laura. "It scares me when I hear that you're drinking and driving. I think that it's very dangerous and that *no one* should do it. You risk your own life and the life of everyone else who's on the road. It even makes me angry, because, you know, I have children and it scares me that they could get hurt by you or someone else who's driving drunk."

Laura assured me that she was a good driver, even after drinking. I explained that alcohol is tricky. It gives a false sense of security, causing people to think that they can drive safely. But research has proven that it slows reflexes and can be very dangerous, especially when something unexpected happens on the road. That's why drunk-driving laws have been passed and are so strongly enforced.

"You know," I said, "you can lose your license if you get caught drinking and driving. And the police are out watching kids cruise. They'll pull you over, even if you haven't violated a law."

This really caught her attention. She valued her driver's license highly. She asked about the legal level of intoxication. I explained it, and I promised to bring her a little cardboard device for calculating the amount of blood alcohol based on consumption, body weight, and time elapsed since drinking. She was interested.

As the session ended, I felt a sense of responsibility for her, her parents, and innocent drivers and pedestrians. I thought about my options, including breaking the confidentiality rule and telling her parents what was happening. What could they do? Not let her use the car again? Keep her at home? She was clever and would get around any punishment they dished out. Eventually it might be necessary to take away the car for good. But at this point it would lead to a monumental power struggle. Laura would probably run away, and she would make sure she was drunk when she drove someone else's car. She was so rebellious and defiant. I decided to trust that beneath her rebellious exterior beat the heart of a reasonably intelligent human being who, *given an opportunity to think*, would make good decisions. I admit to having felt some trepidation.

The next week I brought to my office the device for calculating blood alcohol, and gave it to her. Together we figured out how it worked. She discovered for herself that she had often been clearly over the legal limit of intoxication. She worried about losing her license. She took the device home.

The following week she told me she had decided never to drink and drive again. "It's too dangerous," she said. She stuck to her decision. When she didn't feel threatened by her parents, and cooler heads prevailed, Laura was able to make good decisions on her own. This was a turning point for her. Later that year I proudly attended her high-school graduation.

PROFESSIONAL HELP

The family is one place to confront personal problems, but it's not the only resource. Often families find that they cannot solve their problems alone. If problems are not being solved at home, then it's important to seek help elsewhere, and the sooner the better. Counselors, psychologists, social workers, and other mental-health professionals are an excellent resource. Ideally, they should be consulted before drug dependence develops, to assist with preventive efforts. If serious abuse or dependence has already occurred, the help of professionals is urgent.

Getting to the bottom of a drug problem involves more than self-control or abstinence. The underlying causes must be addressed. Mental-health professionals are trained to help children learn basic life skills—the ones we discussed in the context of prevention—so that they can meet their needs without drugs and without hurting themselves.

Attitudes about psychotherapy have come a long way since the old days, when consulting a professional was seen as a major source of embarrassment, a family secret. And services have become much more accessible with the advent of community mental-health clinics. Free and sliding-fee-scale services are widely available.

When you discuss problems with your children, one of the offers you can make is to seek professional help. You can call it the help of a supportive person trained to deal with problems. Keep it positive and be careful not to present it as a threat: "If you don't shape up, I'll take you to a psychiatrist."

Some children will gratefully accept such an offer, but others will be reluctant. Unless the harm from drug use is serious, rather than trying to force the issue, let professional help remain an ongoing offer as you continue the dialogue. That way, when they finally acknowledge their problems, they won't have to feel that they are giving in to pressure.

Seeking professional help is a family matter. Problems with alcohol and other drugs do not occur in a vacuum. They are affected by the family situation and will have consequences for the family dynamic. As parents, you can benefit from professional help when the family has a drug problem. An ideal offer is:

"Let's all go for some help to deal with this problem. We can start separately or together—whichever makes you more comfortable. I'm sure we [your parents] share some responsibility for what's happening. Let's solve these problems together."

In selecting a professional to help with substance-abuse issues, be aware of two precautions. First, make sure that the professional you select has had experience in working with young people who have problems with alcohol and other drugs. Not all professionals have had this experience, although graduate training programs are increasingly recognizing this as an important area of study. Also, be aware that some substance-abuse and hospital programs tend to see *all* drug use as an indication of addiction. Be sure to inquire whether the program is equipped to work in preventive ways, and to identify and effectively treat less extreme levels of drug use as well.

One of the biggest obstacles to seeking professional help is a culture-wide ideology of super-individualism: "It's my problem, and I need to solve it alone." If you or your child is tied to this belief, I suggest that you rethink it. The argument of the super-individualist is that getting help is a sign of weakness. I think that it's just the opposite. It's a sign of strength to be willing to admit to problems and to use all available resources to confront them.

If a child insists that he or she wants to solve these problems alone, you can encourage him or her to succeed but emphasize the option of help. He may say: "Trust me. I'm gonna change things." A good response is: "I do trust you. Suggesting that you get professional help doesn't mean that I don't. It means that I think you, like anyone else, deserve support in making important changes."

PROMISES, PROMISES

"I'm gonna cut back."

"I'm gonna stop using drugs."

These are sincere promises repeated over and over again by

teenagers who are having serious problems but finding themselves incapable of solving them. Hopeful parents take heart with each new commitment, but at some point they must ask themselves how many times the pledges have been made and then broken.

A good way to keep track of broken promises is by "watching closely" and using the feed-it-back approach. You can offer help:

"If you want, we can set limits and restrictions that would support you. For example, you can agree to come home right after school and to avoid any party where there might be drugs. You can agree to stay away from your friends who use drugs. If you do this, it'll probably be easier for you. What do you think? Or we can get some professional help. Would you like that?"

Each failed attempt to keep a promise is discussed, and each time the need for assistance becomes increasingly clear.

DRASTIC MEASURES

Drastic measures need to be used when drugs have taken over and reasonable discussion simply is impossible. It also makes sense to take drastic measures before dependence has happened, if it is clear that patient and disciplined "watching closely" is not working.

But first a word of caution. Many parents make a serious mistake by *prematurely* using drastic measures. They may, for example, humiliate their teenage child with a urinalysis, or try to keep him "imprisoned" at home during all of his spare time, or place him in a psychiatric hospital against his will, even when drug use has been only minimal.

When reflecting on his teenage years, a young man with a serious drug problem told me about his parents extreme reaction after he first smoked marijuana:

"I was almost perfect compared to other kids. I stayed out of trouble and used to talk honestly with my parents. But they went nuts when I told them I'd smoked weed for the first time. They didn't let me out of the house after school or on weekends for a month. They informed my teachers and basketball coach that I had smoked weed. 'Okay,' I decided. 'If they're going to punish me like that, I won't give them any more information.' My parents became my enemies. I stopped telling them anything. I decided they'd have to catch me."

This left him at the mercy of the "educational influence" of friends. A more moderate response might well have prevented his ultimate problems.

In recent years I've noticed a disturbing tendency to place children who have used drugs in residential treatment centers or psychiatric hospitals as the first alternative, when it really should be one of the last. Seductive advertising by these institutions catches the attention of distracted and busy parents looking for help. Sometimes part of the problem in the first place is that the parents don't have enough time for their children. Hospitals exploit this with advertisements that essentially say, "Turn the responsibility over to us."

Drastic measures should be taken only when all other options have been ruled out. Taking drastic measures to prevent or minimize drug abuse is not the type of prevention we've been talking about in this book. As you will see, however, even though parents sacrifice dialogue for forceful intervention when they take drastic measures, the desired outcome is ultimately the same—to get their child to think about what he or she is doing. We'll talk about this in the next chapter.

PART III
INTERVENTION

9
WHAT TO DO ABOUT
SERIOUS DRUG ABUSE

It shouldn't have been such a shock to Mr. and Mrs. Cooper, considering all the warning signs. Jeremy's grades had fallen dramatically, to the point where this former honor student was failing three classes. The Coopers noticed but figured that it was a passing phase. They kept believing his promises of miraculous improvement, even when time and again these promises were empty. Meanwhile, they wrote notes excusing absences whenever Jeremy "ditched" school.

Jeremy's cheerful disposition had long ago given way to nasty moodiness. Ugly remarks were excused as typical teenage rebellion. Missed curfews were brushed aside as a sign of the times: "Kids aren't behaving as well as they used to."

When Jeremy was fired from his job at a fast-food restaurant, the Coopers believed his unlikely excuse—that he was being hassled unfairly by the boss.

All along, the Coopers gave Jeremy substantial amounts of money, so that he could buy necessities such as lunch and gas for the car. But his needs for money kept growing.

Although the signs of a problem were abundant, Mr. and Mrs. Cooper missed them. Instead, they rescued Jeremy, thus enabling him to consume increasing amounts of marijuana, alcohol, crystal meth, ecstasy, and cocaine.

When he was finally picked up by the juvenile authorities, the whole story came out into the open.

"How could you do this to your family," his father said, "after all we've done for you?"

Jeremy just laughed at him contemptuously.

At this point, Jeremy's parents read an article about getting tough with misbehaving teenagers and decided to lay down the law at home: no alcohol and no other drugs; pass all subjects in school; be home on time for curfew; accept a share of household responsibilities; no more hanging out with druggies—go back to former nice friends; no more supplements to lunch money (he might use them to buy drugs); no more use of the family car.

In getting tough with their son, the Coopers had no self-criticism about their own role in his problems and their own enabling behavior. They also had no sense of how to go from where the problem stood to where they wanted the changes to lead.

Jeremy, who had been the "good boy" protected by loving parents, suddenly became the "bad boy" whose misbehavior could not be tolerated. He had strayed far from being a responsible young man, and now suddenly was being asked to be a model child. Failure was inevitable. Jeremy could not, and would not, meet the new expectations.

He retaliated against the tough regime by blasting his stereo in the middle of the night, sneaking out of windows to be with his friends, and getting into even more trouble with the law.

His condition worsened. His mood changed moment by moment. He became increasingly hostile. His life revolved around getting and using drugs. He didn't seem to care about himself or anyone else.

Now Jeremy is in a drug-treatment center, with an uncertain future. This is a sad story of addiction.

The main thrust of this book is *preventing* drug abuse by empowering children to think clearly and to make wise decisions. One of the effects of addiction is to damage relationships and diminish logical reasoning, making reasonable discussions and wise decision-making almost impossible. When serious drug abuse or addiction occurs, it's too late for prevention. It's time for *intervention*.

Ultimately, however, the cure for drug problems involves the same outcome as prevention—a person learns to think clearly and make good decisions. But the conditions for this must be established. First, you need more drastic measures to cut through the defenses, confusion, and distortions.

This chapter is about meeting the challenge of serious drug abuse or drug dependence once it has already developed, as with Jeremy, or when it seems likely to develop because drug use has been increasing and preventive measures have been ineffective.

Drug addiction is easier to prevent than to cure. There is no sure remedy, so parents must be prepared for a struggle. To help your children, you first need to take care of yourself. It's equivalent to flight attendants' advice to passengers on airplanes to first put on their own oxygen masks before putting them on their children.

TAKING CARE OF YOURSELF

The drug problems of an individual drain the emotional energy of an entire family, arousing anger, depression, fear, and frustration. The experience is also one of confusion: "What went wrong? I don't really understand."

Typically, parents react to serious drug abuse or addiction with extreme blame. Some parents hold themselves personally responsible, saying, "I've failed." Anxious and depressed, they start second-guessing themselves: "If only I had . . . "

Other parents explode with anger and put all the blame on their children, whom they now see as misfits and failures.

Either way, this blaming behavior is, at best, not constructive.

If your children are addicted or are using drugs dangerously, I'm sure you realize that they need help. Regardless of what they do, I recommend that you get professional help for *yourself*, or enroll in a self-help group such as Alanon, Families Anonymous, or Toughlove, or do both. You *need* support, for your own sake and for your children's.

In many respects, the approach of some of the self-help groups is consistent with the philosophy of empowering children on which this book is based. The idea of these self-help groups is that when addiction occurs, you don't stop *loving* your children, but you do stop *rescuing* them. You no longer engage in any enabling behavior, such as providing the personal tolerance, financial resources, phony excuses, or legal help that have allowed drug use to continue. Most self-help groups teach you to draw the line—to clarify the limits of acceptable behavior. Before you start offering help again, your children must take important steps toward helping themselves. They must take responsibility for their own behavior. You cannot, and should not, try to save them.

One problem, however, is that sometimes parents in these groups put *all* the blame on their children and don't acknowledge or fully acknowledge their own mistakes. At most they will say, "We should have been more strict sooner." But drug problems *always* develop within a family context. Therefore, it is important, when drawing the line, to share the responsibility, as the following example shows:

"I'm sure we [your parents] played a part in your problems. I don't think we were as available as we should have been when you were younger. I'm really sorry about that. We also shouldn't have been covering up for you at school. Then we made matters worse by calling you a "druggie" and other names. But that's in the past. We're trying to understand what we've done wrong, so that we can do better in the future. But you've got to do your share of changing, too. Our efforts will be wasted unless you make an equal effort to break your drug habit and learn other ways to meet your needs."

LEARNING FROM PAIN

When your children are on the way to serious drug problems and attempts to reason with them have failed, they can learn from the pain they experience. Pain teaches, and you can be a supportive ally in an effort to promote self-responsibility:

"I see all the problems you're having with friends, in school, and here at home. I hate to see you hurting so much. I don't think it'll get any better without professional help, and it'll probably get a lot worse. How about talking with someone? I'll be glad to arrange an appointment for you, and go along if you want."

Some children will say that they've tried to give up or cut back on drugs but haven't been successful. This, you explain, is all the more reason to get help.

If they won't go for help, make your expectations very clear. At a time when they are not under the influence of alcohol or any other drug, make a gentle yet firm statement:

"I see serious problems. You won't acknowledge the problems or stick with the agreements you've made. I've offered counseling, but you won't accept my offer.

"We have rules at home. We insist that you follow the rules or take the consequences. The rules include keeping your personal living space clean, sharing in household chores, succeeding in school, and showing respect for others who live here. Because of your drug habit, I don't think that you can do this. I don't think that you're capable of making valid agreements, but I'll give you a final chance to prove me wrong."

You and the rest of the family will get angry as your children break rules and behave irresponsibly. It's important to express your resentments, which are the natural consequences of drug abuse by someone you love. (For more information on disciplined ways to express resentments, refer to Chapter 3.)

As Fred, a fifteen-year-old, got out of the car at his friend's house, he was swearing at his father. It was the type of hostile nastiness that often goes with drug dependence. His father didn't get into a verbal power struggle. He simply said, "I'm very angry about what you called me. You'll have to arrange another ride home or take the bus."

When children consistently fail to fulfill their responsibilities because of drug problems, parents should begin to withdraw the benefits and privileges of family membership. Children lose the financial and emotional support that was being misused to perpetuate bad habits. The explanation is not punitive:

"It doesn't feel right to launder your clothing, prepare your meals, or transport you around town while you're being so rude to us. You blast the stereo, lie to us, and don't do your share of the work around the house. Your friends call at all hours. We want to do nice things for you but not under these circumstances. Being thoughtful and cooperative is a two-way street."

A drug problem will create natural consequences not only at home but also in school and possibly with the law. If a teenager is expelled from or flunks out of school, he or she should be asked to get a job and pay rent.

It should be clear that if there is ever a threat of physical violence, you will call the police. Sometimes a single serious encounter with a law-enforcement official is enough to scare a child straight.

As awful as it seems, you can't rescue your children from drug dependence. What you can do is to (1) stop contributing to the problem by rescuing or persecuting, and (2) encourage your children in every possible way to think about what they are doing and to take responsibility for themselves.

As you do your best and suffer with them, remind yourself that you cannot control their behavior.

DRUG TESTING

I used to object to drug testing because I thought that people who were tested became so angry about the indignity that they would never accept help. Dragging your child to a drug test is not likely to inspire feelings of warmth. But I do realize that we must sometimes be pragmatic. There are extreme situations in which children deny drug use with consistent, bold-faced lies, and yet the parents know, in their heart of hearts, that their children are harmfully involved with drugs.

Because most signs of drug use could have other causes, you must allow for other possibilities. But you shouldn't naively believe improbable, repeated lies. When every attempt at communication has failed, and there is no other plausible explanation for harmful events, I think it is essential to test for drugs. Exposing drug use—and, equally important, the fact that your child has been lying—is sometimes the only tactic that can get a young person to engage in an open discussion. Testing also helps parents take the sort of decisive action that must be taken when serious drug abuse is occurring. I have seen numerous cases in which drug tests have brought an adolescent to the negotiating table, led to an admission of significant problems, provided leverage for getting him or her into treatment, and begun to break down huge communication barriers in a family.

However, I have also known many parents who hastily decided on drug-testing and lost significant ground in their relationship with their child. Great caution should be taken to make sure that ordering a drug test is not a panicked response to a mild suspicion, and that exhaustive efforts have been made to communicate about the issue beforehand.

Drug testing is also helpful when young people have exhausted all their excuses for continued drug use and have declared an intention and determination to remain drug-free. Many adolescents have told me that knowing they would be tested helped them to stick with the decision to quit using drugs. Even those who were angry about being tested sometimes admitted that the tests helped.

It is important to bear in mind that adolescents have many ways to beat drug tests, including products that can be bought at "head shops" and drug stores, and other means of flushing the system. Some even smuggle in and heat "clean" urine. Some drugs cannot easily be detected, and some leave the body relatively quickly. You have to rely on good timing and the element of surprise to be effective with drug tests. Be prepared to deal with the angry response you can expect when you start drug testing.

TAKING ACTION

It is wise to intervene in a drug problem before dependence occurs, if it is evident that your children won't agree to give up drugs and they are using drugs dangerously. By this point you have already urged them to go for individual or family counseling. They may have promised to either stop or reduce their drug use. They may have pledged to do better at home or school. But instead of improvement, the situation has worsened. Your children still deny the problem.

It's time for more drastic measures, including the possibility of forcing them to go for drug treatment or reporting their various offenses to the police and involving the juvenile-court system. Involving the police and the courts can be a frightening wake-up call for young people. Learning that their community and a court of law will not tolerate their incorrigible, out-of-control behavior is a powerful educational experience. It is a good lesson to learn before they become adults and face much more serious consequences for their misbehavior. Clearly it is better if someone else reports them, other than you. They will be angry about being reported. However, if they are abusive toward you and will not stop, this is a logical consequence and possibly your only recourse. (Bear in mind, however, that most juvenile-court systems are not highly responsive, because they are already overburdened with huge numbers of young people who have committed serious offenses.)

If the children are of legal age, they can be evicted from the home: "You can't live here and behave this way." Younger children can be sent to live with other relatives or to group homes or residential treatment centers.

These actions will make your children angry and possibly more rebellious. Using this type of power is, at best, a trade-off. You may gain a measure of control. The price you pay is diminished communication and trust. But at this point, you have little alternative. Let your children know that you are considering these drastic measures.

THE WHOLE TRUTH

Drug-dependent teenagers usually get into trouble with many people in their lives—school officials, employers, neighbors, brothers, sisters, friends, and romantic partners. Often these people will come to you with complaints about your child. When they come, it's a good idea to ask them to be candid with your child—to not spare him or her from the truth and also the consequences of such behavior.

In a last-ditch effort to promote voluntary treatment, your strong warning about drastic measures can be complemented by eliciting the candor of other people who are important to your child. You can approach these people and ask them to come forward with their thoughts and feelings—to confront your child, in a tough yet caring and supportive way, with their perspective on what's happening. The idea is that no one should save a drug abuser from hearing the truth about the impact of his or her behavior. This chorus of voices makes it difficult to deny the problem.

The drug abuser may counterattack by offering a string of lies about what's really been happening or even claiming that his or her drug use has already stopped—last week—even knowing that no longer will anyone be fooled. Regardless of what the drug abuser thinks about the situation, a whole group of people close to him or her see things differently. Ideally, the confrontation will break through the denial, and he or she will agree to accept help.

Sometimes families or counselors hold a special meeting to bring significant people together to confront a drug abuser. This encounter is called an "intervention." Such a meeting is an ideal that is not always realizable. However, most people who are concerned will agree to come. Surprisingly, some teenagers endure the confrontational encounter, probably because behind their defensive wall they know something is wrong and are crying for help. They are more likely to attend and stick it out, particularly if an intervention is held right after a drug-related crisis, such as an arrest or the break-up of a relationship. At this meeting, participants are asked to share their observations and feelings with care and concern, and without using put-downs or making accusations. The drug user can answer, but participants are told not to get into arguments.

It used to be said that alcoholics and drug abusers couldn't be helped until they hit rock bottom. This aroused a vision of skid-row bums sleeping on sidewalks with bottles of muscatel in their hands. The idea behind calling people together for an intervention is to stress how bad the situation is for the drug abuser *at this moment*. Whether through a formal intervention or by other means, you want to help identify the seriousness of the problem, so that he or she will get help and do something about it *now*, before hitting rock bottom.

The Cooper family arranged an intervention for their son, Jeremy, in their home, with the help of a local drug-treatment program. Some of what was said at the meeting and over a period of a week after the meeting is condensed and presented below.

A former girlfriend confronted Jeremy: "You stopped being fun. All you ever wanted to do was get high. You kept breaking dates. When you started using cocaine and crystal meth, you weren't fun anymore. You seemed more concerned with drugs than with me. I was very hurt."

A former friend: "You borrowed money from me and never returned it. You called me names because I didn't want to use cocaine. We used to have good times together. We used to be close. Now you've left me."

A teacher: "You don't hand in your assignments. You don't study. You don't come to class anymore. You're failing in my class. This doesn't fit at all with what your previous academic record indicates about your capabilities."

Mrs. Cooper: "You've stopped doing your share at home. You don't keep agreements. Money keeps disappearing. I suspect that you're stealing it. You're rude and insulting to me. This morning you yelled, 'Get lost, bitch.'"

The manager at the fast-food restaurant where he had worked: "I fired you because you came in late and didn't show up for shifts. I gave you fair warning."

Mr. Cooper: "You seem high, either stoned or wired or drunk, almost every day. You don't even look me straight in the eye when we talk."

Jeremy Cooper angrily left the intervention session, threatening to run away. A couple of weeks later he agreed to enter treatment of his own accord.

TREATMENT UNDER PRESSURE

With some children, a hostile, go-for-broke attitude accompanies drug problems. They essentially say, "I don't care what you do. You can't stop me."

In school they say, "Go ahead—send a note home, suspend me, expel me. I don't care."

At home they say: "Go ahead—take away the car, ground me, take away financial support. I'll climb out the window and steal a car if I need to."

If your child won't talk and won't voluntarily go for help, you face a very tough decision about whether to coerce him or her into treatment. You see the problem getting worse. You've stopped enabling. You're not persecuting. What's left?

The idea of young people being forced into treatment is an objectionable one. Most of the time it fails. However, in my experience as a psychologist, I have successfully worked with teenagers who were *initially* coerced into my office by their parents. I tell the parents up front that I won't work with a child who does not ultimately agree that there is a problem and want help. Then I make my position clear to the child:

"It doesn't seem that you really want to be here. It looks as if you were kind of dragged into the office. Is that right?"

"Yes."

"Well, I don't want to be your punishment. It doesn't feel good to me, and I can't be of any value to you if you're here under the gun.

But it does seem that you have at least one problem—your relationship with your parents. I'd be happy to talk about that with you, and I'd be happy to talk about your life and your drug use if you want, so that you and I can reach our own conclusions."

Almost invariably, if the pressure is lifted, these children welcome an opportunity to talk. After all, they usually do have serious problems and many things on their minds, and usually no adult with whom to talk.

I also know of situations in which children do well after being coerced into residential treatment and forced to "detox" from drugs. They get greater clarity of thought once the chemicals are out of their system and sometimes are able to recognize and admit to problems they had been denying. Sometimes, however, they are angrier than before and more determined to defy authority. In part, the outlook of individuals who are pressured into treatment depends upon the way they are received. If mental-health workers function as if they are dealing with a volunteer client, or, worse yet, seem critical or punitive, the outcome will probably be negative.

Treatment under pressure has no guarantees. But when you run out of choices, this is the only one left.

DRUG TREATMENT

The major treatment options for drug abuse are the following:

- once-a-week outpatient therapy
- intensive (three or four times a week or more) outpatient therapy
- day-treatment programs (school plus counseling)
- partial hospitalization (mainly counseling plus school)
- inpatient hospitalization
- residential treatment (long-term living outside the home for treatment in a non-hospital setting)

These options describe settings for treatment. The specific type of treatment varies according to the orientation of the provider.

Another option for confronting alcohol or drug abuse is participation in self-help groups such as Alcoholics Anonymous and Narcotics Anonymous. These peer groups help support individuals in a drug-free lifestyle. Countless numbers of people have benefited from affiliating with these organizations. For some, the strength gained through shared vulnerability in a self-help group is a good complement to professional counseling, which is aimed at uncovering the underlying causes of drug abuse. Sometimes, however, individuals discover contradictions between the orientation of professionals and that of the self-help organizations.

The evaluation of treatment for drug dependence is neither conclusive about what works best nor highly encouraging about outcome. Supporters of each method of treatment claim success, but persuasive scientific evidence to back up the claims is lacking.[1] A variety of factors have confounded the validity of results in terms of evaluating programs.[2] For example, what a reasonable person would consider success is often not what is measured in evaluations. Sometimes the criterion for success is merely completing the program, or remaining abstinent while in the program, or maintaining short-term abstinence after discharge. From the family's point of view, this hardly measures up to what is desired.

The research on effectiveness of treatment is filled with contradictions. Some reports favor residential treatment. Others say that it is costlier but no more effective than outpatient treatment. Some stress longer duration of treatment. Others say that this is not more beneficial.[3]

Anecdotal reports of treatment are sometimes discouraging. Many children go through very expensive inpatient treatment at private substance abuse centers and then use drugs the day they are released. Sometimes drugs are smuggled into treatment centers. Sometimes teenagers who are getting help for a marijuana or alcohol problem learn about heavier drugs, such as heroin and speed, while in a treatment center.

Some residential treatment centers are run by former addicts who have become intoxicated with their new power and cult-like in their practices.

Some counselors offering outpatient or inpatient care have never been trained in dealing with substance-abuse problems. Some of them try to deal with underlying causes without focusing on the drug-abusing or drinking behavior, a naive but still wide-spread approach. Others focus on the drugs but fail to deal with underlying causes.

SUCCESSFUL TREATMENT

Clearly, there is no simple formula for overcoming drug addiction. But there is still hope.

Some teenagers find the power from within to get off drugs.

Some programs work for some people. And sometimes it takes two or three episodes of treatment before success is achieved.

Some teenagers seek help and find relief by joining Alcoholics Anonymous.

In selecting a counselor or a program, I suggest looking for certain characteristics:

Family involvement. Ideally, the whole family system is involved, so that as an individual changes, the system changes as well.

Geared for teenagers. Many programs accept adolescents but were designed for adults with completely different life experiences. An ideal program should be specifically geared to the experiences and needs of teenagers. Counselors should be experienced in working with young people.

Positive peer influence. Because peer influence is so strong, an ideal program should use this force for positive peer pressure.

Focus on positive attitudes and life skills. Some counselors and programs focus only on drugs and addiction. They should also promote the development of healthy attitudes and life skills, helping a young person learn social skills, problem-solving skills, and positive ways to deal with stress. They should promote self-esteem and self-respect, not tear someone apart. These goals are best accomplished in a homey, non-institutional environment. Residential programs should include an array of recreational and educational activities, not merely encounter sessions aimed at confronting drug abuse.

Focus on drugs. Some counselors focus on the underlying psychological causes of drug abuse and fail to empower an adolescent to deal directly with the existing drug problem. It is important that counselors focus directly on the drug habits: aiming for a commitment to abstinence, helping an adolescent to eventually break the ties to the drug-using past, and preparing him or her to prevent relapse.

Understanding the stages of change. Much as we all want a drug-

265

abusing young person to immediately abstain from drugs, a significant body of research has shown that there are important stages of change that precede the "action stage," when someone is ready to make a serious commitment to quit using drugs.[4] When young people are pressured into saying that they will quit immediately, many of them "fake it" by promising to quit, just to get adults off their backs. Many others become increasingly rebellious or defiant. Some make a sincere commitment to quit using drugs. But if they have not laid a solid foundation for success, they are likely to relapse. The result for them is another failure, just what they do *not* need. Therefore, it is important to find counselors and programs that understand the stages of change and base their interventions on this understanding. Instead of the promise of instant abstinence, you want people who will help your child progress steadily through the stages of change.

Transition and after-care. After the program ends, attention needs to be paid to what comes next. Good programs help clients avoid relapse, yet give them the strength to cope with all eventualities. They provide after-care services or a plan for ongoing support. Hospital and residential programs should help arrange a good transition back to home and school.

Philosophy of empowerment. Good counselors in good programs are careful not to take away the power of those who come to them for help. They do not tell young people what is wrong. Rather, they help their clients see it themselves. Good counselors encourage and require young people to use their own power and personal resources in order to take responsibility for themselves. They don't foster dependence.

Professional training in substance-abuse issues. An ideal program is under the direction of a person with extensive professional experience in the field and recognized credentials.

Five years ago I grew impatient with traditional programs for adolescents that (1) used an adult model and (2) pressured them into *saying* that they would quit using drugs. That was the norm. Young people would rebel against these programs or fake their way through them. Then, when released, they would immediately get high. These programs promised the moon (drug-free kids overnight) but delivered little, if anything. I realized that it was important to develop a different approach that would move young people systematically through the stages of change.

The vast majority of young people enter treatment without any intention of quitting. Most of them do not think that they have a problem. Most of them are accustomed to lying to adults and to making phony promises. Most of them have been so busy defending themselves from adult criticism that they have not taken stock of their own lives.

So I developed The Seven Challenges Program and wrote a book, *The Seven Challenges*, and nine workbooks to accompany the text. The idea in this program is the same as in this book. We have to engage young people in a thinking process. We have to create a climate of honesty within which young people can look at what needs they are attempting to meet by using drugs and what harm or potential harm they are suffering as a result of their drug use. Within this context, they can be helped to make wise decisions for themselves. In keeping with what the research indicates, in The Seven Challenges Program, a period of contemplation and preparation precedes successful action.

In making your choices for treatment, I would suggest you talk personally with people who offer the services. I'd be wary of programs making grandiose promises of instant abstinence and claims of 90 percent cure rates. Instead look for programs that are holistic (deal with underlying issues as well as drugs), involve families, understand child development and young people, empower clients, and understand the stages of change.

The treatment of substance abuse has become big business. Like other businesses, profits are sometimes put ahead of concerns for the individual. That is all the more reason for being careful in your choice of the person and place to go for help. You simply can't give up.

It's sad that we have such serious problems with drug abuse in our society. We need to work for social changes that reduce its occurrence. That is the topic of the next chapter. But until those changes occur, we have to use all our power to protect the people we love and to find the help they need.

10
FAMILIES WORKING TOGETHER: COMMUNITY STRATEGIES FOR REDUCING DRUG ABUSE

About thirty years ago I was in a hotel room in Chicago with my college roommate and about fifteen other people, mainly his relatives. We were packed together like sardines. My roommate was recovering from a knee operation. His normally cheerful face was all scrunched up, and his moans sent shivers up my spine. One of his uncles, a physician, suggested Valium and was about to write a prescription.

"No need. I have some," someone said.

"So do I," someone else added.

"Me, too," a third person offered.

Then I witnessed that funny scene you sometimes see when you ask to borrow a pen. Everyone starts fumbling through pockets and handbags to see who can find one first. I didn't count, but about half the people in the room were carrying a supply of psychoactive drugs.

In those days, the mass media were talking about drug problems and a drug culture, referring mainly to marijuana and LSD. When I observed this group in action, I recognized for the first time the full extent to which drugs permeated our entire society.

We live in a drug-filled and drug-oriented world. If you have a headache, you take an aspirin. If your back hurts, you take pain pills. If you feel depressed, you take anti-depressants. Pharmaceutical companies spend billions of dollars promoting their products and promising a drug solution to any problem. We live in a consumer-oriented society in which people buy and consume products to make themselves feel good.

Under these circumstances, it's impossible to isolate children from exposure to drugs and from the consumer mentality. But as you've seen in the previous chapters, with dedicated and sustained effort parents can prepare children for coping with the pressures to use drugs.

To solidify your efforts at home, you can begin to look beyond your own family—to other parents, to schools, and to your community. These are important influences on your children. You want them to be teaching, encouraging, and reinforcing the same healthy behavior and attitudes that you promote at home.

This chapter is about parents expanding their influence and working together with other parents to bring about social changes that reduce the availability and acceptability of drugs in our communities. As an organized force, parents can achieve goals that they could not achieve as individuals.

Every community has a message about children using drugs. The message is what parents, schools, policy-makers, and law-enforcement people *really do* about drugs, not necessarily what they *say* they will do. Until recently, most communities in this country had a message of indifference that went something like this: "We will tolerate children drinking alcohol, smoking or chewing tobacco, and using other drugs as long as there's no serious harm, even though we *say* children shouldn't do it."

This laissez-faire attitude allowed children to start taking drugs at an early age. It allowed recreational use of most drugs, including illegal ones. It even allowed certain types of high-risk behavior, such as driving while intoxicated.

As drug problems escalated, there was an uproar. An enormous movement of activist parents, alarmed by the extent of drug use by children and the indifference of adults, began to change the message in their own communities and around the country. Parents set higher standards of behavior and insisted that their schools and communities do likewise. In response to this grassroots movement, social institutions and government agencies responded with corresponding changes.

The new message about drugs is still evolving, but its leading edge is quite clear: Alcohol and other drugs are *not* for children. We cannot overlook the risks and dangers of children using drugs.

PARENTS HELPING PARENTS

The starting point for cooperating with other parents is getting to know each other. The simplest way to do this is to introduce yourself to the parents of your children's friends. As you get acquainted, you can share experiences and perspectives. At some point you can make the discussion more formal by suggesting that you start talking about the drug issue and other pertinent topics, and that you work toward establishing clear community standards and mutual support in maintaining the standards.

Some of the best results of parents talking with each other have been in making guidelines for parties. Parents have agreed to policies such as these: to have invitation-only parties, to make sure that parties are chaperoned (at least casually), to make it clear that alcohol and other drugs will not be tolerated, and to set an agreed-upon reasonable hour for parties to end.

In some communities, parents make a commitment to call each other if a child is found to be in possession of alcohol or any other drug. That way, the parents are not the last to find out, as is too often the case.

PARENTS AND SCHOOLS

One of the most important ways for parents to take positive action in a community is to make sure that schools have a comprehensive substance-abuse prevention and intervention plan. This should include clear school policy and procedures on drugs, a kindergarten-through-twelfth-grade substance-abuse prevention curriculum, an array of alternative activities, and a system for the identification and referral of drug problems.

Ideally, every school district should establish a community drug advisory committee on which parents are represented. In communities where there were no such committees, parents have been successful in lobbying for them.

Policy and Procedures

One way to create a healthy and safe school climate is by establishing a clear school policy prohibiting drug use and by firmly and fairly enforcing it. The use of tobacco products should be banned on the school grounds. Procedures are needed for handling drug possession, drug use, and the suspicion that someone is under the influence of drugs. The roles and responsibilities of schools and local law-enforcement agencies should be clarified.

Curriculum

Ideally, the school prevention curriculum should be much like the home curriculum discussed in this book, emphasizing the attitudes and life skills that build resistance to substance abuse and providing accurate information about alcohol and other drugs. Some of the curriculum can be included in existing classes. But this type of learning also needs a place of its own. It is *social and psychological knowledge*, and it is as important to an individual's intellectual development as anything else in the established curriculum. Historically, it has been neglected by our schools. Specialized prevention curricula that teach young people how to resist social pressures to smoke or chew tobacco are highly effective and should also be offered in our schools.

Alternative Activities

Alternative activities, so named because they serve as a positive alternative to drug use, are part of a comprehensive prevention program. These activities show that life can be enjoyable and fulfilling without drugs. They provide positive growth experiences, reinforcing the attitudes and life skills in the prevention curriculum. By participating in these activities, students learn leadership skills and are influenced by positive peer role models.

Examples of alternative activities are: Project Prom and Project Graduation (programs in which students plan drug-free celebrations); student retreats; tutorial programs (older students tutoring younger ones); teen leadership training; "Just Say No" Clubs (for students who want to support each other in remaining drug-free); and SADD groups (Students Against Drunk Driving).

Another type of student activity that has been used in preventing drug abuse and other problems is peer counseling. Often students will discuss problems with peers that they would not reveal to adults. Peer counselors offer help or make referrals.

Identification and Referral of Problems

School personnel and peer counselors need to stay alert to the early warning signs of problems and to know how and where to make referrals. Also, students themselves should know where they can turn if they feel that they need help or if they have a friend who they believe needs help.

Ideally, schools should offer support groups or individualized services for students at high risk for drug abuse and for those who have been referred for help. Schools should also designate a staff member to stay abreast of available community resources.

School Climate

The attitudes and life skills that protect against substance abuse do not lend themselves well to brief and simplistic instruction. For example, self-esteem cannot be increased simply on the basis of a few hour-long modules in the classroom. To promote self-esteem and other positive attitudes, and to teach basic life skills, the *entire* school climate must support wellness, self-respect, and respect for others. It must provide opportunities and incentives for success. The whole system must be geared to healthy development. Parents can be a strong force in working for this type of school climate.

COMMUNITY INVOLVEMENT

Parents uniting with each other is the beginning of building a sense of community. Working with schools expands the impact of parents. But to really change the messages about drugs and to fully empower children to resist drug abuse, the *entire* community should be mobilized. This includes local business leaders; law-enforcement personnel; health professionals; elected officials; athletic coaches;

civic groups; youth leaders; the media; and churches, synagogues, and mosques.

In recent years, action-oriented groups have been formed in communities around the country. Some have taken a hit-or-miss approach to creating change, although recently these groups have become much more systematic, in part because professionals have offered team training and other systematic approaches to facilitating community change. Team training pulls together all segments of a community and teaches them to work together. Team members inform themselves about drugs, assess community needs and resources, and examine prevailing attitudes and practices. Then they decide what changes they want and make a collaborative action plan.

Organized communities can influence and change a great deal—attitudes, practices, laws, norms, and behavior. Community groups have used the media to deliver positive prevention messages. They have worked with policy-makers to initiate enlightened legislation about drugs and to increase financial support for substance-abuse prevention and treatment programs. They have raised private funds from businesses to cover the expenses of prevention programs. They have pressured convenience stores and other businesses to stop selling alcohol and tobacco products to minors. They have created alternative activities for young people, such as teen institutes, and recreational and leadership programs. They have opened lines of communication between schools and health professionals, and helped coordinate services.

Some communities have organized effectively to prevent minors' access to tobacco products. Their efforts have put pressure on local merchants to post signs stating that tobacco sales to minors are illegal and have led to the active enforcement of age-at-sale laws, which reduced tobacco purchases by minors. Communities have also lobbied for banning the sale of cigarettes in vending machines. On a state level, grassroots organizing has led to increased tobacco taxes, which have significantly reduced cigarette smoking.

As communities organize, they establish standards for behavior. Children need clear and consistent boundaries. They need to know what type of behavior is accepted in their community and what is not. In the past, as I said before, boundaries about drugs were weak, vague, and inconsistent.

By joining an existing community group or by forming a new one, you demonstrate your personal commitment to preventing drug abuse. You serve as a role model by being a socially concerned, responsible person. You show your children the importance of being involved in social causes, in something bigger than oneself.

THE BIG PICTURE

Drug abuse is not just a personal or family problem. It's a social problem as well. When substantial numbers of children abuse drugs, we have to wonder why. We have to pull back and look at the larger picture.

What we see is that drug abuse is not an isolated problem. It is only one of many problems plaguing children and teenagers. Crime, gangs, school failure, teenage pregnancy, eating disorders, depression, and suicide are others. It is evident that *many* children are having *many* problems growing up.

When I think of drug abuse, I think of people running away from problems. I think of people who can't make a good life for themselves.

Sometimes this happens in prosperous middle-class and upper-middle-class communities. Young people may feel pressured to succeed in ways they find unbearable or suffer from a sense of emptiness, unable to find meaning in their lives. Some of them are highly pessimistic and cynical about the world and their future. Some are exceedingly angry. Many have serious family problems that they have never even addressed. They have stuffed their feelings.

Sometimes adolescents escape through drugs because of lack of opportunity—no education, no jobs, no future. Some children grow up in communities where there are more unemployed adults than adults with jobs. What hope do they see for their future? In these settings it is almost impossible to have a positive attitude. Life skills don't necessarily help. The root cause of drug abuse in this population is the condition of poverty and a sense of hopelessness about the future. Poor people living in the most impoverished and troubled neighborhoods use drugs to seek relief from their struggles. Some of them "deal" drugs because that's the only way they see themselves living above the poverty level.

Even in these extreme situations something can be done right now. We have proven programs that can break the vicious circle of poverty and despair that has been passed on from generation to generation.[1] A national commitment to services aimed at the seriously disadvantaged—high-risk young people—could break the vicious circle. Such a program would include prenatal care, child-health services, child care, and efforts to strengthen families through outside support. Expanded pre-school programs and the prevention of school failure would be a high priority. This would be cheaper by far than the price society now pays for neglected health needs, unemployment, crime, and, of course, drug abuse.[2]

In this book, much of the focus has been on preventing drug problems among people who live above the poverty line. The economic opportunity is there, but still there is a form of impoverishment. We have children who don't know how to enjoy life and can't cope with its pressures. They are deficient in life skills. Their lives are lacking in meaning and fulfillment. They don't feel good about themselves.

In many of these families, economic pressures have forced both parents to work outside the home, even the parents of infants and pre-schoolers. Because of geographical mobility, the support of an extended family and a close-knit neighborhood has been lost. Exhausted parents run out of energy, thus neglecting important aspects of their child-rearing, educational, and nurturing roles. The demands of juggling pressures from work and family sometimes create what psychologist Urie Bronfenbrenner has described as "havoc in the home."[3] Children feel the stress and become insecure, which causes problems in school. Meanwhile, television and the mass media increasingly fill the void left by the disorganized family, taking over the role of transmitter of culture and values.

Economic pressure and "havoc in the home" probably contribute to the problems that lead to divorce, which, in turn, creates additional emotional and economic problems. Many single parents are forced to fulfill the double duties of full-time breadwinner and full-time parent.

The situation is critical. Not only are children being forced to make decisions about drugs at an early age, but they must do it at a time when the family, the chief source of emotional and economic support, is disorganized, fractured, and under severe stress. All of this creates alienation, a lack of connectedness. Alienated children seek acceptance from their peers and affiliate with other troubled youth. As has been suggested throughout this book, children need more links to their parents. They need more time and attention. They need more from their families.

But parents need something, too. They need support. For example, the situation in middle-class homes would be greatly improved if affordable and adequate child care were available and if employers offered flexible work schedules. Much can be done on the social level to improve the situation of families. In a sense, parents need to unite for their own benefit, in order to fight for the type of social support they need from health-care providers, government officials, employers, and educational institutions.

THE VISION

The drug problems we face as a society will be solved only through social change. The process involves building the kind of world in which people don't need to escape. They are happy. They have hope, opportunities, pleasure, and meaningful work. They have a sense of community, belonging, and purpose. They support each other and create positive social institutions. This is *ultimate drug prevention*. By working for these ideals, we teach children a lesson about responsibility and good citizenship. It is the very opposite of the escapism and defeatism that motivate drug abuse.

Meanwhile, empowering our own children and working in our own families, schools, and communities is a good first step toward making the type of world that we can now only imagine. Raising intelligent, loving, self-confident, and fulfilled children who can make wise decisions about drugs is an attainable goal and an accomplishment worthy of high praise.

References

CHAPTER 1

1. J. Michael Polich, Phyllis L. Ellickson, Peter Reuter, and James P. Kahan. *Strategies for Controlling Adolescent Drug Use.* Santa Monica, Ca.: The Rand Corporation, 1984.
2. National institute on Drug Abuse. *Adolescent Peer Pressure: Theory, Correlates, and Program Implications for Drug Abuse Prevention.* Rockville, Md.: DHHS Publication No. ADM 84-1152, 1984.
3. Daniel Goleman. "Parents' Oh-So-Subtle Influences." *San Francisco Chronicle,* August 8, 1986, p. 28.

CHAPTER 2

1. Andrew Weil and Winifred Rosen. *From Chocolate to Morphine.* Boston: Houghton Mifflin, 1993.
2. Ibid.
3. Ibid.
4. Ibid.
5. Barbara Critchlow. "The Powers of John Barleycorn: Beliefs About the Effects of Alcohol on Social Behavior." *American Psychologist* 41 (1986): 751–762.
6. National Institute on Drug Abuse. *Let's Talk About Drug Abuse: Some Questions and Answers.* Rockville, Md.: DHHS Publication No. ADM 81-706.

7. D. B. Kandel. "Drug Use by Youth: An Overview." In D. J. Lettieri and J. P. Ludford, eds., *Drug Abuse and the American Adolescent*. Rockville, Md.: National Institute on Drug Abuse Research Monograph No. 38, 1981.

8. National Institute on Drug Abuse. *Cocaine*. Rockville, Md.: DHHS, Publication No. ADM 83-1304. *Inhalants*. Rockville, Md.: DHHS Publication No. ADM 83-1305. *Hallucinogens and PCP*. Rockville, Md.: DHHS Publication NO. ADM 83 1306. *Marijuana*. Rockville, Md.: DHHS Publication No. ADM 83-1307. *Opiates*. Rockville, Md.: DHHS Publication No. ADM 83-1308. *Sedative-Hypnotics*. Rockville, Md.: DHHS Publication No. ADM 83-1309.

9. Clay Roberts and Don Fitzmahan. *Yellow Pages Resource Supplement for "Here's Looking at You, 2000."* Seattle: Comprehensive Health Education Foundation, 1986.

10. Weil and Rosen, op. cit.

11. Kenneth S. Schonberg, ed. *Substance Abuse: A Guide for Health Professionals*. Elk Grove Village, Il.: American Academy of Pediatrics, 1988.

12. Steven Riedell. "Inahalants: A Growing Health Concern." *Behavioral Health Management*, May–June 1995, 28–30.

13. Terry Todd, cited in Louis Lasagna. "Breakfast of Champions." *The Sciences* 24, no. 2 (1984): 61–62.

CHAPTER 3

1. Claude Steiner. *Scripts People Live*. New York: Grove Press, 1974.

CHAPTER 5

1. American Academy of Pediatrics. *Smoking: Straight Talk for Teens*. Elk Grove Village, Il.: 1990.

2. Ferguson, Tom. *The No-Nag, No-Guilt, Do-It-Yourself Guide to Quitting Smoking*. New York: Ballantine Books, 1987.

3. Peggy Riccio. "Campaigning for Tobacco-Free Kids." *Prevention Pipeline*. (Center for Substance Abuse Prevention) July–August 1996: 16–17.

4 Michael Meyers. "Saving the Children." *Professional Counselor* 2, VI (December 1996): 41–44.

5. Media Influence is the public health concern, by David Pines, *Prevention Pipeline* July/August 1996 Center for Substance Abuse Prevention

6. "Cool Fools." *Newsweek*. July 21, 1997: 60–61.

7. John Slade. *Facts on Nicotine and Tobacco*. New Jersey Alcohol/Drug Resource Center and Clearinghouse Fact Sheet. Piscataway, NJ: Rutgers University, Center of Alcohol Studies: 1992.

8. Pines, op. cit.
9. *Preventing Tobacco Use Among Young People: A Report of the Surgeon General.* Washington, D.C.: Department of Health and Human Services, 1994.
10. American Academy of Pediatrics, op. cit.
11. Surgeon General, op. cit.
12. Ibid.
13. B. R. Flay. "Youth Tobacco Use: Risks, Patterns, and Control." In J. Slade and C. T. Orleans, eds. *Nicotine Addiction: Principles and Management.* New York: Oxford University Press, 1993.

CHAPTER 7

1. Anderson C. Johnson. "Project Smart: A Social, Psychological, and Behavioral Based Experimental Approach to Drug Abuse Prevention." Paper presented at the annual convention of the American Psychological Association, Anaheim, Ca., 1983.

CHAPTER 9

1. Polich, op. cit.
2. Chad D. Emrick and Joel Hansen. "Assertions Regarding Effectiveness of Treatment for Alcoholism." *American Psychologist* 38 (1983): 1078–1088.
3. William R. Miller and Reid K. Hester. "Inpatient Alcoholism Treatment: Who Benefits?" *American Psychologist* 41 (1986): 794–805.
4. J. O. Prochaska, C. C. DiClemente, and J. C. Norcross. "In Search of How People Change." *American Psychologist* 47 (1992): 1102–1114.

CHAPTER 10

1. Lisbeth Schorr. *Within Our Reach: Breaking the Cycle of Disadvantage.* New York: Doubleday, 1989.
2. Carnegie Corporation of New York. "Bringing Children Out of the Shadows." *Carnegie Quarterly* 33, II (1988): 1–8.
3. Urie Bronfenbrenner. "Alienation and the Four Worlds of Childhood." *Phi Delta Kappan* 67 (1986): 430–436.

Index

position on drug use, 10–11, 107, 159, 187–88

reacting to knowledge of drug use, 193–94. *See also* subhead exchange-of-information process

reasons for, 159–62

specific drugs, talking about, 110–11

starting discussions, 101–6

suspicions, communication of, 93, 192–93

taking care of bodies, 104–5

tobacco use, 140–47. *See also* tobacco

word–association game, 104

drastic measures, 249–50

drug testing, 258–59

forced treatment, 259, 262–63

guidelines for treatment programs or counseling, 265–67

interventions, 260–62

juvenile–court system, involving, 259–60

law enforcement, involving, 259–60

options in drug treatment, 263–64

pain, learning from, 256–57

responsibility and consequences, 256–58

support for parents, 255–56

truth–telling confrontations with others, 260–62

drugs. *See also* specific subject headings

abuse of. *See* abuse of drugs

addiction. *See* dependence

age of user, 38–39

availability of, 3–4

clear message about, 10–11, 107, 230, 231–32

combinations of, 36

consumer society of, 13–14, 269–70

definition, 107

delay in use of, 14

discussion with children. *See* discussion of drugs and drug use

effects of use, 39–40

emotional damage caused by, 14

experimental use, 44

first use of, 3–4

good and bad drugs, opinions on, 30–35

harmful use, 44–45, 111–14, 217–19

health of user, 39

identity, effects on sense of, 11–12, 14

ingestion, methods of, 37–38

legality of, 36–37, 111, 113

limits on behavior, setting, 11

medications, use of, 104–5

mood swing, seeking, 44

patterns of use, changes in, 37

personality of user, 38–39

pervasiveness of, 269–71, 275–77

pharmacology of, 36

physical evidence of use, 47

quantity, frequency, and length of use, 37

reasons for use, 39, 66–67

scare approach to, 64, 101–2

setting for drug use, 38

signs of drug use, 45–47, 155–56, 192, 253–54

social problem, scope of, 275–77

stages of use, 43–45

statistics on, 10, 114

tolerance to, 37, 42

types of drugs, 48–50. *See also* specific drug names

anabolic steroids, 63

depressants, 55–58

explaining to children, 110–11

hallucinogens, 58–59

inhalants, 60

marijuana. *See* marijuana

narcotics, 58

stimulants, 50–55

use defined, 40

war on, 4

withdrawal syndrome, 37, 42, 43

E

ecstasy, 55

emotional damage, 14, 46

empowerment of children, 6–7, 15, 22, 277

activities to promote. *See* activities

agreements with children. *See* agreements with children

clear thinking, 69–70, 79–84

constructive criticism and, 76–78, 93–95

discussion and exchange of information. *See* discussion of drugs and drug use

giving and asking for love, 71–74

limits, setting of, 84, 85

negative feelings, expression of, 91–92

negotiation of differences, 95–96

problem-solving abilities, 70, 86–90

relationship values and skills, 70–71, 90–96

Index

About the Author

Robert Schwebel, Ph.D., has worked for more than twenty-five years in the prevention and treatment of alcohol, tobacco, and other drug problems. His experience includes developing drug-prevention programs for schools, public agencies, and families; developing drug-treatment programs for various agencies; working in private practice with youth and famlies; and presenting lectures and workshops to professional and community audiences.

After receiving a doctorate in clinical psychology from the University of California at Berkeley, he moved to Tucson, Arizona, where he lives with his wife and two sons. For three years he directed the largest drug-prevention program in Arizona, and for five years he served as clinical director of drug treatment at a facility with a broad continuum of services. He wrote *The Seven Challenges* and the nine *Seven Challenges Workbooks*, which are part of the Seven Challenges Program, an innovative drug-treatment program now widely used across the country.

Dr. Schwebel has been actively involved in public-policy matters, serving on various policy and advisory boards, including as U.S. chair of the Binational Task Force on Substance Abuse with Mexico. Dr. Schwebel has also been active in the mass media. For eleven years he wrote a weekly column on families and relationships for *The Arizona Daily Star*. He has hosted a local NBC-TV talk show about relationships called "Good Loving." He has also appeared on the "The Oprah Winfrey Show," "The Today Show," and CNN interview programs, as well as on national radio programs and local television and radio programs across the country. He wrote *Who's on Top, Who's on Bottom: How Couples Can Learn to Share Power* and is a co-author of *A Guide to a Happier Family*. Schwebel's newest book for Newmarket Press focuses on the dangers of tobacco for kids.

PARENTING/CHILDCARE BOOKS FROM NEWMARKET PRESS

Ask for these titles at your local bookstore or use this coupon and enclose a check or money order payable to: **Newmarket Press**, 18 E. 48th St., NY, NY 10017.

Baby Massage
____ $11.95 pb (1-55704-022-2)
How to Help Your Child
Overcome Your Divorce
____ $14.95 pb (1-55704-329-9)
How Do We Tell the Children?
____ $18.95 hc (1-55704-189-X)
____ $11.95 pb (1-55704-181-4)
Inner Beauty, Inner Light:
Yoga for Pregnant Women
____ $18.95 pb (1-55704-315-9)
In Time and With Love
____ $21.95 hc (0-937858-95-1)
____ $12.95 pb (0-937858-96-X)
Loving Hands: Traditional Baby Massage
____ $15.95 pb (1-55704-314-0)
Mothering the New Mother, Rev. Ed.
____ $16.95 pb (1-55704-317-5)
My Body, My Self for Boys
____ $11.95 pb (1-55704-230-6)
My Body, My Self for Girls
____ $11.95 pb (1-55704-150-4)
My Feelings, My Self
____ $11.95 pb (1-55704-157-1)
Raising Your Jewish/Christian Child
____ $12.95 pb (1-55704-059-1)
The Ready-to-Read,
Ready-to-Count Handbook
____ $11.95 pb (1-55704-093-1)

Saying No Is Not Enough, Rev. Ed.
____ $23.95 hc (1-55704-324-8)
____ $14.95 pb (1-55704-318-3)
The Totally Awesome Business Book
for Kids (and Their Parents)
____ $10.95 pb (1-55704-226-8)
The Totally Awesome Money Book
for Kids (and Their Parents)
____ $18.95 hc (1-55704-183-0)
____ $10.95 pb (1-55704-176-8)
The What's Happening to My Body?
Book for Boys
____$18.95 hc (1-55704-002-8)
____$11.95 pb (0-937858-99-4)
The What's Happening to My Body?
Book for Girls
____ $18.95 hc (1-55704-001-X)
____ $11.95 pb (0-937858-98-6)
Your Child at Play: Birth to One Year, Rev.
____ $24.95 hc (1-55704-334-5)
____ $15.95 pb (1-55704-330-2)
Your Child at Play: One to Two Years, Rev.
____ $24.95 hc (1-55704-335-3)
____ $15.95 pb (1-55704-331-0)
Your Child at Play: Two to Three Years, Rev.
____ $24.95 hc (1-55704-336-15)
____ $15.95 pb (1-55704-332-9)
Your Child at Play: Three to Five Years, Rev.
____ $24.95 hc (1-55704-337-X)
____ $15.95 pb (1-55704-333-7)

For postage and handling, please add $3.00 for the first book, plus $1.00 for each additional book. Prices and availability are subject to change.

I enclose a check or money order payable to **Newmarket Press** in the amount of _____

Name_____

Address _____

City/State/Zip_____

For discounts on orders of five or more copies or to get a catalog, contact Newmarket Press, Special Sales Department, 18 East 48th Street, NY, NY 10017; Tel.: 212-832-3575 or 800-669-3903; Fax: 212-832-3629.

p:\newmarke\bob's\saynobob.qxd--2/11/98